D0849133

Writing Broadcast News

Writing Broadcast News

Shorter, Sharper, Stronger: A Professional Handbook

THIRD EDITION

Mervin Block

CQ PRESS

A Division of SAGE
Washington, D.C.

CQ Press
2300 N Street, NW, Suite 800
Washington, DC 20037

Phone, 202-729-1900; toll-free, 1-866-427-7737 (1-866-4CQ-PRESS)

Web: www.cqpress.com

Cover design: Jeff Everett/El Jefe Designs
Composition: C&M Digitals (P) Ltd.

♾ The paper used in this publication exceeds the requirements of the American National Standard for Information Sciences—Permanence of Paper for Printed Library Materials, ANSI Z39.48-1992.

Printed and bound in the United States of America

14   13   12   11   10   1   2   3   4   5

Library of Congress Cataloging-in-Publication Data

Block, Mervin.
   Writing broadcast news: shorter, sharper, stronger: a professional handbook / Mervin Block. — 3rd ed.
      p. cm.
   Originally published: Chicago: Bonus Books, 1987.
   Includes bibliographical references and index.
   ISBN 978-1-60871-417-9 (alk. paper)
   1. Broadcast journalism—Authorship. 2. Broadcast journalism. 3. Report writing.
I. Title.
   PN4784.B75B56 2011
   808'.06607—dc22

2010037394

Dedicated to the memory of my parents

CONTENTS

PART III: BEST PRACTICES

A NOTE ON SCRIPTS AND EXCERPTS

Most scripts in this book were submitted to me over the years by news directors who were preparing for newswriting workshops I held in newsrooms across the country. I had asked the NDs to send me about 200 pages so we could discuss them at the workshop. I'd read the scripts in advance and set aside those with common or unusual mistakes. At the station, I'd project the scripts onto a screen without the name or initials of the writer. Then I'd point out the mistakes to the staff. With no ID on the scripts, no one was put on the spot—except me.

riting well isn't merely important—it's imperative. Whether writing for TV, radio, new media or for print, we all need to write better.

If you're a writer or want to be one, any kind of writer—reporter, producer, anchor, newswriter, blogger, intern—and you absorb the tips and pointers in *Writing Broadcast News*, you're bound to write better.

Over the years, surveys have shown that most news directors say the skill they prize most in job applicants is writing. No matter what kind of work you do in any kind of newsroom (broadcast, digital or print), good writing is a boon.

This new edition is better organized than the previous edition. And this edition does a better job of highlighting important points. It's expanded in key areas, and it has a more comprehensive index, making it easier for readers to find what they're looking for. As a result, this edition is shorter, sharper, stronger.

The suggestions I passed along in the previous edition are still pertinent, helpful, timely—and timeless. And this new edition provides even more suggestions.

Do you want to strengthen your scripts? Streamline them? Know more about attribution? Question leads? Quotation leads? *Quote* and *unquote*? And other quotidian questions? Want to learn more about broadcast newswriting in general? About news judgment and journalism? This professional manual offers clear, simple guidance.

Writing Broadcast News is intended for two kinds of writers: broadcast professionals who want to enhance their skills and students who want to acquire those skills. Whichever group you're in, newbie or oldbie, or you don't know where you stand, you've come to a place I trust is worth your while. And even if you want to focus on writing for print or the new digital media rather than for radio or television, this book can help.

Writing Broadcast News reviews the basics briskly, then deals with other elements of broadcast newswriting. The book presents scripts and excerpts that have been broadcast, along with my corrections, objections and suggestions. I've collected the scripts over the years at newswriting workshops I've held in TV and radio newsrooms in about 45 states, 3 Canadian provinces and elsewhere.

Because mistakes are often our best teachers, I point out flaws in these scripts. After I correct a script, I often provide my rewrite. The scripts are the same as those displayed in the previous edition, and my rewrites offer countless clues on how to revise effectively.

Writing Broadcast News starts with the Dozen Deadly Don'ts, and it follows with a raft of Venial Sins. I don't just list the sins; I elaborate on each one. Then I pivot to what I call the Top Tips of the Trade. I've polished them and added several new ones.

Two new features in this edition are pull quotes and WordWatcher boxes. This book's boxes and pull quotes emphasize and illuminate especially important points. These typographical devices are used to draw you into the text and enable you to add more arrows to your quiver.

For 13 years, I wrote a column, WordWatching, for the Radio-Television Digital News Association (formerly RTNDA). The Word-Watcher boxes in this book, based on my monthly column in RTDNA's *Communicator*, focus on the differences between writing for the eye and writing for the ear.

This book is full of tips—tips about words, about grammar, about writing, about journalism. Sounds like an advertisement, doesn't it? Well, *Writing Broadcast News* speaks for itself, and you can see for yourself.

To write well, we need to read a lot, write a lot and think a lot (but not of Camelot). Write as often as possible. And show your scripts to someone who's a better writer than you. If you're already the best writer in your class or shop, it's probably time to move on to a tougher class or a bigger shop.

The English writer Hilaire Belloc said, "Of all fatiguing, futile, empty trades, the worst, I suppose, is writing about writing." I disagree. Writing about writing is challenging. I get a real kick when readers tell me my book has helped them get the hang of writing news for broadcast—or helped them write better.

But in spite of my disagreement with Belloc's remark, I do agree with something else he wrote: "When I am dead, I hope it may be said, 'His sins were scarlet, but his books were read.'"

I'm more than happy to see *Writing Broadcast News* back in print. Its absence pained me. After all, I fathered the book. And mothered it. Till fate smothered it. Now CQ Press has rescued it, revived it and renewed it.

ACKNOWLEDGMENTS

I thank Charisse Kiino, editorial director of CQ Press, who thought it desirable to reissue all my books.

Thanks, too, to Lorna Notsch, production editor, and Pam Suwinsky, copy editor. I also want to thank three other stalwarts at CQ Press: Erin Snow, Linda Trygar and Chris O'Brien.

I wish to acknowledge another author, Scott Travers, who insisted that I see his agent, Bill Corsa, several years ago, even before I needed an agent. So I saw Bill. And retained him as my agent. I thank Bill for his belief in *Writing Broadcast News* and his unrelenting efforts to find a new publisher. Bill's expertise worked the magic that kept this book from disappearing.

My thanks, too, to my superb editor through the years, Julia B. Hall. She edited the second edition of this book, and it bears her hallmark of quality. Her skills also strengthened this edition.

PART I

RULES

Dozen Deadly Don'ts
Mistakes that mar scripts

ny writer who knows a lot knows there's a lot to know. And every writer should know that what counts most is what you learn after you know it all.

When I began to write broadcast news, I had already mastered three basic rules: (1) write on only one side of the paper, (2) don't write more than one story on a page and (3) keep the keys clean. With the advent of the computer, rule 1 no longer applies. Even so, over the years, I've digested some other valuable rules while working for old pros in broadcast newsrooms; I've recalled some rules from a class in broadcast newswriting; and I've devised some rules from insights gained through writing day after day after day. Also, I've assimilated rules laid down by various writing experts, especially Strunk and White—and *they* call them rules. I've learned a lot from my mistakes. As you probably know, mistakes are often our best teachers. So the sooner we make our first thousand mistakes, the sooner we can correct them.

Often, the right thing to do is not to do the wrong thing. The Ten Commandments tell us mostly what *not* to do. According to the Talmud, the Old Testament sets forth 365 negative commandments and 248 positive commandments. Not that I want to turn a script into Scripture. But if the Good Book sees the positive purpose of the negative, so should we.

In a burst of creativity, I've labeled the most important no-no's the "Dozen Deadly Don'ts." You may already know some of these how-to techniques. But though we're taught once, we must be reminded many times. These reminders are omnidirectional: They cover radio and television; a.m. and p.m.; AM and FM. And they apply to all kinds of scripts: from 20-second stories to two-hour specials, from anchors' "readers" to reporters' "wraps."

A writer who understands the Don'ts can see why they may be even more important than the Do's. Walter Cronkite was so impressed by the ability of Maine lobstermen to find their way through thick fog he once asked a laconic local, "How do you know where the rocks are?" "Don't," the man replied. "I know where they ain't."

Just as a jazz musician performs his magic by knowing which notes not to play, the careful writer knows what not to write. Here are the Dozen Deadly Don'ts, not necessarily in order of sinfulness. Remember: Our scripts will suffer from—if not die for—our sins, so don't commit any of them.

▶ 1. Don't scare listeners.

And don't scare them away. A prime—but not prime-time—example is this first sentence of a broadcast script:

> This is a very complicated and confusing financial story.

Why start with a turn-off? No matter how complex or confusing the story, our job is to simplify and clarify, not scarify. We're often faced with stories that seem impenetrable. But we need to get a grip on ourselves—and on our notes or source copy—and plow ahead. And not tell our listeners that we're baffled or buffaloed (even if we are). "The world doesn't want to hear about labor pains," the pitcher Johnny Sain said. "It only wants to see the baby."

That scare was probably not intentional; we certainly don't want one that is:

> How does the thought of 10 percent ground bones and other meat remnants in hot dogs, sausage or bologna sound to you?

I'd tell the weenie who wrote that, "Don't try to upset me or my stomach. And please don't question me."

Many scripts are scary for another reason: They've been put on the air apparently untouched by human hand—or mind.

▶ 2. Don't give orders.

Don't tell listeners to do this or do that. Don't tell them to listen, or watch, or stay, or fetch. Just give them the news. When a radio anchor says, "Don't touch your dial," I wonder, "Why, is it radioactive?"

▶ 3. Don't bury a strong verb in a noun.

Instead of writing a lead about a "bomb *explosion*" write, "A bomb *exploded*." Nouns are the bones that give a sentence body. But verbs are the muscles that make it go. If your first sentence lacks a vigorous verb, your script will lack go-power.

▶ 4. Don't characterize news as *good, bad, interesting* or *shocking.*

Just report the news. Let the listener decide whether it's good, bad, interesting, amazing, surprising, disturbing or shocking. What's good news for some is bad for others. What seems, at first glance, to be good can turn out to be bad. What's good for a city dweller may be bad for a farmer. What's good for Luke Skywalker may be bad for Lucy Streetwalker. A steep fall in oil prices seems like good news. But in many places in this country, it turns out to be bad news. The best course: Just tell the news.

Also undesirable for newswriters is the good news–bad news combo: "Governor Gibson had good news and bad news today. He said he's going to push for a tax cut—but not this year." What's objectionable is that the phrase "good news and bad news" is worn out—like old news.

In fact, the "good news–bad news" coupling has been traced back to biblical times. When Moses came down from Mount Sinai with the Commandments, he reportedly told his people, "I have good news and bad news. The good news is that I got them down from 40 to 10. The bad news is, adultery is still in."

I said "reportedly" because a news director who reads that may muse, "If a camera wasn't there to shoot it, did it really happen?"

But it's not wrong to use the "good news" approach when the news is indisputably good for a *specific* group or person: "The IRS had good news today for taxpayers." Or "Governor Boodle received good news and bad news today. His good news: He was put on probation. His bad news: He has to make restitution." Otherwise, the time-consuming, subjective "good news" label is bad news. And please don't call a story "unusual." We don't report the usual, do we? Not usually.

▶ 5. Don't start a story with: *As expected.*

When I hear an anchor say "As expected" at the top, it's usually a story I had *not* expected. Hadn't even *suspected.* Most listeners tune in to hear the unexpected. Even seers have no idea of what to expect. *As expected?* By whom? Not by your average listener. When listeners hear a story begin with *as expected* and the story turns out to be something they did not expect, they probably feel they don't know what's going on.

Often, when newswriters start with *as expected,* they do so because *they* have been expecting a development. Or their producer has told them to keep an eye peeled for the story a news agency says will be moving shortly.

So they've been scanning the wires. After hours of expectation, the story finally arrives. Without thinking, without considering their listeners— listeners who aren't newshawks, listeners whose reading is limited to the program listings—the writers rush to type the words that have been on *their* minds. So they start with that deflating phrase *as expected*, which takes the edge off any story.

Even more of a turn-off than *as expected* is a negative version that I've heard with my own ears. It went something like this: "*Not unexpectedly,* Senator Blather said today he's going to run for reelection." Another variation: "The *long-awaited* appointment of Judge Michael Mutton to the State Supreme Court was made today by Governor Grosvenor." It certainly wasn't *long-awaited* by listeners. Probably only by Mutton. (And his Li'l Lamb Chop.)

That's not the only phrase considered a nonstarter. Here are more than a dozen more ways not to start a story:

Don't start a story with: *In a surprise move....*

A network broadcast this lead:

> In a surprise move, the Interstate Commerce Commission rejected the proposal to merge the Santa Fe and Southern Pacific railroads.

I had long forgotten about the proposal. The ICC had been considering it for two and a half years, so how could I be surprised about the decision when I wasn't aware it was pending? For whom was the rejection a surprise? People in the transportation industry, perhaps. But for the rest of us, news is full of surprises.

Don't start a story with: *A new development tonight in the....*

Every item in a newscast is supposed to be fairly new, based on something newly developed. Some writers try to go beyond that wasteful opening with "A *major* new development tonight. . . ." What's to be gained by telling people, "I've got news for you"? Friends may say that on the phone, but professionals don't proclaim it in a newscast.

And don't start a newscast by saying, "We begin with. . . ." As soon as you open your mouth, listeners know you've begun. Equally useless: "Our top story tonight is. . . ." If it's the first story, it should be the top story. Top stories run at the top. Skip that needless opener and go straight to the news. And don't write, "Topping our news tonight. . . ." Makes me think of Reddi-wip.

Don't start a story with: *Someone is news, is in the news, is making news* or *is dominating the news.*

Without ado or adornment, go ahead and tell the news. That's what a newscast is for. That's why they call it a newscast. Everyone who's mentioned in a newscast is "making" news. When writers say someone "is making news" or "making headlines," they're wasting time, time better spent reporting news.

> *Without ado or adornment, go ahead and tell the news.*

Another waste of time is the lead that says someone "made history today." Or "entered history books today." Only historians will decide what was historic. And they won't decide today.

Equally pointless is this lead: "They're rewriting the record books today in. . . ." That script is what needs rewriting. Just tell the news. If someone has broken a record worth reporting, say so—simply.

Don't write a first sentence that uses *yesterday* or *continues.*

Both words are bad news. Listeners tune in expecting to hear the latest news, the later the better. They want to hear news that has broken since they last heard or read the news. Imagine tuning in to a newscast and hearing an anchor start talking about something that happened *yesterday.* Yesterday? I thought yesterday was gone for good. Who cares about yesterday? I want to hear what happened today. *Yesterday* is still common in newspaper leads, but for broadcasting, it's too old, too dated, too rearview-mirrorish.

But a script mustn't deceive listeners by substituting *today* for *yesterday,* and it mustn't try to pass off yesterday's news as today's. Use ingenuity in figuring out how to write a first sentence without harking back to yesterday. You don't need to be a historian to know that nowadays, yesterday is history.

A worse sin than using *yesterday* in a lead is using yesterday's

WORDWATCHER

PRINT *Mayor Hudson's wife was reported missing yesterday.*

BROADCAST *Mayor Hudson's wife has been reported missing.*

If you must lead with a story that broke yesterday, update it so you can use a *today.* Or use a present tense verb with no *yesterday* or *today.* Or if you find out, just before tonight's broadcast, that the mayor's wife was kidnapped last night, you can write around *last night* or *yesterday* by making use of the present perfect, as above. The present perfect tense expresses an action carried out before the present and completed at the present, or an action begun in the past and continuing in the present. In a subsequent sentence, you can slip in that dirty word *yesterday.*

news. Steer clear of *continues* in an opening sentence. In a second or subsequent sentence, *continues* isn't objectionable, but it's meaningless to end a story with "the controversy continues." Or "the investigation continues."

The problem with *continues* is that it doesn't tell a listener anything new. Worse, it tells listeners that nothing's new. *Continues* doesn't drive a sentence or story. It merely says something that has been going on is still going on. It tells the listener this is going to be a story that's not news—just olds.

Find a verb with verve.

News is what's new. When you have to write about a long-running story—a siege, a drought, a hunger strike—search for a new peg. If you can't find a new peg, find a different angle of attack, move in from a different direction. Focus on whatever has occurred today or is going on today, something you can report for the first time, something that you didn't know about yesterday. Find a verb with verve, says Merv.

Don't start a story with: *Another, More* or *Once again.*

With few exceptions, those words are turn-offs. If we start a story with *another,* it sounds as if whatever the story turns out to be, it's bound to be similar to a story told previously, one that's not much different. Perhaps just more of the same.

A broadcast script:

> Another jetliner tragedy in Britain today. A chartered airliner caught fire on takeoff in Birmingham, and 54 passengers were killed.

The crash is newsworthy on its own merits, not because it was the third airline accident within a month. To punch up that fact, I'd give it a sentence of its own: "A British jetliner caught fire on takeoff in Birmingham, England, today, and 54 passengers were killed. It's the third airline disaster in less than a month."

Also, starting a story with *more* signals the listener that what's coming may be more of the same—what some pros call "the same old same old." Usually, it's better to skip *more* and go straight to whatever the new *more* is. One reason many broadcast writers start with *more* is that it's an easy way to go: "More headaches for the president today," "More wrangling in City Hall today," "More arrests in the Acme Power case." Want more?

Don't start a story with: a sentence that has a *no* or *not*.

At least, try not to. Rewrite your negative lead to make it positive. Instead of saying, "The president is not going to take his planned trip to

Tahiti," you'll have a stronger opening by saying, "The president has canceled his trip to Tahiti." A basic rule of writing or speaking is, Put your sentences in a positive form. In *The Elements of Style*, Strunk and White say that, generally, it's better to express even a negative phrase in a positive way: "did not remember" = "forgot"; "did not pay any attention to" = "ignored." Not for nothing do they stress that.

Another argument for avoiding *not*: in some cases, a listener may confuse *not* with *now*. We shouldn't go overboard worrying about listeners' hearing problems, but it's the reason some broadcast newspeople write "*one* million" instead of "*a* million"—lest a listener mistake *a* for *eight*.

> *Rewrite your negative lead to make it positive.*

A similar concern leads many newsrooms to report that a defendant was found *innocent* rather than *not guilty*; they fear that some listeners might not catch the *not*. Or that the newscaster might inadvertently drop the *not*. But many writers (and I'm one) prefer writing *not guilty*—because it's clear and correct. Juries don't find people *innocent*. How could a jury find someone *innocent*, which means without sin?

Don't start a story with: a participial phrase or a dependent clause.

It's not the way we talk. It's not the way anyone talks. And it's not the way to help listeners latch onto a story. Would you say to a friend:

"*Needing new shoes*, I'm going downtown tomorrow to buy some"?

No. You'd say, "I need new shoes, so tomorrow I'm going downtown to buy some."

A lead that backs into a story with a participle is weak and murky. And it requires too much of listeners. The participle, or participial phrase as in the example, takes a verb and turns it into an adjective by tacking on *ing*. The participial phrase with secondary information that listeners hear at the start means nothing until they hear the next cluster of words and discover the subject of the sentence. Then they have to rearrange the word clusters to make sense of what they just heard. How many listeners have the time, energy and aptitude to do that while the wordathon rolls on and on?

Try making sense of this lead, written for a local broadcast:

> Saying their project could never be compatible with the river which bears its name, the Regional Planning Council denied approval of the massive 1800-acre Wekiva Falls Complex in North Orange and Lake County.

If you were listening to that, could you tell what the subject of the sentence is—or is going to be? After such a clumsy approach, would you care?

Second, if you put a subordinate clause *after* the subject, you separate the subject from the verb. Try to avoid subordinate clauses that separate subject and verb. The greater the distance between subject and verb, the greater the difficulty for the listener. Listeners hear only one word at a time. By the time they hear the verb, they have to rewind mentally and figure out who's doing what. While listeners are puzzling over it, they can lose their train of thought. And if they do lose it, they probably won't be able to get back on board.

> *The greater the distance between subject and verb, the greater the difficulty for the listener.*

To make the subject of the story clear and unmistakable, the best pattern for writing your first sentence is subject-verb-object: Start with the subject, go directly to the verb and follow with the object. The closer the verb follows the subject, the easier for the listener to follow. So go with S-V-O.

Don't start a story with: a quotation.

Listeners can't see quotation marks, and they can't examine your script. So when an anchor starts with a quotation, listeners assume the words are the anchor's own. It's especially confusing for listeners when the anchor opens with an assertion that's bold, startling or open to question—and then gets around to telling us who first spoke those words.

> *Attribution precedes assertion.*

Likewise, if a story needs attribution, the way to proceed—the *broadcast* way—is to put the source, or attribution, first. Remember: Attribution precedes assertion.

When we talk to one another, we automatically put attribution first. We don't stop to think about it. Our conversations follow the subject-verb-object pattern naturally and spontaneously: "Jim told me, 'Blah, blah.' And Jane replied, 'Hah, hah.'" Is any other word order preferable? Nah, nah.

In the unlikely event your boss rebukes you, you might complain to a friend, "The boss told me today I have to learn how to park my bike straight." Without thinking twice, you'd put the attribution first. You sure wouldn't blurt out, "'You have to learn how to park your bike straight.' That's what the boss told me today." Yet, we hear anchors start a story with a quotation—or an indirect quotation or a stunning statement—that sounds as if they're expressing their own views.

Don't start a story with: a question.

Why not? Question leads tend to sound like quiz shows or commercials. Questions can be hard to deliver, draw an answer you don't want and trivialize the news. Also, questions delay delivery of the news. And listeners are looking for answers, not questions. No one hurries home to catch a newscast to find out the latest questions.

Don't start a story with: the name of an unknown or unfamiliar person.

Names do make news, but only if they're recognized. An unknown name is a distraction. It can't be the reason you're telling the story; you're telling it because that person figures in something unusual. If the name means nothing to listeners, they're not likely to pay close attention, and they'll miss the point of your story.

The best way to introduce an unknown is with a title, or a label, or a description: "A Milwaukee milkman, Gordon Goldstein [he took that name because it's a blend of Guernsey and Holstein], was awarded five-million dollars in damages today for. . . ."

Many stories don't need the person's name. Without a name, a story flows better and runs shorter. What does an unknown name in a distant city mean to you? Or your listeners? But, if you're writing about a runaway or a fugitive, the name may be essential.

What's in a name? It depends. Before using a person's name, ask yourself whether the story would be incomplete without it. It is standard, though, to start a story with the names of people who have titles, prominent people who are in the news constantly: President Whoever, Secretary of State Whatever, British Prime Minister Hardly Ever. Omit their first names. The same style applies to mention of your mayor, police chief, governor and maybe a few other public officials when you use their titles.

We can also start a story with the name of someone who has star quality, a person whose name is widely known—in almost every nook and cranny by almost every crook and nanny. But we use that person's first name and precede the name with a label: "The actress Meryl Streep," "the painter Pablo Picasso," "the author John Updike."

We don't use anyone's middle name—unless. Unless we're writing about someone who has long been identified with a middle name, like John Paul Jones. Or Martin Luther King.

Skip initials, too—unless the person you're writing about has long been identified with an initial: Michael J. Fox, J. Edgar Hoover, Edward R. Murrow. Another exception: an initial may be desirable if you are trying to avoid a mix-up with someone widely known who has the same (or a similar) name.

Broadcast newswriters customarily omit "Junior" and "the Second" after someone's name—unless *not* using them could cause confusion with prominent sound-alikes. But there's no need to include someone's first name *and* a nickname. Go with one or the other. But *not* both together. We don't have time, especially for those silly uses of first names with standard diminutives, like Thomas "Tom" O'Connor. Besides, have you ever heard of a Thomas called Joe?

When you do use names, try to use as few as possible so listeners can keep their eye (or ear) on the ball. Overuse of names—sometimes any use—leads to clutter. Don't diffuse the focus of a story; keep the listener's mind out of the clutter.

Don't start a story with a personal pronoun.

This script started with a personal pronoun, *he,* and kept *he-heing:*

> He walked out of a New York prison today looking a little slimmer and slightly grayer. But one thing has not changed. He's still followed everywhere he goes.

Who *he?* I want to know from the get-go who or what a story is about. So when I hear a script start with *he,* I wonder whether I missed the first sentence, the one that identified the subject. Withholding the identity of the subject stumps listeners. I don't like newscasters to play games with me. And I won't waste time with newscasts that don't present news in a clear, understandable manner. I'm not alone.

A print feature can start with *he* because a reader can spot who *he* is from a headline or a photo or a caption; but we don't open a conversation with a pronoun. If we rely on the best pattern of all, subject-verb-object, we'll avoid premature pronouns.

Don't start a story with: *There is, There are* or *It is.*

They're dead phrases—wordy and wasteful. The power of a sentence lies largely in a muscular verb. A sentence gets its get-up-and-go from an action verb like *smash* or *shoot* or *kill*—or hundreds of other verbs that express action.

Although *is* and *are* are in the active voice, they aren't *action* verbs. And they don't convey action. They—and other forms of *to be*—are *linking* verbs. They link the subject of a sentence with a complement—another noun or adjective, a word that identifies or describes the subject. Other linking verbs include *have, seem, feel* and *become.* Not one of them has the power to drive a sentence—they only keep it idling. So when you start a sentence with *there is,* you're just marking time until you introduce the verb that counts.

A network evening newscast:

> There is a major power failure in the West affecting perhaps as many as 17 states. Utility company officials say a power grid that delivers electricity from the Pacific Northwest went down today. The cause of the blackout is not yet known, but it happened on a day when power resources were being stretched by record hot temperatures, including 102 degrees in Salt Lake City.

The *weather* was hot, not the temperatures. The script should read "record *high* temperatures." And let's make that lead read right, or at least better: "A power failure has blacked out a large part of the West."

Another *there* lead, this on local television, needs corrective surgery:

> There's a train rolling through town tonight. But this is one you definitely won't mind missing.

By deleting *there's,* we make the sentence shorter. By making it shorter, we make it stronger. The story is about a train, not about *there.* After we lop off *there's,* let's write it right: "A train is rolling through town tonight. . . ." There are instances, though—as in this sentence—when *there are* may be appropriate.

Don't write a first sentence in which the main verb is any form of *to be,* such as *is, are, was, were* and *will be.*

It's not necessarily wrong, just weak. Sometimes it's acceptable, even desirable. But it's better to search for an action verb. An exception to avoiding *is* in a first sentence: when *is* serves as an auxiliary or helping verb, as in: "Mayor Glom is *going* to Guam." But *is,* alone, is usually a nerd word.

A sentence we often hear on the air:

> "The president is back in the White House."

Factually and grammatically, the sentence passes muster, but it doesn't cut the mustard. The *is* lacks movement. It merely expresses a static condition, not action. The next sentence is better because it has an action verb indicating someone has *done* something: "The president has returned to the White House." Or "The president has arrived back at the White House."

The use of *is* in a first sentence is all right when the sentence is short and the story big. For example: "The teachers' strike is over." Or "Mayor Smiley is dead." The second sentence gets its impact from *dead.* Which leads to another tip: Certain one-syllable words that end with a hard consonant—like *dead* (or *drunk*)—gain impact when used at the end of a sentence. (No, I'm not suggesting you write *dead drunk.*)

One of the biggest weaknesses in broadcast news stories is the opening sentence. Too many limp—or just lie there. Every lead can't be a grabber, but what listeners hear first can be crucial as to whether they keep listening. So newswriters should choose action verbs.

This network script shows how *not* to do it:

> There was another clash in Britain tonight between police and gangs of youths. The latest incident was in the northern London district of Tottenham, where hundreds of youths overturned cars, threw gasoline bombs and set fires. Several policemen were reported injured. The incident followed the unexplained death of a West Indian woman during a police search of her home.

Let's see where that lead went wrong. The story had plenty of action that could have been reported with vigorous verbs. Instead, the writer began with the flabby *there was.* And then further weakened the sentence with *another.* When *another* is so high up, it often makes a story less newsy. After all, the main point of the story isn't that the two groups clashed *again.* The story is that they *clashed.* And if it weren't a sizeable clash, it probably wouldn't be worth reporting. The writer sapped the strength of a good verb, *clash,* by using it as a noun. Also, *youth* isn't a conversational word, not in schoolrooms, not in living rooms, not in newsrooms.

One way to pep up that script: "Hundreds of young people in London *went* on a rampage tonight. They *set* fires, *overturned* cars and *threw* gasoline bombs."

▶ 6. Don't cram too much information into a story.

Too many facts, too many names, too many numbers, too many words are just too much for too many listeners. They can't process such a steady flow of facts. Brinkley said the ear is "the worst, least effective way to absorb information." That's *David* Brinkley, not Christie.

No matter how complex the story, our job is to condense the facts and give the listener not just the essence but rather a highly concentrated essence—the quintessence. The architect Ludwig Mies van der Rohe, a minimalist, used to say, "Less is more." When it comes to lead sentences, "More is less." Moreover, more is a bore.

▶ 7. Don't write for broadcast the same way you'd write for print.

Print and broadcast are two far different critters. Because of these differences, you need to set aside habits formed when you wrote an essay or a term paper. Or when you wrote an article or a book. In writing a broadcast script, you mustn't take a tiresome trudge. Instead, focus on brevity, clarity and simplicity. The rest is electricity.

Newspaper readers can rip an article out of a paper, fold it, put it away and read—and reread it—at their convenience. They can show it to a friend and ask what something means. Your listeners have only one chance to hear your script. One time only. They can't phone you and ask you what you meant. You have to write in a way that enables listeners to understand your script instantly.

Newspaper reporters often construct their stories on the scaffolding of the Five W's—*Who? What? When? Where? Why?* And another question: *How?* They squeeze the most important facts into the top of an article, with succeeding paragraphs presenting facts in descending order of importance. But broadcast newswriters bypass that pattern. They skimp on the Five W's; they might write a script with only a few W's.

> *Think listeners, not readers.*

For writers with a newspaper background, a reminder: Don't write in inverted pyramid style. Leave that to print people. If you don't know what an inverted pyramid is, don't ask. You'll have one less print habit to kick.

Keep this in mind: Think listeners, not readers. Be sure to write right. And write tight.

▶ 8. Don't use newspaper constructions.

Here's an example of a common newspaper construction: "The chairman of the Senate Foreign Relations Committee said today Beijing should stop threatening Washington. Senator John Kerry said. . . ."

Newspaper readers would probably see that Kerry is the committee chairman, the person described in the first sentence. But in broadcasting, the nature of the medium leads many listeners to assume that the Kerry in the second sentence is another person and that Kerry is adding *his* voice to the chairman's. In broadcasting, this is better: "The chairman of the Senate Foreign Relations Committee, John Kerry, said today. . . ." Or else "The chairman of the Senate Foreign Relations Committee said today. . . . Chairman John Kerry told. . . ." That makes Kerry's identity unmistakable. (P.S. Don't call anyone a chair. Or a couch.)

Another common construction ends a sentence with "according to . . ." or "she said." But that's not *our* style. We in broadcasting never end a sentence with attribution. Or never should. When attribution is needed, keep this in mind: Attribution precedes assertion.

In journalism school, a class in *broadcast* newswriting taught me not to use *newspaper* terms. When that instruction sank in, it struck me as sensible. Why should we in broadcasting use the language and style developed over centuries for another medium, a medium that broadcasting tries to distance itself from—and distinguish itself from?

A few print phrases and words to avoid:

▶ *in the headlines:* What headlines? Why are those newscasters plugging newspapers?

▶ *front page, sports page, people page, back page* or *cover story:* Cover for TV? Pages? The only pages in broadcasting run errands.

▶ *up* as a verb: "The workers want to up their pay." Reminds me of a *Reader's Digest* title: "How We Upped Our Income; How You Can Up Yours."

▶ *slay: Slay* is a good Anglo-Saxon word, but *slay* is not so strong as *kill* or *murder.* Don't use *slay* unless you're talking about dragons. Or Santa.

▶ *youth,* when writing about a young person: It's not uncouth to say *youth.* But *youth* is a print word. Have you ever heard anyone use it in conversation? If so, please report him to the Bureau of Youth Abuse.

▶ *former, latter, respectively:* Few listeners remember names or items mentioned even moments earlier; and they certainly can't look at your script to see what you were referring to.

▶ 9. Don't reach for big words when small words can do the job.

"Short words are the best," said Winston Churchill, "and the old words when short are the best of all." The author Richard Lederer said, "Small words cast their clear light on big things—night and day, love and hate, war and peace, and life and death." As they say (not Churchill and Lederer), Save the big words for Scrabble.

▶ 10. Don't pluck a clever word or phrase from your source copy and use it in your script.

Listeners who heard a newscast or visited an Internet news site an hour before your newscast and then heard your borrowed words may figure that you got your gems from that earlier newscast or news site. So they'll regard you or your anchor as copycats. Use your own words; say it your own way. After all, you're a writer, right?

▶ 11. Don't lose or fail to reach a listener.

The best way to keep a listener is by talking *to* the listener, not *at* the listener. And by working at your job, not forcing the listener to do your work. She won't, so you must. Writing is hard work; it's easy only for those who haven't learned to write. Compressing a long, complex story into 20 seconds is a challenge. Telling that story well is even harder. As Confucius should have said, "Easy writing, hard listening. Hard writing, easy listening."

▶ 12. Don't make a factual error.

That's the deadliest sin of all. It causes you to lose your credibility. And eventually your listeners. Perhaps even your job.

If you want to win a Peabody and not wind up a nobody, here's another important rule: Don't be intimidated by rules. Newswriting isn't an exact science. To improve your scripts, go ahead: bend a rule or break one—if you must. But only when you can improve a script.

First, though, you must *know* the rules and *know* when you're breaking them. As the poet T.S. Eliot said, "It's not wise to violate the rules until you know how to observe them."

Venial Sins
Words that hurt copy

A notch or two down the scale from the "Deadly Don'ts" are the "Venial Sins." They may not be deadly, but they are sinful.

▶ 1. Don't start stories with prefabricated phrases.

Among the most trite: "This is the story of," "It's official," "Once upon a time," "Now it can be told," "It shouldn't come as any surprise," "It had to happen eventually," "Mayor Mozzarella made it official today," "The mayor fired the opening shot today in the . . . ," "When was the last time you . . . ?" "Believe it or not!" "[Lebanon] is no stranger to violence," "Oliver Orville is no stranger to politics," "For City Hall today, it was the best of times, it was the worst of times," "It was business as usual today at . . . ," "What we know now is . . . ," "It's that time of year again," "This story may surprise you," "This story may make you angry," "Here we go again."

▶ 2. Don't *end* stories with prefabricated phrases.

Shun: "Now the ball is in the mayor's court," "Don't count him out yet," "As Yogi Berra put it, 'It's not over till it's over,'" "It'll probably get worse before it gets better," "The full story is yet to be told," "So he's on safe ground—for the foreseeable future" (in contrast to the *un*foreseeable future?), "Police are investigating" (since when is that news?), "No one knows what the outcome will be," "What happens next is anyone's guess," "The outcome remains to be seen," "Only time will tell," "No one knows for sure," "In the final analysis," "There's no end in sight"—and variations without end.

▶ 3. Don't use prefabs anywhere.

Most of these word clusters are the kinds that secretaries can type on a word processor with one keystroke, like "In response to your letter" and "Very truly yours." Lawyers call these word-strips "boilerplate," and they are extruded into deeds, wills and contracts, with little thought or effort. Among prefabs used in broadcast news: "At a hastily called news conference," "At a crowded news conference," "In a prepared statement," "In an abrupt about-face" and "In a bloodless, pre-dawn coup."

▶ 4. Don't waste words.

Not only do excess words waste time; they also dilute the impact of what we say. Some words are usually excess baggage. Watch out for:

in order: as in, "They went to the White House *in order* to protest the president's action." In most cases, when we delete *in order,* the sentence means the same.

in the process of: as in, "The mayor is now *in the process of* deciding whether to run for another term." When you delete *in the process of,* the meaning is the same, and the sentence is improved.

literally, actually, really: as in, "The umpire *literally* walked off the field." Or "The sheriff *actually* saw the crash." Those adverbs don't help. So they hurt. *Really.*

suddenly, gradually, finally: as in, "*Suddenly,* he fell off the roof." No one falls gradually. Remember that scene in Hemingway's *The Sun Also Rises* when Bill asks, "How did you go bankrupt?" And Mike replies, "Two ways. Gradually and then suddenly." *Finally,* those adverbs add nothing to a sentence but bulk. *Usually.*

flatly: as in, "She *flatly* denied it." and "He *flatly* refused." A denial is a denial. A refusal is a refusal. So *flatly* falls flat. In *The Careful Writer,* Theodore M. Bernstein calls *flatly* "almost always superfluous."

personally, officially: as in, "The governor *personally* favors taking steps to stop the project." *Unofficially,* those adverbs only delay delivery of the news. Another adverb that's usually unnecessary is *formally. Seriously.*

miraculously: Leave miracles to ministers. If you get the urge to write "Miraculously, no one was killed," try "Somehow, no one was killed."

local and *nearby:* as in, "The injured were taken to a *local* hospital." Or to "an *area* hospital." (*Area* is rarely an adjective, except in "area code" and "area rug.") Where else would the injured be taken? To an out-of-town hospital? If someone is taken to a distant hospital, it may be worth reporting. Otherwise, listeners assume the injured were taken to the nearest hospitals. If someone is taken to a hospital across the street from an accident, that may be part of the story. (Note: Ambulances *take* people; scripts shouldn't *rush* them. Ambulances do rush; so do fire trucks. That's their job. But in copy, *rush* sounds breathless.) But please don't write that the injured were taken to three *different* hospitals. All hospitals are different. And separate.

separate: as in, "The indictment says the defendants met on seven *separate* occasions." Of course the occasions were separate. Otherwise the defendants would have met only once. Better: "The indictment says the defendants met seven times."

a total of: as in, "*A total of* 50 people were hurt." A total waste.

then: as in, "After he was arrested and charged, he was *then* freed on bond." When the chronology is obvious, *then* tends to be unneeded: "After he was arrested and charged, he was freed on bond."

the fact that: as in, "The marchers were protesting *the fact that* the sheriff refused to release the two prisoners." Better: "The marchers were protesting the sheriff's refusal to release the two prisoners." When you eliminate *the fact that* from a sentence, you almost always improve your script. That's a fact.

meanwhile: as in, "*Meanwhile*, the White House said it's studying the problem." I hesitate to say there's never an occasion to use *meanwhile*. But the use of *meanwhile* to tie two items together shows listeners the stitches. By directing attention to itself, *meanwhile* gives away our M.O. Transitions should be unnoticeable. A skillful cabinetmaker joins his panels neatly. Leaving the joints exposed is considered poor craftsmanship.

▶ **5. Don't use *in other news* as a transition.**

Every story on a newscast is other news. Each story differs from all other stories. If the first five minutes has been devoted to one big story, shift to the next story by going to a commercial. Or pausing. Or changing tone. Or changing camera. Or anchor. Or writer.

According to an able transition team, Arthur Wimer and Dale Brix, the best transitions are word bridges. At least, when they seem helpful and logical and the words aren't wasted. "Otherwise," they say in their *Workbook for Radio and TV News Editing and Writing*, "don't use [transitions] if they seem forced, illogical or awkward."

After many a tragedy, we hear this transition: *on a lighter note,* which implies that what we just heard was light and what we're going to hear is even lighter. After a tragedy, anything is lighter, including a lesser tragedy. After a bombing, a local anchor said,

> On a much lighter note. . . .

On a heavier note: Please weigh your words.

Speaking of strained segues—and *speaking of* is another type of transition to trash—this was broadcast on a New York City TV station: After an anchor described John Glenn (erroneously) as "the first man to orbit the Earth," his co-anchor said,

> And speaking of the Earth, the Earth has weather, and here's our weatherman.

Speaking of weathercasters, they, too, can chill me. A weatherman on another station said,

> we're sitting under a convective flow.

Huh? What's that? And a Los Angeles meteorologist reported

> a split flow in the 500-millibar chart.

Whatever that is. Made me think of splitting for Malabar. Or Malibu. But let's not use as a transition that old Monty Python line: "And now for something completely different."

▶ 6. Don't use nonbroadcast words.

A nonbroadcast word is one not readily understood by most listeners. A listener who's baffled by a word on a newscast isn't going to reach for a dictionary. How many listeners understand *infrastructure?* Or *draconian?* Or *byzantine?* How many *writers* do?

I remember a network anchor's asking me the meaning of *evanescent.* I knew, and I told him. But I didn't know whether he knew and was testing me or just was avoiding a trip to the dictionary. Maybe he figured that if I knew, everyone knew. So he went ahead and used *evanescent* in his newscast. What we write is indeed evanescent, *fleeting.* But *evanescent* is a nonbroadcast word. So is *vagaries.* How many listeners know what they are? Or confuse them with vagrants?

I won't give you a list of nonbroadcast words, but here are some warning signs: If you suspect that a word is a nonbroadcast word, you're probably right. If you've never run into the word before, never used it and never heard anyone else use it and if you have to look it up in the dictionary, it's probably a good word *not* to use. Some newswriters think that by slipping in a big word or an off-beat word they'll make a big impression. On whom? Their boss? Their audience? Well, they do make an impression—but it's unfavorable.

> *If you have to look it up in the dictionary, it's probably a good word not to use.*

▶ 7. Don't use hollow words.

Steer clear of hollow words. They just take up time, space and energy. In a word, they're nothing but padding. These extraneous words, when used in certain combinations, include *incident, activity, condition* and *situation.* Newscasters talk about "the shooting *incident*" when all they should say is "the shooting." (Incidentally, a shooting is hardly an incident. An incident is usually a minor event, such as a jostling on the bus.) Also, don't write about "the famine *situation.*" A famine is a famine. And everything is a situation. We're in one right now.

Some weathercasters refer to "thunderstorm *activity*" when they should say only "thunderstorms." They may say "the storm *condition*" will last several hours. That sentence, too, would be stronger if it were *unconditional;* just say "the storm." We hear weathercasters talk about the temperature reaching "the 45-degree *mark.*" By itself, *45 degrees* is enough. And "the temperature's falling to zero *degrees.*" Zero is on the thermometer, but zero is not a degree. Zero is zero.

Newscasters also talk about a trial that has been "one month *long.*" Better: "The trial has lasted a month." We hear about an attorney who needs *one month's time.* But we have no time for *time.* Some newscasters say, "The test will run for a three-month *period.*" Better: "The test will run three months." Period!

▶ 8. Don't use vague words.

One of the most popular is *involved.* When I hear that someone was involved in a crime, I don't know whether he committed the crime or was a victim. Or a witness. Whenever possible, be specific.

▶ 9. Don't use vogue words.

These buzzwords and fad words shouldn't find their way into your copy: *accessorize, arguable, high profile, icon, interactive, interface, meaningful, methodology, paradigm, parameters, parenting, prioritize, proactive, scenario, supportive, viable.*

▶ **10. Don't use weary words.**

A weary word is one that's exhausted from overuse. The first one that comes to mind, and it comes to many minds, is *controversy*. That's why so many newscasters refer to a *new controversy,* or to a *controversial* candidate, a *controversial* bill, a *controversial* plan, a *controversial* move, a *controversial* movie, a *controversial* action, a *controversial* faction. Almost everything is controversial. Even Santa Claus. Some people object to him because they regard Christmas as a sacred day, one not to be desecrated by Santa and his commercial ties.

So who or what is *not* controversial? Congress debates bills, people argue over candidates, objectors circulate petitions and pickets protest. Broadcast newswriters who want a strong word for a lead quickly may reach for *controversy* or *controversial* because they think it's the best and fastest way to go. But they don't realize that the more they use *controversy* and *controversial,* the less they mean.

▶ **11. Don't use weasel words.**

You may think you're being more solemn and respectful by saying someone *passed away.* Or *passed.* Or *passed on.* Or *succumbed.* No. Those euphemisms may be well intended, but they're wordy and indirect. So hereafter, when dealing with the hereafter, just let people *die.* And if you're tempted to use *expired,* perish the thought. Save *expired* for contracts and subscriptions.

▶ **12. Don't use windy words.**

Some newswriters use windy words to inflate their stories because they're not aware of simple synonyms. They use *commence* when they could say *start.* Maybe they think *start* is too common and that they ought to give their copy a touch of class. But there's no point in putting on airs. Windy words just slow down listeners' comprehension, add length to a story and dilute its impact.

Other highfalutin words that we hear too often: *utilize* instead of *use; implement* (verb) instead of *carry out* or *put into effect; implement* (noun) instead of *tool.* And please don't use *initiate,* unless you're writing about a fraternity. We have no need to say *approximately* when all we need is *about.* Mark Twain said, "I never write 'metropolis' for seven cents when I can get the same . . . for 'city.'"

▶ **13. Don't use wrong words.**

Make sure you know what a word means before you use it. The best way to make sure is to check a dictionary. One of the most frequently misused words in scripts is *dilemma*. It doesn't mean *problem, plight* or *predicament*. A *dilemma* is two alternatives that are equally undesirable.

The ten other most misused words, according to a *Los Angeles Times* survey: *egregious, enormity, fortuitous, hopefully, ironically, penultimate, portentous, presently, quintessential, unique*. Another word often misused is *heroics*. Dictionaries define *heroics* as "talk or behavior that is excessively dramatic and intended to seem heroic." So *heroics* shouldn't be confused with *heroism*.

Words we should steer clear of include *pled*, misused as the past tense of *plead*. The preferred form is *pleaded* (consult your *Associated Press Stylebook and Libel Manual*). And use the preferred past tense of *sink* (*sank*), *shrink* (*shrank*), *fit* (*fitted*), *broadcast* (*broadcast*), *dive* (*dived*) and dozens of other verbs. Watch out for regular *and* irregular verbs—and other irregularities.

And keep an eye out for words with contrary meanings, like *sanctions*. When newscasters say the United Nations "imposed sanctions," they mean "penalties." But in most dictionaries, the first definition of the noun *sanction* is permission or approval. The fourth or fifth definition, depending on your dictionary, is "a penalty." The verb *sanction* means "allow." So the use of *sanctions* in a script can leave listeners in a quandary.

Another word to watch out for is *depose*, which means "to remove from office or power." But *depose* also means "to take a deposition from." So if you write that an official was deposed, your sentence may be ambiguous; and an editor who sanctions ambiguity should be deposed.

Also watch out for sound-alikes, words that sound the same but have contrary meanings, like *raze*. To raze a building is to tear it down. But a listener hears *raise* and thinks a building is going up, not coming down. And "to *halve* pollution" is far different from "to *have* pollution."

▶ 14. Don't use foreign words and phrases.

Not everyone classified as literate is a prospective Ph.D. So writers should stick to English, the only language we require listeners to know. Most listeners don't read the *New Yorker* and don't work the *New York Times*'s crossword puzzles. And except for non-native English speakers, most of us don't use or hear foreign words in conversation. The people we're writing for are people who understand plain English. That doesn't include Olde English. So let's stick to everyday words. Every day.

I don't want to seem persnickety, but we should also avoid *per*. No, that's not a peremptory command. As with other tips, rules, pointers, principles or whatever you call them, I'm not saying, "Never, ever, under any circumstances whatsoever." All I'm saying is, whenever possible, avoid *per*.

Most experts oppose the use of *per* where *a* or other familiar words will do. For example, instead of writing "55 miles per hour," write "55 miles an hour." Instead of *per week, per pound,* write *a week, a pound.* And avoid *per se, per annum, per capita, per diem* and *per Deum*—unless you write with divine inspiration. Also avoid *amicus curiae, caveat emptor, en route, gratis, ipso facto, quid pro quo, status quo, via, vis-à-vis,* etc., especially *et cetera.* Avoid almost all other Latin words and terms. I say *almost* all because a few, such as *percent,* are so deeply rooted in our common speech that they are acceptable. *Percent* comes from the Latin *per centum,* meaning "by the hundred." But use *percent* only *after* a number. Not "A large *percent* of cooks were out of work." Rather "A large *percentage* of cooks were out of work."

A few Latin words may be acceptable *in extremis* when no English equivalent is available or when the Latin can be readily understood. The Latin term *in absentia* may be acceptable to report the case of a defendant who was sentenced when not present. At least, *absentia* sounds like *absence.* But I think it would be better to say, "He was sentenced although [he was] not present." Or "although he didn't show up." Another acceptable Latin term is *persona non grata,* the diplomatic term for someone declared unwelcome—not to be confused with *persona au gratin,* a diplomatic big cheese. Otherwise, foreign words are just not *apropos.*

The columnist Mike Royko once took a swipe at Americans who use foreign words: "Just as irritating as restaurants are books and magazines that slip French words in and expect us to understand them. That's why I gave up reading the *New Yorker,* which is one of the worst offenders. I don't know why that magazine does it. Half of all New Yorkers I've known can't speak understandable English, much less the language of the bwah and fwah."

Another language to steer clear of is the language of lawyers, exemplified by *therefore* and *nevertheless.* No need for a newswriter to use any of them. Here are the basic English equivalents: *therefore* = so; *nevertheless* = even so; *notwithstanding* = despite. Also, skip *however.* Instead, use *though, yet, still* or, most often, *but.*

▶ **15. Don't use clichés.**

One cliché is not worth 10,000 pictures. A cliché usually brings to mind a lazy or weary writer. So much copy is clotted with clichés it curdles the mind. A Los Angeles TV newswoman reported that an executive was confident that the movie industry, stung by an investigation, would get a

clean bill of health.

I'd like to see one of those bills of health, clean or soiled. And I'd like to see one of those "bargaining tables" I hear about so much. Or a "bargaining chip." Or even a bargain.

A New York City TV reporter, covering a double murder, said,

The police have their work cut out for them.

Made me wonder whether the victims had been dismembered. Another reporter said three fugitives had everyone on

pins and needles.

That script should have been spiked.

Often, when a blackout, blizzard, flood or shutdown hits a community, a newscaster says residents are "taking it in stride." I've never heard that anyone is *not* taking it in stride.

A network newsman keeps calling gold "the yellow metal" and silver "the gray metal." But 1 haven't heard him call copper "the red metal" or U.S. currency "the green paper." Yet.

Another cliché: *met behind closed doors.* As in, "The president and his national security adviser *met behind closed doors.*" Where else would they meet? On a bench in Lafayette Park? Some writers even have people *huddling behind closed doors.* If the secrecy of a meeting is unusual or significant and worth mentioning, you can say, "The committee met in closed session." Or "met in secret." Or "met privately." But don't let people *huddle* unless there are 11 of them and one is a quarterback.

Avoid—almost all the time—song titles and lyrics.

Also objectionable in news scripts are catchphrases lifted from commercials: "As for your umbrella, don't leave home without it." My advice: Don't reach out and touch any of them. And avoid—almost all the time—song titles and lyrics. How many times have you heard this lead-in to a voice-over, "It rained on the city's parade . . ."? How many times have you written that?

The most cliché-clotted copy I've ever heard on the air:

[A candidate] dropped the other shoe today and threw his hat into the ring for president, and now it's a whole new ball game.

As Shakespeare put it, "They have been at a great feast of languages, and stolen the scraps."

When it comes to scrapping clichés, experts disagree. Several experts say some clichés have *a saving grace.* In *The Careful Writer,*

Theodore M. Bernstein of the *New York Times* said, Use a cliché "only with discrimination and sophistication and . . . shun it when it is a substitute for precise thinking."

But many other writing experts say clichés cause air pollution. For them, all clichés are *dead as a doornail.* The columnist Colman McCarthy told how, as a college English major, his required reading list was crushing. He adopted a method suggested by the writer John Ciardi: "Read a writer's essay, poem, story or column until the first cliché. At that collision, stop. Then drop."

The grampa of good grammar, Henry W. Fowler, also condemned clichés. But he said writers would be needlessly handicapped if they were *never* allowed to use, among others, *white elephant, feathering his nest, had his tongue in his cheek.* In *Modern English Usage,* he observed, "What is new is not necessarily better than what is old; the original felicity that has made a phrase a cliché may not be beyond recapture." (As George Burns put it, "If you stay around long enough, you become new.")

▶ 16. Don't substitute synonyms for words that are easily understood.

Many writers dread using the same word twice in a 20-second story, not to mention twice in one sentence. Perhaps they fear that someone in charge might think that using *said* twice in a story indicates an anemic vocabulary. So they figure the best way to dispel any such notion is to find a different word for *said.* But in writing broadcast news, the best verb to express oral communication usually is *said* (or *says*).

Says—along with *said*—is part of natural speech. You tell a friend, "Jim says he's going to lunch early." You don't say, "Jim stated—or commented, or observed, or announced, or related, or remarked, or any of dozens of other verbs of utterance—that he's going to lunch early." The word *says* has been compared to a skillful stagehand: he does his work well, moves the show along and stays out of sight.

Some synonyms for *said* cause copy to be either stilted or tilted. Copy that sidesteps *said* is stilted when it uses *stated* or *declared.* Those two verbs are best reserved for formal statements or declarations. And copy may be tilted when, as a synonym for *said,* the writer uses a verb that might reflect on the person who was doing the saying or call into question his veracity: *admit* ("He admitted having a car"), *claim* ("He claims he wrote the book himself"). Other verbs that should be used with caution: *insist, maintain, complain, concede.*

Several other verbs are often used as the equivalent of *say,* but they don't have the same meaning. One is *explain,* as in, "He explained that the

Bulls won." That's hardly an explanation. *Explain* should be reserved for explanations. *Explain* is not to be used as Ring Lardner did in *You Know Me, Al:* "'Shut up,' he explained."

Point out is another verb that shouldn't be substituted for *say*. Save *point out* for pointing to facts, not assertions that may or may not be true. It's wrong to write, "He pointed out that his contract is still valid." He says it is. But maybe it isn't. A correct use for *point out:* "He pointed out that the largest state is Alaska."

Laugh is also used incorrectly as a synonym for *say*. "She *laughed* that losing isn't everything." People do laugh, but they don't laugh words. Better: "She said with a laugh that she would try again" or "She laughed and said she'd try again." And don't let anyone *chirp* even if you're quoting a jailbird who has turned canary.

Another problem crops up when a writer uses *said* before mentioning the person who's doing the saying: "Said one official: The mayor is disheartened by the outcome. . . ." The writer might have been trying for a change of pace or what he thought was streamlining. But by placing *said* before the subject, he's transgressing against the fixed word order of the normal sentence and violating conversational style. People don't talk like that. They don't tell a friend, "Said the magazine renewal letter: '*Time* is running out.'" It's unnatural. Says who? Says me.

But don't just take it on my say-so; listen carefully to what people say and how they say it. Wolcott Gibbs of the *New Yorker* once wrote a profile of *Time*'s co-founder, Henry Luce, and parodied *Time*-style of yore. It often ran counter to standard English: "Backward ran sentences until reeled the mind. . . . Sitting pretty are the boys. . . . Where it will all end, knows God!"

Enough *said*?

Some writers who shy away from short words or avoid using a simple word more than once in a story look for what's called an "elegant variation." If they were writing about bananas, they would, on second reference, talk about "elongated yellow fruit." It's easier for a listener if we use *banana* twice in 20 seconds. Or even three times. Just don't slip on an appealing variation.

▶ **17. Don't hotrod.**

Hotrodding is high-powered writing. Hotrodders pepper their copy with words like *special, major, important, extra, crisis, unique, unprecedented.* In some stories, those words may be apt. But everything can't be special. "Where everybody is somebody," Sir William S. Gilbert wrote, "nobody is anybody."

Hotrodders exaggerate a spat between two public officials into a *clash.* The officials *lash out* at each other. When the two officials meet, it's at a *summit.* Or it becomes a *confrontation* or *showdown.* When an official announces a drive or a campaign against almost anything, it becomes a *war.* So we have a *war* against crime, a *war* against drugs, a *war* against illiteracy, a *war* against pornography, a *war* against scofflaws. After being bombarded by all these *wars,* listeners lose their understanding of war. So far, I haven't heard of a *war* against potholes. Or crabgrass. But at this very moment a newscaster in West Overshoe may be preparing to launch another such war.

When hotrodders write about experts, the experts are described as *respected.* Awards are *prestigious.* Fads or trends become *revolutions,* disclosures *shockers,* increased costs *astronomical* (because they've *skyrocketed*). Two other popular words in the lexicon of hotrodders: *mystery* and *mysterious.* When I was a newspaper cub (an inkling), I learned that rewritemen used those words when they were short on facts and long on fancy.

No discussion of hotrodding can ignore *spectacular.* Broadcasters often apply it to fires or to fire footage (and they're not all fire buffs—or firebugs). Hotrodding sportscasters apply *spectacular* to a baseball player's catch, a football player's run, a tennis player's serve or a golfer's drive, not to mention the Amalfi Drive. In fact, *spectacular* seems to be an all-purpose adjective, one that some writers use whenever they can't think of anything else to try to hold their audience.

One way to avoid hotrodding is not to write on a hypewriter. We want our copy to be calm, clean, clear and crisp, true and trustworthy. And free from all sin.

Top Tips of the Trade

40 pointers that lead to better scripts

ow that we've looked at the Don'ts, let's look at the Do's. Even among the Do's are a few tips that reinforce the Don'ts.

I call these the Top Tips of the Trade. And no matter what you call them—tips, pointers, principles, reminders, guidelines or rules—they'll help you develop as a writer, not just improve your scripts. Also, they'll help your listeners.

▶ **1. Write the way you talk.**

The two basic rules in writing news for broadcast:

Rule 1: Write the way you talk.

Rule 2: Never forget rule 1.

If you don't talk the way a good writer should, perhaps you should become a Trappist (and shut your trap).

No one writes exactly the way he talks or talks the way he writes. Writing for broadcast is a compromise. Keep in mind that you're writing for people who can't read your script. They only hear it. And they hear it only once. One way to make sure they get it the first time around—and they get only one crack at it—is to use workaday words and phrasing.

No need to stoop to the style of Dick and Jane. But you should write in a straightforward, linear fashion—without detours or zigzags—so that ordinary listeners can grasp your script word by word, word for word, word after word. It is unswerving directness—along with your adherence to rules—that enables listeners to follow the thread of your story.

When you're writing, don't think about telling *all* those people out there. Don't write your script for legions of listeners. Write as if you're telling *one* listener. Think of a friend sitting in your den (if you have a den *and* a friend). Or think of a friend on the phone. Or tell it the way you'd like to have someone tell it to you. The skills you bring into play at this point are selecting, summarizing and storytelling. Always remember that you're writing for the ear, not the eye. And remember, too: "Think listeners, not readers."

You're writing for the ear, not the eye.

▶ **2. Start strong. Well begun is half done.**

The most important words you'll write in a story are those that come first—what Mitchell Stephens calls in *Broadcast News* "the lead's lead." Bear down on your first sentence. "Start strong" doesn't mean make the story stronger than the facts warrant, and it doesn't mean to distort, exaggerate or misrepresent. It means to put all your mental power into the start. Your first words may determine whether your listeners keep listening. So focus on your first words and your first sentence. If you set sail with even a small compass error, and if it's uncorrected, you can wind up way off course, even on the rocks or at the bottom. As Euripides once told me, a bad beginning makes a bad ending.

TO GRASP THE STORY

▶ **3. Read—and understand—your source copy.**

Read it to the end. Carefully. Don't write a script after reading only two or three paragraphs of the source copy. If you don't understand something, don't use it. Because, if *you* don't understand it, how can you write it so that your listeners will understand?

Too many writers lift words and phrases from source copy and transplant them into their own copy without knowing what they mean. When an editor or producer asks what something in the script means, many a writer replies, "Well, that's what the wire copy says." Don't be a copycat.

▶ **4. Mark key facts.**

By marking your source copy—preferably with a red or orange pen—you'll see instantly what's important and what you should consider including in your script. This can help you boil down the important and interesting to the essential. Your markings will also help you check the facts in your completed script against your source material. You can make your marks by circling, underlining or highlighting.

As you develop your news judgment, you'll do a better job deciding which facts to use and in which order. And which facts to omit. The more you learn about what makes news, the better you'll be able to write news. So it helps to ponder the question, "What is news?" One of the best answers is provided by an authority on journalism, Melvin Mencher. He says, "Most news stories are about events that (1) have an *impact* on many people, (2) describe *unusual* or exceptional situations or events or (3) are about widely known or *prominent* people." In *Basic News Writing* (6th ed.), he goes on to say that other elements, including *conflict, proximity* and *timeliness,* heighten the news value of an event. "Boiled down to its essentials," Mencher says, "every story is about either a *person* who has said or done something important or interesting or a *person* to whom something important or interesting has happened." Or the story is about "an *event* of importance or interest to many people."

▶ 5. Tell it in *your* words.

When a wire story has a clever play on words, or an unusual combination of words, avoid borrowing that language. Why? Because if we do borrow, a listener who recalls hearing those same words in the same order on an earlier newscast on another station may say, "So that's where that guy gets his news!"

Even though some broadcast wires are supposed to be written for the ear to accommodate broadcasters, the quality of the copy is uneven. Not all of it is written by people who are adept or experienced. Why parrot what *any* writer has said? Aren't you a better writer? Or trying to be one? We should rewrite source copy and use our own words and phrasing.

▶ 6. Think. Don't write yet. Think.

Don't do something; just sit there! Allow time for incubation and meditation. Even if you're fighting the clock, you may be able to take as much as 30 *seconds* to think. And if you're working on a script for tomorrow, you can afford more than that.

I had a producer who'd snap: "Write. Don't think." Wrong message. Think what the story is all about; think what the heart of the news is; think of the best way to tell it. Think.

▶ 7. Translate the journalese.

Our source copy doesn't always play by our rules. Wire copy generally crams the Five W's—*Who, What, When, Where* and *Why*—and *How* into the first paragraph or two. And for good reason: when a newspaper sets a story in type and it's too long for the allotted space on the page layout, an editor is most likely to trim from the bottom, often lopping off entire paragraphs.

We broadcast writers don't usually have room for the Five W's and How. We ignore the inverted pyramid. But we can't ignore the flaws of some wire copy written in wirese or journalese. *Journalese* is defined in *Webster's Unabridged Dictionary* (2nd ed.), as "writing marked by triteness, oversimplification, verbal distortion, unwarranted exaggeration, and coloring for persuasive or sensational effect."

Journalese is a quaint tongue we have to translate into English while we write. As newspaper style developed over the centuries, it deviated further and further from the way people speak. People who read newspapers can give them their full attention. They read whatever they wish and at their own speed. And they can reread and mull over whatever interests them. Listeners can't do that with broadcast stories, so we must adjust our language to allow for the peculiarities of listeners' hearing apparatus, which processes information slowly. That's why we must make our copy simple and direct.

An approach for this kind of lean, clean, clear writing is described by Strunk and White: "Vigorous writing is concise. A sentence should contain no unnecessary words, a paragraph no unnecessary sentences, for the same reason that a drawing should have no unnecessary lines and a machine no unnecessary parts. This requires not that the writer make all his sentences short, or that he avoid all detail and treat his subjects only in outline, but that every word tell."

Set your mental processor to adjust every sentence until it conforms with broadcast rules. Writers who have mastered the rules know that rules help make their writing work. Yet, the ultimate test for any kind of writing isn't whether it follows the rules but whether it works.

▶ 8. Develop the courage—and the competence and the confidence—to write simply.

How simply? Don't worry, we're not writing for simpletons. But we are writing for a general audience, comprising listeners at all levels of interest, knowledge and brainpower. Which means we would do well to heed the advice of Edward R. Murrow. During World War II, he reported from Europe and directed the CBS News staff there. He told them: "Imagine yourself at a dinner table back in the United States, with a local editor, a banker, and a professor, talking over the coffee. You try to tell what it was like, while the maid's boyfriend, a truck driver, listens from the kitchen. Talk to be understood by the truck driver while not insulting the professor's intelligence."

DEVELOPING THE SCRIPT

▶ **9. Avoid wordy warm-ups.**

Get to the point. But what if you don't get the point or don't even see the point? If you've read the source copy, marked it, thought it through and are still stumped, put your source copy face down and tell the story to your keyboard in your own words. If you do that without glancing at the source copy, you'll probably confine yourself to the highlights, which is just what you're supposed to do. Don't fret about producing perfect copy; just get it down in rough form. You may not be sure what you want to say until you see what you've said. Read your script and reread it. Delete any unnecessary words. If you don't need to keep them in, you do need to keep them out.

If that approach doesn't work, pretend you're telling the story to a friend by phone. Let's say your friend is out of town and you're in a hurry. You wouldn't rattle on. You wouldn't digress or say any more than it takes for your friend to get the gist. You'd tell your story hurriedly, and you'd hit only the high points. You wouldn't talk in the curt style of a nine-word telegram (isn't the tenth word usually *Love*?). You'd speak in a conversational style. Once you've deleted the unnecessary words, you'll have your lead. Or at least a good framework for your script.

If you find that that doesn't do the trick, try to visualize tomorrow morning's newspaper and its front page: How would the banner stretching across the top of the page capsulize the story? Which few words would a headline writer choose to condense a complex event? When you put your mind to it, you can often get a handle on a story that way.

When I'm stumped in deciding what a story is all about, I use the technique I just laid out: I try to picture the front page of tomorrow morning's newspaper. Some newswriters begin by shutting their eyes; some stare into space, as if they expect to

WORDWATCHER

PRINT   *Fifty people are dead in the explosion of a gas tank in Hackville.*

BROADCAST   *A gas tank in Hackville blew up today and killed 50 people.*

As soon as you say, "Fifty people *are* dead," the story starts sliding downhill. *Are* is weak, as is any form of *to be; explosion* obscures *explodes;* and the place name is mentioned last, so the listener doesn't have the slightest idea where the explosion happened until the end of the sentence.

For broadcast writers, it's best to set the scene first and tell what happened. The second and third sentences of a script usually answer questions raised by the first—How many people were hurt? What caused the explosion? Any homes damaged?—and the fourth sentence (if your story runs that long) answers anything unanswered. Ideally, your sentences hold hands: they flow smoothly and seamlessly. And listeners aren't aware of your hard work and careful construction.

see cue cards; some hop right to it and bat out a story one, two, three. Some imagine the event in their mind's eye. The mind's eye can see plenty: from a nuclear explosion to a sunset in Sarasota. The best way is the one that works for you. If you haven't found your way, keep at it anyway.

▶ **10. Put attribution before assertion.**

This is one hard-and-fast rule a writer mustn't play fast and loose with. If you're sure your information is factual, you may be able to go ahead without using attribution. Or at least you may defer identifying the source. But if you're writing a story that seems iffy, or at least not solid, let your listeners know who's behind those assertions at the outset. We don't usually attribute stories to wire services because, in a sense, they work for our news department.

If a wire service moves a big story that seems improbable, a network will try to pin it down. If a networker cannot verify it and the story is too big to ignore, a newscaster may start the story this way: "The Associated Press says the Chief Justice of the United States is going to undergo a sex change." (The title is not "Chief Justice of the U.S. Supreme Court.") If the story were less startling, or less unlikely, the broadcaster might delay identifying the source but would make it clear that the information is not in the realm of established fact: "The Chief Justice of the United States *reportedly* plans to retire soon." The next sentence would justify *reportedly* by linking it to the people doing the reporting: "The Associated Press also reports he's going to move to Hawaii. The AP says the Chief Justice has told associates he wants to. . . ."

That's the same way we handle big stories broken by newspapers: "The Chief Justice of the United States reportedly is going to enter a monastery. The *New York Times* also reports he plans to. . . ." No responsible news organization wants to say, on its own authority, with no confirmation: "The Chief Justice of the United States is entering a monastery." Nor is it good enough to start by telling about the Chief's impending departure and then saying, "That's what the *New York Times* reports today." Not good enough because you've presented the departure as fact, then told the listener, in effect, it may not be a fact.

An offense against good judgment occurs when the newscaster presents a shocking assertion in a way that implies it represents the newscaster's fact-finding or thinking: "Good evening. The United States should bomb Moscow back to the Stone Age." The second sentence then pulls the rug out from under the opening: "That's the opinion of Councilman Tom Troy." The opinion of a councilman? Listeners should know up front who's doing the saying so they know how much weight to give the opinion. And so they don't assume the anchor himself is sounding off. All of which underlies an immutable—and oft-repeated—basic of broadcast newswriting: Attribution precedes assertion.

▶ 11. Humanize your copy.

Write about *people*, not about *personnel*. Whoever wrote this wire-service story should be reported to the Missing People's Bureau:

> Tribal factions angered over a beer hall dispute fought with sticks and iron bars Sunday at Kloof gold mine west of Johannesburg, killing seven black miners and badly injuring 39, police said.

For use on the air, this wire story needs major surgery. *Faction* is an abstraction. Listeners can't see factions; but they can see people. So we should talk about people: blacks, or black miners, or black tribesmen—but not about factions. And we don't hang attribution on the end.

Another type of story that often needs humanizing is a statistical release. Instead of writing about "a decline in births," we should, when possible, write about "fewer babies." Instead of writing about "unemployment," we should, when

Write about people, not about personnel.

time and context permit, talk about "people out of work." Instead of talking about "deaths," we should, where appropriate, write about "*people* killed" or "*people* who died." People want to hear about *people*. Abstractions don't breathe—or bleed. Besides humanizing stories, we should also be on the alert to localize them. Bring a national story down to a local level by way of its local effects.

▶ 12. Activate your copy. Use action verbs and active voice.

If your copy lies there limply, give it some get-up-and-go with verbs that move. When you write in the active voice, the subject of the sentence acts. The passive voice is weak because the subject of the sentence doesn't act but is acted upon. Use of the passive conceals the actor: "Mistakes were made." And "A cherry tree was chopped down."

Another fault: Besides concealing the actor (also known as the doer or agent), the passive voice is wordy. And dull. In some cases, though, the passive may be better: "Mayor Byrd was hit by an egg. . . ." You wouldn't write, "An egg hit Mayor Byrd" or "A protester threw an egg that hit Mayor Byrd."

> *Join the action faction. Avoid the passive.*

I won't say, as a passivist would, "The passive is to be avoided." Nor will I say passively, "Action must be taken." But as an activist, I do say, "Join the action faction. Avoid the passive." Act now.

▶ 13. Use familiar words in familiar combinations.

Using familiar words is not enough. You have to use them in ways that listeners are accustomed to hearing. A broadcaster said,

The economy shows growth signs.

All good, plain words—but. But we don't talk that way. And, I hope, we don't write that way. We'd say straight out, "The economy shows signs of growth."

▶ 14. Omit needless words.

Thank you, Strunk and White. Rid your copy of most *that*s, *which*es, *who ise*s, *of*s and other space-eaters. As you read your script, you may spot a few of them sneaking in. In most cases, they can be deleted with no loss of meaning—and with a gain in clarity. Needless words lengthen your sentences and force your listeners to work to extract the substance. The fewer (but well-chosen) words you use to tell a story, the clearer and more forceful the story.

The importance of examining the need for every word is pointed up by Harold Evans in *Newsman's English:* A London fishmonger had a sign that said: FRESH FISH SOLD HERE. A friend persuaded him to rub out the word FRESH; he wasn't expected to sell fish that wasn't fresh. Then the friend persuaded him to rub out HERE; he's selling the fish, naturally, in his shop. Then the friend urged him to rub out SOLD; he isn't expected to give it away. Finally, the friend persuaded him to rub out FISH; you can smell it a mile off.

▶ 15. Go with S-V-O: subject-verb-object.

Start your lead with the subject, go straight to the verb, then the object. That's the standard pattern of sentences for people who speak English. The closer the verb follows the subject, the easier for the listener to follow. Yes, I've said that before, and I reserve the right to say it again.

Avoid subordinate clauses. In rereading your script, if you find a subordinate clause that contains essential information, give it a sentence of its own. Or parcel out that information in other sentences.

▶ 16. Limit a sentence to one idea.

This makes it easier for listeners to understand a story they can't read, let alone reread. By limiting a sentence to one idea, the writer serves listeners by uncomplicating stories—by simplifying (but not oversimplifying) them, by reducing difficult, complex stories to their crux.

▶ 17. Think small. Use short words and short sentences.

The words that people use most frequently tend to be short. We don't want to lapse into baby talk, but we do want to make ourselves understood by people who may be only half-listening, people who may be listening amid distractions, people on the go, people who have a lot on their minds, people who have no opportunity to check your script, people who can't rip out your story and go over it at their leisure—or ask you what you mean. People are accustomed to hearing words the same way they absorb them in an ordinary conversation, in a linear fashion and they are best able to understand them that way: short words in short sentences. People are more comfortable with short words. That's why some big words have been bobbed: "telephone" (*phone*), "airplane" (*plane*), "parachute" (*chute*), "automobile" (*auto* or *car*), "refrigerator" (*fridge*), "television" (*TV*), "air conditioning" (*AC* or *air*).

▶ 18. Avoid *may, might, could, should, seems.*

They, too, are linking verbs, but they're even wimpier than *is:* they wobble. And they waffle. They don't say anything for sure. Whenever possible, make a definite statement, not one that has the ring of *maybe yes, maybe no.* Can you imagine a strong script that starts with a sentence riding on *seems?* That's even weaker than *is.* At least, *is* says something is. *Seems* says only that it *may* be. So another word to avoid in a lead is *may.* Even softer is the verb *might,* which in the present tense (*might* is also the past tense of *may*) indicates a possibility that is even less likely than *may.*

   If the facts of a story suggest that something *may* occur, think through the lead carefully to find a way to say something definite. Instead of "The space shuttle *Pegasus* may finally get off the ground today," I'd say, "The space shuttle *Pegasus* will try again today to get off the ground." The second lead may be only marginally better, but it has more strength than *may,* which carries the burden of an implicit *may not.*

▶ 19. Put your sentences in a positive form.

Try to avoid *not* and *no.* That old song says it best: "Accentuate the positive, eliminate the negative, latch on to the affirmative, don't mess with Mister In-Between."

▶ **20. Use present tense verbs where justifiable.**

The verb that can be used most often in the present tense is *say.* You may even be able to use the present tense throughout your story. In the second or third sentence, you can shift to the past tense. Example: "Governor Smiley says he's going to visit China. His goal, he says, is to push for business for the state's farms and factories. The governor told a dinner audience in Middletown tonight that he plans to leave next month." *Note:* In the second sentence, the attribution is delayed. That's all right because the first sentence led with attribution. It is allowable to defer attribution until after the first few words; but it's definitely a no-no to defer attribution until the end of any sentence.

A newspaper or wire service reporter might end a sentence with "the governor said" or "according to the governor." People don't talk like that, and we broadcasters don't write like that. The second sentence in that example does need attribution because we don't really know what his true goal is; it may be no more than a free vacation.

▶ **21. Use *and, also, but, so, because* to link sentences.**

Connectives join sentences and allow listeners to see how they're tied together in one fabric. Using connectives makes it easier to follow the thread.

No matter what your eighth grade teacher might have told you, feel free to start a sentence with a connective. Example: "Mayor Collins was indicted today. A grand jury charged him with grand larceny—stealing more than 10-thousand dollars from petty cash. Because of the indictment, the mayor said, he's taking indefinite leave." *Because* connects that sentence to the one before. And *indictment* also helps the listener even though *indicted* was used in the first sentence.

Use possessives—*his, her, its, their*—to tie sentences and facts together. Instead of talking about "*the* car" make it "*her* car." If you think listeners could have any doubt about who *he, she* or *it* refers to, don't hesitate to repeat the name or noun. Problem: "The car crashed into a home, and *its* roof caved in." The antecedent of *its* is *home,* but some listeners might take it to mean that it was the *car* whose roof caved in. To remove all doubt, delete *its* and substitute *the home's.* Although we have to be frugal in using words, don't hesitate to repeat a word to make sure a sentence is clear. You must write not only so that you can be understood but also so that you can't be misunderstood.

▶ **22. Try to put the word or words you want to emphasize at the end of your sentence.**

A periodic sentence creates tension, interest and emphasis as it goes along by placing the most important word or words at the end. So don't take the edge off by ending a sentence with weak, incidental or irrelevant words.

One expert says books about writing have not given the element of emphasis enough emphasis. According to Theodore A. Rees Cheney in *Getting the Words Right,* "A word or idea gains emphasis (and is therefore remembered) if it is positioned right before the period that ends the sentence...." The type of construction suggested by Cheney builds tension and suspense by saving its impact or meaning until the end. F.L. Lucas writes in *Style:* "The most emphatic place in clause or sentence is the end. This is the climax; and during the momentary pause that follows, that last word continues, as it were, to reverberate.... It has, in fact, the last word."

In *The Elements of Style,* Strunk and White also tell us how to deal with emphasis: "The proper place in the sentence for the word or group of words that the writer desires to make most prominent is usually the end."

And David Lambuth says in *The Golden Book on Writing:* "Unless you have good reason for doing otherwise, put your most important word or phrase at the end of the sentence. The most important word is usually a substantive [a word or group of words having the same function as a noun] or verb. Don't sacrifice the strategic final position to a preposition or even to an adverb, unless it really is the most significant word—which it sometimes is. The well-known advice against ending a sentence with a preposition is valid only [with] unimportant prepositions. In certain cases, a preposition is the most emphatic word to end a sentence with."

In contrast to the periodic sentence, the cumulative (or loose) sentence makes a statement and keeps on going, adding subordinate elements, like modifiers, clauses and phrases, as it rolls all over the place, which is what this sentence is doing before your very eyes, accumulating more add-ons. It could have ended after any of the last few commas.

"There is a slackness to a loose sentence, a lack of tension," Thomas Whissen says in *A Way With Words.* He calls it comfortable and easy to write. But he observes, "There is no real build-up, no anticipation, no excitement."

One of the benefits of the periodic sentence is that it builds up to the main point. Unlike the loose sentence, it doesn't make its point and then run downhill. As Lambuth writes, "Build *up* to your big idea, not *down* from it."

Most sentences in newspapers and wire copy are loose. And most of us, when chatting, use loose sentences. If we had time to think through our thoughts thoroughly, we'd use far more periodic sentences. They carry the most impact and are the most *rememberable.*

▶ **23. Place the time element, if you need one, *after* the verb.**

The listener who turns on your newscast tonight has every reason to believe that all your stories are today's news, not yesterday's. What will catch the listener's ear and prompt him to keep listening is an action verb, not a *today* or a *tonight.* And please don't use a phony *tonight.* **It's wrong to say something happened *tonight* when the story broke four hours earlier.**

▶ **24. Use contractions—but cautiously.**

> ## A common
> ## hazard is can't.

Although contractions are conversational and time savers, some contractions can cause confusion. The most common hazard is *can't.* Even careful listeners—and careful listeners are not plentiful—can miss the final *t;* they think they heard *can,* which is contrary to what the script is trying to stress: *cannot.* We risk misleading listeners when we use a negative contraction, if loss of the final letter(s) leaves the positive form of the verb reverberating.

Some contractions are safe to use: among them, *don't* and *won't.* If a listener misses the final *t,* he's not going to mistake *don't* for *do.*

▶ **25. Pep up your copy with words like *new, now, but, says.***

Not only does *new* signal listeners that they're hearing news, but it can also compress a mouthful into one short word. Instead of writing, "The government issued a report today that says . . . ," we can start speedily, "A *new* government report says. . . ."

Now has two good uses: it can show that an event is going on at this very moment, or it can indicate a reversal in course. For example: "Sheriff Gooch is now on his way to the district attorney's office." The *now* makes the sentence more vivid, more current, more newsy. And *now* is also effective in pointing up a change: "Sheriff Gooch has denied he knew of. . . . But *now* he says. . . ."

▶ **26. Watch out for *I, we, our, here, out, up, down.***

When *I* is used in a direct quotation in a story, it's open to misunderstanding: "The mayor said, 'I need to take off weight.'" The listener has good reason to believe the mayor is referring to the anchor. So paraphrase: "The mayor said he needs to take off weight." Use as few quotations as possible. Say it in your own words. Paraphrase.

I'm also puzzled when a newscaster uses *we.* Is the newscaster using *we* to avoid *I?* When she says *we,* is she referring to her newsroom, her community or what? *Our* is too possessive unless you're writing about something that is yours, something that belongs to you or your station. Avoid "*our* troops" unless your station maintains its own militia. As newspeople, we report from the sidelines, not as partisans or participants.

Here should almost always be deleted from copy. *Here* causes the listener to wonder whether the speaker means "here in our newsroom" or "here in our town." Newscasters also start stories like this: "*Here* in Hicksville. . . ." Hicksvilleans know they're in Hicksville. They don't need to be reminded.

Up and *down,* as directions, are often objectionable for similar reasons. In conversation, when talking about the town to our north, we'd say "*up* in Hangtown." When writing for broadcast, don't say "*up* in Hangtown." For folks north of Hangtown, Hangtown is *down.* Another adverb to watch for is *out,* as in "*Out* in Far Corners." People out there regard themselves as insiders. In their worldview, every other place is *out.*

▶ **27. Hit only the main points; trash the trivia.**

Just because the wires carry something doesn't mean we need to use it. Some wire service reporters write long because they haven't learned to write short. Some write long because newspaper clients have plenty of space to fill. And some papers with news holes shovel in wire copy by the yard.

Broadcast newswriters must be highly selective. The minutiae that a newspaper or magazine might print are, for us, useless. Be sure every word you use is essential and nothing is superfluous. Whatever you say, say it only once. Life's too short for repetition—except for my suggestions.

▶ **28. Don't raise questions you don't answer.**

Don't insert a fact that cries out for clarification. A local script about a fire in a trailer park said a man was killed in a trailer "where he lived with a companion." But the script didn't tell listeners whether the companion survived, nor whether the companion was a colleen or a collie.

WRITING RIGHT AND RIGHTING THE WRITER

▶ **29. Read your copy aloud. If it sounds like writing, rewrite it.**

What counts is not how it looks but how it sounds. If it sounds unconversational (as if written for the eye), rewrite it. When you read it aloud, you can also catch any unfortunate combination of words. For example: a BBC news reader or presenter (as the Beeb calls anchors) said—so the story goes—that, in a golf match, Lord Hampton "had been playing a round" with Lady Fairfax. If the writer had read his script aloud, he might have caught that double meaning. I'm not saying a writer should have a dirty mind, but it sure helps. It also helps to have a mind that's nimble enough to catch a single word that seems safe on paper but can cause trouble. For example: *query.* You may never be tempted to use *dastard,* but be careful of *duck, funk, shift, finger, morass, Uranus* and *horticulture.*

The network broadcaster who wrote the following news item should also have listened to his script:

> An Interior Department report on Teton Dam is still pending. So are Congressional studies of the Bureau of Reclamation and other dam-building agencies.

The writer should have caught *dam-building agencies.* The listener can't see the hyphen, so the phrase sounds like a curse. If you read your script aloud to yourself before turning it in, you'll catch innocent combinations of words that sound damning.

▶ **30. Rewrite. The art of writing lies in rewriting what you've already rewritten.**

Check all names, dates, amounts and facts with the source copy. Take time—and make time—to give your script a good going-over. Is every word necessary? If it's not necessary to put it in, it *is* necessary to keep it out.

After you get rid of any clutter and trim the flab, ask yourself: Are the words right? And in the right order? And does it read right? Also: Is every bit of information right? Accuracy is imperative. As one news agency used to say, "Get it first, but first get it right." (The agency had trouble getting it either way—and went the way of all flash.)

Spare time is scarce in newsrooms, particularly as air time approaches. When you get to work, go to work. If you skip the chitchat and bear down on writing, maybe you can save enough time to rewrite your copy. And then re-rewrite it. The importance of rewriting is illustrated in George Plimpton's interview with Hemingway for the *Paris Review.* Plimpton was the editor of the quarterly literary journal. And Hemingway was, well, Hemingway, an author who spoke earnestly.

Plimpton: How much rewriting do you do?

Hemingway: It depends. I rewrote the ending of *Farewell to Arms,* the last page of it, 39 times before I was satisfied.

Plimpton: Was there some technical problem there? What was it that had stumped you?

Hemingway: Getting the words right.

GETTING THE WORDS RIGHT! Broadcast newswriters don't have the time Hemingway had. We write in haste and can't revise at leisure. But if we're working on a piece that doesn't need to go on the next newscast today, we can let our script sit overnight and cool off. The next day, having forgotten the precise wording, we can read our script as if

> *Listeners don't need a perfect lead, or even a great lead. Just a good lead.*

it's new and written by someone else. We can go over the script energetically and enthusiastically. With fresh eyes and refreshed mind. Maybe this time, after another rewrite or two, we'll get the words right.

The perfect is the enemy of the good. The writing coach Don Fry sees it like this: Listeners don't need a perfect lead, or even a great lead. Just a good lead.

▶ 31. When in doubt, leave it out.

Go with what you know. Just before air time, when we handle so much copy, we probably can't find answers to all our questions about the source material, or resolve ambiguities, or reconcile discrepancies. Yet, we can't assume. Or speculate. We deal only in facts, not in conjecture. The wires are not infallible. Their stories are gathered, written and edited not by superhumans but by imperfect humans like us. (Isn't *that* a scary thought!)

▶ 32. Rewrite a release.

You must be even more careful if your source copy is a press release. Wire service stories are written by newspeople who work for news agencies; in effect, they work for us. They're hired for their journalistic skills, and they're trained to report objectively. Press agents aren't journalists. They're not disinterested parties, and they don't work for us; they work for someone else.

Whether they call themselves press agents, press information officers or public relations managers, they still work for private parties. And, as the adage has it, "Who pays the piper calls the tune." The press releases they write, which they often label *news* releases, are written for the benefit of their private interests. Sometimes we find a release worth using. But that release may or may not be accurate. It may or may not be complete. It may or may not be fair. It may or may not be true.

If you decide to use a press release or a part of one, rewrite it. But first, make sure that the person named as the sender did in fact send it and that it's not a hoax. Even if it's not a hoax, remember that the release comes from someone who is, in effect, a salesperson, trying to "sell" you a story, one written to advance her interests, not yours.

If you doubt any key points in the release, pick up your phone and verify them on your own. If you can't verify them but decide to go ahead anyway, be sure to attribute them to someone named in the release. Many press agents are honorable people, and they write releases that are reliable. But some press agents slip in a few curves. It's your job to detect them—and reject them. "The most essential gift for a good writer," as Hemingway put it so elegantly, "is a built-in shockproof shit-detector."

▶ **33. Confirm your tips.**

Another source of problems—and opportunities—is tips. People with all sorts of motives phone newsrooms: some callers are looking for kicks, some for rewards, some for vengeance. Any caller—or e-mailer—can identify himself as just about anyone else. Listen carefully, ask questions and treat each call as potentially newsworthy. But when you hang up, or hit delete, don't go straight to your keyboard. Verify everything you want to use. But don't try to verify a tip simply by phoning the tipster and talking to him again.

Some pranksters delight in phoning in phony obituaries. Never use an obit before first checking with the undertaker. And watch out for mischief makers. I remember a cub reporter who was refused service by a Chicago nightclub because he wasn't wearing a tie. So he walked across the street to a saloon, where a TV set was carrying a telethon. In a twinkling, he got an inspiration. He phoned the telethon and said he was the manager of the nightclub that had denied him service and wanted to make a contribution to fight some dreaded disease: $5. The TV host's on-air announcement of the measly gift made the famous club look like a den of scrooges, and the reporter got his revenge. Yes, I did. (Thinking about it makes me want to hum "Pranks for the Memory.")

Yet, you shouldn't take my cautionary words as advice to hang up on unfamiliar or anonymous callers. Or to ignore them. Or to make prank calls of your own. Another Chicago reporter, Martin J. O'Connor, used to say he didn't care if a tip came from Judas Iscariot. If Marty could confirm it, he'd run with it. Once you have confirmed a story, it's yours.

▶ **34. Know your city.**

Many, if not most, people who work in broadcast newsrooms grew up in places other than where they live. And many hope to move up and go else-where. (Where else?) Until then, though, they should do their utmost to learn their current city so that they don't talk about the intersection of two streets that run parallel.

▶ 35. Follow current events.

Read a local newspaper every day. And one good national newspaper—in print or online. Keep abreast of what's going on in your city, your county, your state, your country, your world. Social media sites such as Twitter do more than help you keep up with your friends. You can track news outlets and widen your media diet—and your horizons. Your mental database needs daily uploading.

▶ 36. Improve yourself.

Read, read, read. Newspapers, magazines, books. As Mark Twain said, "The man who doesn't read good books has no advantage over the man who can't read them." If Twain were writing today, I'd e-mail him and ask him to revise that to include women. And if he listened to me, I'd also ask him to include newspapers and magazines.

▶ 37. Build your vocabulary.

Focus on learning small words, not big ones.

▶ 38. Listen to newscasts whose writing is good.

You can identify good writing by listening carefully and noticing which anchors and which writers comply with the basic rules and also shun the sins. If possible, record those newscasts, replay them and listen carefully.

▶ 39. Find a good writer in your newsroom and ask her or him for guidance.

That assumes, of course, that you don't know everything. Ask that person to look over some of your scripts and tell you what's wrong.

Sir William S. Gilbert said, "I never read favorable criticism; I prefer reading unfavorable [criticism]. I know how good I am, but I do not know how bad I am." (If you think Gilbert and Sullivan is a law firm, you'd better go to Google—or Gondoliers.)

I wouldn't ask that good writer to be my mentor. I wouldn't utter the word *mentor:* if you did, the writer might be reluctant to take on any additional burden or responsibility. So don't scare her (or him). You don't need a formal connection. Just ask that writer to look at one script at a time.

Also: You can make a first impression only once. So on your first day, at least, show up early. Everyone who works on putting together a newscast knows that you gotta get on on time, and you gotta get off on time. That's another reason punctuality is paramount. As my grandmother taught me, "Better an hour early than a minute late."

▶ **40. Give it all you've got.**

Absorb all these Top Tips. After you read a wire story or other source copy, apply the tips automatically. You can't take the time to review each one step by step, like an airline pilot going down his checklist for takeoff. Absorb those tips so they become second nature and you can apply them on auto-pilot. Then your scripts will be all set for the air.

(As for my combining *have* and *got* in *Give it all you've got,* your eighth grade teacher might object. But in his authoritative *Modern American Usage,* the grammarian Bryan A. Garner says *got* adds emphasis and *have got* is "perfectly idiomatic.")

∗

Murphy's Law is true: "If something can go wrong, it will." But Mervy's Law says: "If something *can't* go wrong, it will." So when you finish a script, reread it, recheck it and turn it in. Then reflect and relax. Next, pray. And polish your résumé.

PART II

STYLE

Writing Well with Orwell
What style is—and isn't

George Orwell himself might have been at a loss for words over 1984's orgy of Orwelliana, but as a resolute wordwatcher, he still has much to tell us. Not only did he coin words that have become catchwords—*Big Brother, doublethink, newspeak, unperson*—but he also wrote knowingly about using words.

Orwell worked in radio for the BBC as a writer, producer and broadcaster, so he knew broadcasting. His goal was to write plainly and clearly, to produce "prose like a window pane." In 1946, after writing *Animal Farm* and before writing *1984*, he set down some basic rules that are still sound and equally useful when writing for print or broadcast. These rules may not enable us to write as well as Orwell, but they can help:

▸ Never use a metaphor, simile or other figure of speech which [that was Orwell's word, but "that" is preferable] you are used to seeing in print. ["What a good thing Adam had," Mark Twain said. "When he said a good thing, he knew nobody had said it before."]

▸ Never use a long word where a short one will do.

▸ If it is possible to cut a word out, always cut it out.

▸ Never use the passive where you can use the active.

▸ Never use a foreign phrase, a scientific word or a jargon word if you can think of an everyday English equivalent.

▸ Break any of these rules sooner than say anything outright barbarous.

Although Orwell presented these rules in an essay more than half a century ago, they're just as pertinent today. In the essay "Politics and the English Language," he offered this advice:

"A scrupulous writer, in every sentence that he writes, will ask himself at least four questions, thus: What am I trying to say? What words will express it? What image or idiom will make it clearer? Is this image fresh enough to have an effect? And he will probably ask himself two more: Could I put it more shortly? Have I said anything that is avoidably ugly?"

Orwell condemned slovenliness, vagueness and the use of ready-made phrases. He warned against "gumming together long strips of words already set in order by someone else." Once a writer falls into that habit, Orwell said, it's easier and quicker for him to say, "In my opinion it is not an unjustifiable assumption that" than to say, "I think." One question I am asked time and again is, "Mr. Block, how do I develop a style?" By following the rules we've presented in this book and in the many books that came before mine, including *The Word*, also published as *Associated Press Guide to News Writing* by Rene J. Cappon; *The King's English* by Henry W. Fowler and Francis G. Fowler; *Simple & Direct* by Jacques Barzun; The Ten Principles of Good Writing in *The Technique of Clear Writing* by Robert Gunning; and Gary Provost's *100 Ways to Improve Your Writing*.

STARS OF STYLE

Style is not like fast food. You can't walk in and say, "I want a style. To go."

Sorry, it's no go. Style is intangible. You can't pick it up or buy it. And you can't borrow a writing style, one that stamps your copy as something special. Although style is not yours for the asking, style *is* gettable. But first, you have to get a handle on it.

> *Style is not like fast food.*

When I say "style," I mean *what* you say and *how* you say it, the words you choose, how you use them, the way you construct your sentences. That's *writing* style. It's not the kind of style that style manuals deal with, the basic work rules for a newsroom, designed mainly for uniformity.

Most writers are individualists. They want personal styles. They want their scripts to differ from other people's scripts. And most of those other people want a distinctive style to make *their* scripts—*and* themselves—stand out. Many new writers who yearn for a style shoot for the stars; they try to pattern their writing after that of star newscasters widely known for their style. Some newscasters do have fine writing styles. But some establish their reputation for style through a combination of elements that have nothing to do with writing: presence, personality, performance and presentation. If you want to develop *those* qualities, you'll have to read another chapter. In another book. By another writer.

Style is more than an unusual or unique way to say something. Trying to define style, a Frenchman said, is like trying to put a sack of flour in a thimble. But if you can't put your finger on style, how can you get your hands on it? Put thimbly: from reading, from listening and from learning. And from writing, writing, writing.

A dictionary defines *style* as "distinction, excellence, originality and character in any form of artistic or literary expression."

Distinction. Excellence. Originality. That's a lot to aim for. Sure, we write about momentous events, but we spend more time writing about crashes, crimes and coroner's cases. It's hard to make copy about the commonplace interesting, let alone distinctive, excellent and original. And if we all write about the same things, follow the same rules and use the same basic language, how in the world can we develop a style that's noticeable? And recognizable? And admirable?

The answer: Don't worry about developing your own style. Don't even think about it. Work on your craft; hone your skills, and your style will come to you. The development of style may be a process of decortication, a stripping or peeling away. As a writer learns to get rid of nonessentials, she discovers that what's left is style. But a writer shouldn't work too hard at attaining a style or else the excessive effort will show.

The attainment of style mustn't be our main goal. Our most important goal is to communicate clearly, to tell a story well, so well that a listener understands it instantly and easily. To do that, we must write simply. We must not stretch and strain to strut our stuff—and that's the sort of sentence to scrap, a succession of hissing sibilants. Alliteration and other devices of rhetoric do work on occasion, but they should be used with care. Anyone searching for a personal style should keep in mind that style is no substitute for substance and a writer should not sacrifice substance for style. According to my publisher, Aaron Cohodes, the best way for a writer to be different is to be better.

We shouldn't labor to draw attention to our scripts. And we shouldn't draw attention to ourselves. Our focus should be on our listeners. They are the people we should direct our attention to. Those people out there. Them.

Still, you might say, there must be more to style than that platter of platitudes. Right you are when you are right. There's far more. And the more we learn about writing, and the more we write, the more we realize that style is not easy to come by.

To say that style is elusive is not to say what it is. Perhaps some of the world's best stylists can tell us—and tell us how to find a style. They've said it far better than I can. So let's turn to these guest lecturers, who clearly prize clarity above all else:

"First, clarity; then again clarity; and, finally, clarity."

Anatole France

"A good style must, first of all, be clear."

Aristotle

"Words, like eyeglasses, blur everything that they do not make more clear."

Joseph Joubert

"If any man wishes to write in a clear style, let him first be clear in his thoughts."

Johann Wolfgang von Goethe

"Clear writers, like clear fountains, do not seem so deep as they are; the turbid looks most profound."

Walter Savage Landor

"In language, clearness is everything."

Confucius

"Clearness is the most important matter in the use of words."

Quintilian

"Whatever we conceive well we express clearly, and words flow with ease."

Nicholas Boileau

"People think I can teach them style. What stuff it is. Have something to say and say it as clearly as you can. That is the only secret to style."

Matthew Arnold

"When you can with difficulty say anything clearly, simply and emphatically, then, provided the difficulty is not apparent to the reader, that is style. When you can do that easily, it is genius."

Lord Dunsany

"Nothing is so difficult as the apparent ease of a clear and flowing style. . . . Those graces which, from their presumed facility, encourage all to attempt to imitate them, are usually the most inimitable."

Charles Caleb Colton

"Lucidity is the soul of style."

Hilaire Belloc

"The indispensable characteristic of a good writer is a style marked by lucidity."

Ernest Hemingway

"Style is the dress of thought; a modest dress,
Neat, but not gaudy, will true critics please."

The Rev. Samuel Wesley

"Style is not something applied. It is something that permeates. It is of the nature of that in which it is found, whether the poem, the manner of a god, the bearing of a man. It is not a dress."

Wallace Stevens

"Style is organic, not the clothes a man wears, but the flesh, bone, and blood of his body. Therefore it is really impossible to consider styles apart from the system of perceptions and feelings and thoughts that animate them."

J. Middleton Murry

"Style is the dress of thoughts; and let them be ever so just, if your style is homely, coarse, and vulgar, they will appear to as much dis-advantage, and be as ill received, as your person, though ever so well-proportioned, would if dressed in rags, dirt, and tatters."

Lord Chesterfield

"I am well aware that an addiction to silk underwear does not imply that one's feet are dirty. None the less, style, like sheer silk, too often hides eczema."

Albert Camus

"Style is neither an involuntary matter nor something you add to the text to 'dress it up.' Style should not be thought of as an end

unto itself. It is a series of choices—of voice, tone, diction, structure, grammar and usage—that depend on purpose and appropriateness. Putting style in almost always clutters writing up; removing clutter gives writing style."

Mitchell Ives

"Those most likely to talk about it [style] are least likely to have it. Style in writing compares to intonation in speaking. It may be harsh; shrill; nasal; affected; a soft Southern timbre, or a cockney vivacity. It is as personal as clothes or complexion. It can be controlled and educated, but beneath control it must partly remain instinctive, unconscious and organic. As in clothes so in literature it is most admirable when least obtruded. Its very plainness implies high cost; the cost of thinking and study."

Christopher Morley

"Style is a sort of melody that comes into my sentences by itself. If a writer says what he has to say as accurately and effectively as he can, his style will take care of itself."

George Bernard Shaw

"True ease in writing comes from art, not chance,
As those move easiest who have learned to dance."

Alexander Pope

"He that will write well . . . must follow this counsel of Aristotle, to speak as the common people do, to think as wise men do."

Roger Ascham

"When you doubt between words, use the plainest, the commonest, the most idiomatic. Eschew fine words as you would rouge, and love simple ones as you would native roses on your cheek."

August W. Hare

"Crisp writing usually has a good deal of shortening in it."

Anonymous

"Only great minds can afford a simple style."

Stendhal [Henri Bayle]

"To write simply is as difficult as to be good."

W. Somerset Maugham

"The chief aim of the writer is to be understood."

John Dryden

"I am unlikely to trust a sentence that comes easily."

William Gass

"There is no way of writing well and also of writing easily."

Anthony Trollope

"What is written without effort is in general read without pleasure."

Samuel Johnson

"Ready writing makes not good writing; but good writing brings on ready writing."

Ben Jonson

"You write with ease to show your breeding, but easy writing's curst hard reading."

Richard Brimsley Sheridan

"In what he leaves unsaid I discover a master of style."

Friedrich von Schiller

"Style is what gets left out."

Bertholt Brecht

"There is but one art, to omit."

Robert Louis Stevenson

"Proper words in proper places, make the true definition of style."

Jonathan Swift

"A man's style is his mind's voice. Wooden minds, wooden voices."

Ralph Waldo Emerson

"A pen may be just as usefully employed in crossing out as in writing."

Quintilian

"In composing, as a general rule, run your pen through every other word you have written; you have no idea what vigor it will give to your style."

Sydney Smith

"No style is good that is not fit to be spoken or read aloud with effect."

William Hazlitt

"Writing, when properly managed, is but a different name for conversation."

Laurence Sterne

"The style is the man himself."

Georges de Buffon

"Montesquieu had the style of a genius; Buffon, the genius of style."

Baron Grimm

"Words are like leaves; and where they most abound,
Much fruit of sense beneath is rarely found."

Alexander Pope

"A good style must have an air of novelty, at the same time concealing its art."

Aristotle

"Intense study of the Bible will keep any man from being vulgar in point of style."

Samuel Taylor Coleridge

"There is such an animal as a nonstylist, only they're not writers— they're typists."

Truman Capote

"Simple style is like white light. It is complex but its complexity is not obvious."

Anatole France

"A pure style in writing results from the rejection of everything superfluous."

Albertine-Adrienne Necker de Saussure

"A good style should show no sign of effort. What is written should seem a happy accident."

W. Somerset Maugham

"Everyone recognizes it, everyone describes it, but no two people agree as to its exact nature."

Henry Seidel Canby

"Without style there cannot possibly be a single work of value in any branch of eloquence or poetry."

Voltaire

"There is nothing more dangerous to the formation of a prose style than the endeavour to make it poetic."

J. Middleton Murry

"The greatest possible merit of style is, of course, to make the words absolutely disappear into the thought."

Nathaniel Hawthorne

"There is no such thing as good style or bad style. The question is, does it accomplish its intention?"

Christopher Morley

"The secret of the style of the great Greek and Roman authors is that it is the perfection of good sense."

John Stuart Mill

"A man's style is nearly as much a part of himself as his face, or figure, or the throbbing of his pulse. . . ."

François Fénelon

"The best style is the style you don't notice."

W. Somerset Maugham

"One should not aim at being possible to understand, but at being impossible to misunderstand."

Quintilian

"You do not create a style. You work, and develop yourself; your style is an emanation from your own being."

Katherine Anne Porter

"The first rule of style is to have something to say. The second rule of style is to control yourself when, by chance, you have two things to say; say first one, then the other, not both at the same time."

George Pólya

"To achieve style, begin by affecting none—that is, place yourself in the background. A careful and honest writer does not need to worry about style. As he becomes proficient in the use of the language, his style will emerge, because he himself will emerge, and when this happens he will find it increasingly easy to break through the barriers that separate him from other minds, other hearts—which is, of course, the purpose of writing, as well as its principal reward."

William Strunk Jr. and E.B. White

"We are surprised and delighted when we come upon a natural style, for instead of an author we find a man."

Blaise Pascal

"I've been called a stylist until I really could tear my hair out. And I simply don't believe in style. The style is you."

Katherine Anne Porter

"A strict and succinct style is that, where you can take away nothing without loss, and that loss to be manifest."

Ben Jonson

"As for style of writing, if one has anything to say, it drops from him simply and directly, as a stone falls to the ground."

Henry David Thoreau

"The style of an author should be the image of his mind, but the choice and command of language is the fruit of exercise."

Edward Gibbon

"Whatever is translatable in other and simpler words of the same language, without loss of sense or dignity, is bad."

Samuel Taylor Coleridge

"The virtues of good style are more negative than positive. The man who knows what to avoid is already the owner of style."

Henry W. Fowler

"The first and most important thing of all, at least for writers today, is to strip language clean, to lay it bare down to the bone."

Ernest Hemingway

"I notice that you use plain, simple language, short words and brief sentences. This is the way to write English—it is the modern way and the best way. Stick to it; don't let fluff and flowers and verbosity creep in."

Mark Twain

"I know of only one rule: style cannot be too clear, too simple."

Stendhal [Henri Bayle]

"Obscurity in writing is commonly a proof of darkness in the mind; the greatest learning is to be seen in the greatest plainness."

John Wilkins

"Our taste in style matches our taste in corned beef. Lean is keen."

William Safire

"Carefully examined, a good—an interesting—style will be found to consist in a constant succession of tiny, unobservable surprises."

Ford Madox Ford

"The fundamental rule of style is to keep solely in view the thought one wants to convey. One must therefore have a thought to start with."

Jacques Barzun (quoting an unidentified French stylist)

"Your writing style is yourself in the process of thought and the act of writing, and you cannot buy that in a bookstore or fix it up in a seminar."

William Safire

"For a man to write well, there are required three necessaries: to read the best authors, observe the best speakers, and much exercise of his own style."

Ben Jonson

"A good narrative style does not attract attention to itself. Its job is to keep the reader's mind on the story, on what's happening, the event, and not the writer."

Leon Surmelian

"To me style is just the outside of content, and content the inside of style, like the outside and the inside of the human body—both go together, they can't be separated."

Jean-Luc Godard

"It is by the use of familiar words that style affects the reader. People feel that using them is the mark of a man who knows life and its daily concerns, and maintains contact with them."

Joseph Joubert

"Words in prose ought to express the intended meaning; if they attract attention to themselves, it is a fault; in the very best styles you read page after page without noticing the medium."

Samuel Taylor Coleridge

"[The beginner should shun] all devices that are popularly believed to indicate style—all mannerisms, tricks, adornments. The approach to style is by way of plainness, simplicity, orderliness, sincerity."

E. B. White

"A style, representing the sum total of choices made in daily speech and writing, expresses our individual connection with that vast and confusing body of knowledge known as language."

Charles W. Ferguson

"To write in a genuine familiar or truly English style is to write as any one would speak in common conversation, who had a thorough command and choice of words, or who could discourse with ease, force and perspicuity, setting aside all pedantic and oratorical flourishes."

William Hazlitt

"Obscurity and affectation are the two great faults of style. Obscurity of expression generally springs from confusion of ideas; and the same wish to dazzle, at any cost, which produces affectation in the manner of a writer, is likely to produce sophistry in his reasoning."

Thomas Babington Macaulay

"The way of speaking that I love is natural and plain, as well in writing as speaking, and a sinewy and significant way of expressing one's self, short and pithy, and not so elegant and artificial as prompt and

vehement. Rather hard than harsh, free from affectation . . . not like a pedant, a preacher or a pleader, but rather a soldier-like style. . . ."

Michel de Montaigne

"The first rule of all writing—that rule to which every other is subordinate—is that the words used by the writer shall be such as most fully and precisely convey his meaning to the great body of his readers. All considerations about the purity and dignity of style ought to bend to this consideration."

Thomas Babington Macaulay

"You want to fix up your writing, parse your sentences, use the right words? Fine, pick up the little books, learn to avoid mistakes, revere taut prose and revile tautology. But do not flatter yourself that you have significantly changed your style. First, straighten out yourself so that you can then think straight and soon afterward write straight."

William Safire

"He who thinks much says but little in proportion to his thoughts. He selects that language which will convey his ideas in the most explicit and direct manner. He tries to compress as much thought as possible into a few words. On the contrary, the man who talks everlastingly and promiscuously, who seems to have an exhaustless magazine of sound, crowds so many words into his thoughts that he always obscures, and very frequently conceals them."

Washington Irving

"To eliminate the vice of wordiness is to ensure the virtue of emphasis, which depends more on conciseness than on any other factor. Wherever we can make 25 words do the work of 50, we halve the area in which looseness and disorganization can flourish, and by reducing the span of attention required we increase the force of the thought. To make sure our words count for as much as possible is surely the simplest as well as the hardest secret of style."

Wilson Follett

"Style is hard to pin down. The difficulty recalls Justice Stewart's remark about obscenity; he couldn't define it, but he knew when he saw it. Whatever it is, style provides the individual hallmark that writers stamp upon their work—but that metaphor is inapt, for it suggests that style is something you put onto a piece after you've finished it, as

if it were ketchup on chili, or lemon on fish. Style doesn't work that way. It's more of a marinade, permeating the whole composition."

James J. Kilpatrick

"While one should always study the method of a great artist, one should never imitate his manner. The manner of an artist is essentially individual, the method of an artist is absolutely universal. The first is personality, which no one should copy; the second is perfection, which all should aim at."

Oscar Wilde

"Style is everything and nothing. It is not that, as is commonly supposed, you get your content and soup it up with style; style is absolutely embedded in the way you perceive."

Martin Amis

"Style is the hallmark of a temperament stamped upon the material at hand."

Andre Maurois

"Style is the image of character."

Edward Gibbon

"Style is effectiveness of assertion."

George Bernard Shaw

"Style is the essence of thinking."

Robert Louis Stevenson

"Style is the physiognomy of the mind."

Arthur Schopenhauer

"Style is what gives value and currency to thought."

Henri Frederic Amiel

"An honest tale speeds best being plainly told."

William Shakespeare

"Be plain and simple, and lay down the thing as it was."

John Bunyan

"Style comes only after long, hard practice and writing."

William Styron

"Get your facts right first; that is the foundation of all style."

George Bernard Shaw

Accuracy. Brevity. Clarity. They're our ABCs. But they're not so simple as ABC.

Accuracy depends on our dedication to facts: finding facts, focusing on facts and sticking to the facts.

> *Accuracy. Brevity. Clarity. They're our ABCs.*

But how can we achieve brevity and clarity? The paths are many, but the surest guidance comes from old pros. Our first advice comes from a master, Anton Chekhov, who spelled out the virtues of brevity and clarity in a letter to another Russian writer:

> "Take out adjectives and adverbs wherever you can. . . . You understand what I mean when I say, 'The man sat on the grass.' You understand because the sentence is clear and there is nothing to distract your attention. Conversely . . . 'A tall, narrow-chested man of medium height with a red beard sat mutely, looking about timidly and fearfully' . . . doesn't get its meaning through to the brain immediately, which is what good writing must do, and fast."

But a word to the wise is often insufficient. Next I pass along more advice from more old pros, words that can guide us to brevity and clarity—with vitality. Not that advice or rules can make us better writers instantly—or even eventually—but they can point us in the right direction.

Some of the best rules for writing have been set down by Writer's Digest School. Like other rules quoted in this chapter, they're reprinted here word for word. Although all these rules were intended for people who write for the eye, in almost every case they also help us write for the ear. *Writer's Digest* advises:

▸ Prefer the plain word to the fancy.
▸ Prefer the familiar word to the unfamiliar. [And use familiar words in familiar combinations.]
▸ Prefer the Saxon word to the Romance.
▸ Prefer nouns and verbs to adjectives and adverbs.
▸ Prefer picture nouns and action verbs.

▶ Never use a long word when a short one will do as well.

▶ Master the simple declarative sentence.

▶ Prefer the simple sentence to the complicated.

▶ Vary your sentence length.

▶ Put the words you want to emphasize at the beginning or end of your sentence. [The end is usually preferable.]

▶ Use the active voice.

▶ Put statements in a positive form.

▶ Cut needless words, sentences and paragraphs.

▶ Use plain, conversational English. Write the way you talk.

▶ Avoid imitation. Write in your natural style.

▶ Write clearly.

▶ Avoid gobbledygook and jargon.

▶ Write to be understood, not to impress.

▶ Revise and rewrite. Improvement is always possible.

Now do it—with style.

Mervin Block

Lead-Ins, Lead-Outs, Tags, Teases, Voice-Overs

How to get a handle on them

The tips and rules that guide us to writing better stories also serve in writing other elements of a newscast. But each of the elements has its own peculiar needs.

An anchor reads a lead-in to lead into a reporter's narrative or a natural sound cut, perhaps of a shouting match. The lead-in sets the scene and identifies the reporter—or the people who are the loud speakers.

The lead-in's job is to alert listeners and prepare them for what's coming—the important, fascinating, exciting, startling, horrifying or amusing story that's about to unfold. Yet the lead-in is more than a billboard for the coming attraction. It sets up what follows so it makes sense to a listener. And it supplies a crucial fact or two that may be missing from what follows. Generally, a lead-in should supply the *where*. On the other hand, if the reporter immediately says where he is, a lead-in needn't include the *where*.

Lead-ins must do more than just lead in. They should keep listeners listening, either through the impact of hard facts told well or through the engaging grace of a light touch. A lead-in should grab a listener by the throat, or by the ears—but gently, politely. Not an easy assignment, especially if the reporter's story is a 97-second weakling. And not if we comply with the truth-in-advertising laws, never promising more in the lead-in than the piece delivers. All we need are the same skills we use in writing "readers" (or "telling" stories)—scripts unaccompanied by video.

Lead-ins come in many varieties, but, in general, they can be classified as hard or soft. A hard lead-in is usually used to introduce a hard-news story. Ideally, the reporter writes his script as if he were telling the whole story. Then, before the newscast, he gives his first sentence (or two) to the anchor to use as her lead-in. After the anchor goes on the air and delivers that lead-in—or a rewrite that retains the essence of the original—the reporter picks up the narrative with the second (or third) sentence of his script. That way, the story flows seamlessly. No maddening repetition, no gaps, no flaps, no traps.

When an anchor doesn't have the benefit of a proposed lead-in from the reporter, the anchor (or writer) should write a lead-in that sets up the story—almost like a newspaper headline. But with sentences that don't sound like headlines or use headline words. If the writer has the opportunity to read the reporter's script in advance, he can include any essential facts missing from the script. Or he can give one or two of those facts to the anchor for a tag at the end of the reporter's piece.

A soft lead-in is usually reserved for soft news. (One kind of lead-in that you don't want to write is *squishy* soft.) Soft lead-ins intro features, human interest and semi-soft stories. Good soft-news lead-ins are hard to write. But, by writing and writing and writing, you can learn to get it right.

As with the Deadly Don'ts in Chapter 1 of this book, Don'ts are especially important in writing lead-ins:

ADVICE ON LEAD-INS

▶ **Don't use the same key words the reporter uses.** Don't introduce him or her with the same words he or she starts with. Violation of that rule produces "the echo-chamber effect." It sounds—and resounds—like this, with the anchor speaking first: "Governor Goober warned today he's fed up with state employees who loaf on the job." Then we hear Goober say, "I'm fed up with state employees who loaf on the job." Or instead, we hear the reporter say, "Goober said he's fed up with state employees who loaf on the job." Listener: "Haven't I heard that somewhere before?"

Or the anchor leads in with something like this: "Old MacDonald said today he's going back to his farm. Steve Simpson reports he's pining for his pigs, ducks and cows." Then Steve begins, "MacDonald is pining for his pigs, ducks and cows." This leaves the listener higgledy-piggledy, and the duplication wastes time and crowds out other material.

Instead of starting the second sentence with the reporter's name and stepping on the reporter's lines, the anchor could say, "He [MacDonald] has been working as a bricklayer, but now he has decided to throw in the trowel. Steve Simpson has the story." By saying Steve has the story, the anchor suggests that the best is yet to come.

If possible, a writer should prepare a lead-in only after reading the text of the cut or the reporter's script. Or at least talking with the reporter so the writer knows what the reporter is going to say. Or so the reporter knows what the lead-in is going to say.

▸ **Don't steal the reporter's thunder.** Although the lead-in for a hard-news story should hit one or two highlights, the anchor shouldn't skim off all the good material. Otherwise, the reporter's account will be anticlimactic. It will sound as if the reporter got his news from the anchor. Or, as they say so delicately in the barnyard, the reporter will be left sucking hind teat.

Right after the anchor's lead-in, too many reporters start by saying, "That's right." But don't we expect the anchor to be right? When a reporter starts by saying, "That's right," he's not advancing the story; he's delaying it. And the reporter comes across as a simp or a sycophant.

▸ **Don't write a soft lead-in for a hard-news story.** A soft lead-in may work for a feature story, but a hard-news story calls for a hard-news lead-in. A lead-in is like a store's display window. A dime store doesn't dress a window with diamonds. And a diamond merchant doesn't display dimes. Hard news, like diamonds, deserves an appropriate showcase.

> *A lead-in is like a store's display window.*

▸ **Don't write a lead-in that conflicts with the reporter's script.** This may seem abecedarian (no kin to ABC's Sid Darion), but every so often we hear an anchor's lead-in that's at odds with something the reporter is about to say. That's a mislead-in.

▸ **Don't overstate or oversell.** The lead-in shouldn't promise—or suggest—more than the reporter can deliver. It should adhere to standards of journalism, not descend to hucksterism.

▸ **Don't be vague.** Sometimes, though, because of the way newscasts are put together, we don't know exactly what the reporter in the field is going to be saying or which segment of a speech is going to be used. So we have to write "blind"—without saying anything specific. And we put down only enough words in the lead-in to allow the control room to take control: "The new chairman of the city transit agency, Lionel Train, spoke out today on the agency's problems." But that's flat. Writing blind—like flying blind—can be risky. So we don't want to say something that turns out to be wrong. Or conflicts with what follows. Whenever possible, say something explicit and substantive: "The new chairman of the city transit agency, Lionel Train, said today he'll clean up the agency's problems within six months."

▸ **Don't use a faulty throw line at the end of the lead-in to introduce a reporter.** You confuse a listener by saying, "Jerry Jarvis has the story," if the next voice we're going to hear is not that of the reporter but of a woman taking an oath of office. One way to handle that throw line is to say, "Jerry Jarvis looked on as Mary Barton took the oath."

Most lead-ins run less than 20 seconds, and a few run barely 5 seconds. No matter what it takes to do the job, no matter what the length, every word counts. And the shorter the lead-in, the greater the need for every word to carry its weight.

▸ **Don't write a tag in haste.** Tags are used by anchors to add a fact or a comment or a correction or a brief wrap-up after a reporter ends a report. A tag—also known as a cap, button, lead-out or write-out—requires the same care as the newscast's lead story. Otherwise, you might produce a lead-out as wishy-washy and silly as this one, broadcast by a major market TV station:

> Relations between the U-S and the Soviet Union could get much better . . . or worse, possibly depending a great deal on today's events.

The tag is supposed to add a bit of information, perhaps an important fact that couldn't be fitted into the lead-in. Or perhaps it's an updated casualty figure. Or late news that should accompany the story just reported. Or it can be a P.S. that rounds out the story. Or a correction of something that the reporter had recorded. Or it might be an anchor's comment or aside. Whatever you call it or whatever you put into it, keep it short and to the point.

Some anchors begin their tags by saying, "Incidentally" or "By the way." But it's best to refrain from those transparent efforts to be casual. If an item is indeed incidental, it doesn't deserve valuable air time. And if the item is not incidental, it shouldn't be minimized by being called incidental.

You may also be assigned to write crawls, the ribbon of news that scoots along the bottom of a TV screen. Many crawls give me the creeps. The problems include misspellings and misstatements. Writing for the crawl requires the same skills needed to write regular news scripts. But crawls are highly condensed. So you need to have sharp news judgment and an ability to boil down complex stories to a short sentence or two. In crawls, abbreviations are standard. Spelling correctly is a must. As with any kind of writing or performing, improvement comes through doing it. And reviewing it.

If you're in radio, you don't have to worry about voice-overs (V/Os), the scripts that are read over silent video. And if you're in TV, you don't have to worry either, as long as you observe these pointers:

▸ **View the footage before writing.** If that seems obvious, think of all the V/Os you've heard on the air that didn't fit the picture. If previewing the video is out of the question, try to get a shot list (aka shot sheet, shot card, spot sheet and breakdown sheet). That list itemizes the scenes in chronological order, describes the contents in a few words and provides the running time of each shot as well as the cumulative time. If you do pre-view the footage, make your own shot list. Without such a list, by the time you get back to your keyboard, you may forget whether the third scene shows injured people or overturned trailer homes, and you may need to know for sure.

Your words don't need to match the picture every step of the way. But they should supplement what viewers see—and, if necessary, help them understand what they're seeing. If need be, identify the setting and the main characters an instant or two before each new scene comes up. In some pieces, "spotting" a new character—by name or description—is imperative. We call this "keying," "writing to picture" or "cuing words to picture." If we write about something the camera didn't shoot or the video doesn't show but that's pertinent, we "write away from picture."

To establish what it's all about at the start of a V/O, it's usually best for the script to match the picture. After the viewer is told what it's all about, it may be all right to write away from picture. But don't get carried away. Don't describe in detail what viewers can't see for themselves.

▶ **Don't state the obvious.** For too many writers, this is not so obvi-ous. That's why we hear lines like "This is the man," "This is the lake," "This is the man jumping into the lake." Viewers can see that. We serve them by supplementing what they see by putting the picture into perspective. We inform them that the water temperature was 35 degrees, that the man weighed 250 pounds and that he didn't know how to swim.

Avoid "Here we see," "shown here" and "seen here." If we're seeing an overturned mobile home, the script needn't whack viewers over the head with a "here." If something needs to be explained or spelled out, do it unob-trusively and without fanfare.

▶ **Don't tell viewers to "watch this."** If you wish to direct your view-ers' attention to something that's about to occur in a long shot, do it subtly. Let's say that in a few seconds a man in the crowd is going to pull a gun and fire. Unless viewers know in advance, they might not be focusing on that part of the screen and could miss the critical part of the action. We can alert them without issuing orders: "A man on the far right, the man in a khaki jacket, pulls out his gun and prepares to fire at a policeman."

▶ **Don't fight the picture.** Our words shouldn't be at odds with the picture. We shouldn't say zookeepers recaptured two monkeys at the moment viewers see someone holding two children.

▶ **Don't identify people in a video by using the newspaper phrase** *left to right.* If several people are on the screen and you need to direct the viewers' attention to someone, you can refer to "the man in the ten-gallon hat" or "the woman with the parasol."

▶ **Don't overwrite.** Don't squeeze too much copy into the script, making the voice-over run longer than the footage. If you have a feature or a soft-news story and don't have to "hit" any scenes, write loose. That way, the words don't overwhelm or drown out the picture.

▶ **Don't overload your listeners with facts.** Viewers are busy viewing. They're not giving their undivided attention to the words. And too many facts—or words—can cause sensory overload.

▶ **Make use of natural sound and silence.** Don't feel required to cram words into every single second. If the footage has natural sound, like a gurgling brook, let the picture and sound carry the scene. Even when the footage is silent, you can sometimes skip the narrative. Pause. A few seconds of silence can be eloquent. And, depending on the scene, the anchor's (or reporter's) silence can underline the drama. What kinds of scenes? Perhaps a fireman breathing life into a baby, a lottery winner exploding with joy, a pole vaulter flinging himself over the crossbar.

▶ **Be sure the *where* is at or near the top of the V/O.** If the anchor's lead-in doesn't identify the place, be sure it's identified promptly. Sometimes, though, it's acceptable to identify the place with only a super—the superimposition of characters that spell out the name. Viewers should know right away what they're looking at, where it was shot and when (if it's not fresh).

▶ **Read your V/O against the footage while an editor or deskmate watches and listens.** This is the best way to catch mistakes and weaknesses. If you time each segment of your copy as you write it, the final run-through should be all right. But don't take any chances: Read your V/O aloud against the footage.

The most frequent weakness in voice-overs written by newcomers, according to Charles F. Cremer, Phillip O. Keirstead and Richard D. Yoakam in *ENG: Television News* (3rd ed.), is overwriting. These authors say the problem is not only that the text exceeds the running time of the video but also that viewers drown in the words and don't get a chance to mesh words and pictures in their minds.

LEAD-INS GONE WRONG

What's wrong with this lead-in?

> One person is hospitalized and another is headed to Lynn District Court after an alleged home invasion in Lynn. _____ _____is live from Lynn District Court with the latest.

Let us count the ways:

1. Is that person a man, woman or child? If we know, let's say so.

2. Saying that someone is hospitalized—or that many people are hospitalized—is not news, newsy or newsworthy. Tens of thousands of people are in hospitals.

3. An *alleged* home invasion? Do the police suspect that the homeowner wants to file a false insurance claim? Does the writer mean an *alleged* home invader? Or an invader of an *alleged* home (what the police used to call a disorderly house)?

4. *Invasion:* The writer has buried *invade,* a good action verb, in a noun, *invasion.* Halfway down that lead-in, *invasion* gives off the first whiff of action in the story. And what follows *after* in that lead should precede *after.* After all, if you phoned a friend about the story, you wouldn't say, "One person is hospitalized and another is headed. . . ." You'd start with the action—not the reaction. You'd talk about the thug(s) who stormed into a home.

5. Why call the reporter *live*? We wouldn't switch to a dead reporter. Some reporters may seem dead, but if they're standing by, they should be alive. They'd better be alive. ("Live at Five," they say of some newscasts, "Dead by Six.")

6. While we're counting, let us count the *Lynns:* three in that script. Too many.

7. The *latest*? Presenting the latest is what newscasts are all about. Remember, news is what's new. And what's new is the latest. (So what else is new?)

Who edited that script? *Was* there an editor? Did a newsroom invader (a Darth Vader) abduct the editor? Unfortunately (perhaps fortunately), that leaden lead-in is the only part of the script that fell into my clammy claws. I have only a few facts to work with, so my rewrite is a product of speculation, interpolation, extrapolation and desperation:

"Two men with guns forced their way into a Lynn home today and beat a woman guest. A passerby who saw the break-in called the police, and they caught one intruder. The injured woman is in the hospital, and the suspect is on his way to Lynn District Court. Jane Jones has the story."

If the invasion of the booty-snatchers had been broadcast hours earlier, I might have written the lead-in this way: "Police are searching for a gunman who broke into a Lynn home and beat a woman guest. Another gunman was caught by the police at the scene, and he's now on his way to Lynn District Court. Jane Jones has the story." Or, depending on the extent of previous coverage and the time elapsed since the crime, I'd write this: "A suspect arrested in a home invasion is now being taken to Lynn District Court, and Jane Jones has the story." To which many anchors would add, under their breath: "We hope."

> That's it for the weather. Just one reminder. Sunday is Daylight Savings Time. Don't forget to turn your clocks forward one hour on Sunday.

The first two sentences are a waste of time. When the weathercaster stops talking about the weather, everyone knows that's it for the weather segment. No need for the anchor to proclaim the obvious. In fact, there is a need for the anchor *not* to do so. And no need to say, "Just one reminder."

Better: "Daylight *Saving* [not Savings] Time starts Sunday. Remember (more emphatic than *Don't forget*), at two ayem, Sunday, set your clock ahead one hour."

Let's look at another snippet:

> Investigators are trying to find out what caused Wednesday's deadly helicopter crash.

Instead of *deadly,* make it *fatal. Deadly* can mean either "causing death" or "capable of causing death." But *fatal* is unambiguous; it describes something that has already caused death or dire consequences, or will do so—inevitably. But writers *are* correct in referring to a *deadly* disease, a *deadly* enemy and a *deadly* weapon.

> The probe into Monday's deadly gas attack on a Tokyo subway has lead to an arrest and a second dramatic raid on a Japanese religious cult.

Probe is a newspaper headline word. Print editors use *probe* as a synonym for *investigation* because *probe* can be fitted into a one-column head. But *probe* is not a spoken word, not unless you're speaking about a doctor who probes a wound. And did the writer mean an attack with deadly gas or an attack that caused death? *On* a subway? The writer was on the wrong track.

Either an event occurs *in* the subway, which is the underground tunnel, or *on* a subway train. And that writer should get the *lead* out and make it *led*.

Dramatic? Aren't most raids dramatic? Writing coaches say, "Show, don't tell." So, instead of calling something dramatic, tell us what happened that makes it dramatic.

The script about the Tokyo story goes on:

> **In a full** [as opposed to partial?] **military-type mission today, specialists seized more containers of potentially noxious chemicals.**

What is a *military-type* mission? One with air cover? *Noxious* chemicals? *Noxious* means harmful to living things. The writer might have meant *toxic*, which means capable of causing injury or death. But many listeners (and writers) are unsure of the meaning of *noxious* and *toxic*. A better word for those chemicals, closer to the tone of the terror in Tokyo, is *poisonous* or *deadly*. And no need for *potentially*. In our line of work—and it *is* work—words count. So let's work on being deadly accurate.

A TEASE IS TERSE

A tease is designed to inform viewers what lies ahead, to pique their curiosity and tempt them into staying tuned. A tease needs more than compression; it needs crushing. Or squashing. What you might call minimalism to the max. With only several seconds to work in, a writer needs a big vocabulary of short words. Also: creativity, imagination and a discriminating disdain for the rules. Often, there's not enough room for a complete sentence, so she needs to write her line like a headline: "Murder at the Waldorf." Good tease. Lacks a verb but packs a punch.

> *A tease needs more than compression; it needs crushing.*

Yet one of the dangers in condensing a story into a headline is that by reducing and rounding it off, we can easily warp it. And warping can lead to slanting. And distorting. So no matter how catchy the tease you've written, no matter how clever, ask yourself: Is it misleading? Or deceptive? Does it hint of more than the newscast is going to offer? If your answers are no, no, no, then go, go, go.

How often are you annoyed to find that a newspaper headline isn't supported by the story? Often we see that kind of headline in tabloids at supermarket checkout counters. But the headlines are beyond checking out: "Siamese Twin Girls Born Pregnant" and "Man Gives Birth to Test-Tube Twins." Although I haven't heard anything that phony in broadcast tease(r)s, I have heard some that flirt with fraud. The kind of tease that brings teases into disrepute is exemplified by this broadcast tease:

> California's on fire.

But California was not on fire. A few hundred acres were on fire. Lesson: Don't get carried away—or *you* will get burned.

Apply the same standards to teases that you apply to news stories. We can't always follow writing rules in writing teases, but we must pursue the paramount goal to be fair and factual. We mustn't overstate or overpromise. (Unless we don't mind being the target of a comedy sketch, we shouldn't write a tease that's a parody of itself: "TV teases taken to task. Tape at ten.")

One-minute newscasts usually run less than a minute. Whatever their length or brevity, they represent a challenge that's anything but minute. Jamming four or five stories into 40 seconds or so is like trying to stuff six pounds of suet into a five-pound sack. It's tough. I know. I've written one-minute newscasts (at three networks), and I've even stuffed seven stories into 50 seconds—a series of short bursts.

Writers who do these 'casts frequently develop a knack for ultra-compression. Oops; that *frequently* is a squinting modifier. It seems to be looking in two directions at the same time: it might modify *do* or *develop*. I edit myself as I go along, almost unconsciously, so I'll redo that sentence to read, "Writers who frequently do these 'casts develop a knack for ultra-compression." And that's part of what it takes to develop any skill: frequency. Not to mention a competent editor. Unfortunately, editors in many newsrooms have been deleted.

QUESTION LEADS

What do you think of question leads? And of these broadcast examples?

> The *Achille Lauro* is docked safely in Port Said this morning. But where are the hijackers? Have they already gone free?

You're asking us? We tuned in to find out.

> First, amazement. Then, outrage. Tonight, above all, confusion. Who, if anyone, has custody of the four *Achille Lauro* hijack murderers who took partly paralyzed 69-year-old Leon Klinghoffer from his wheelchair, shot him, killed him and tossed him overboard? Who, if anyone, will bring the murderers to justice?

Why the time-consuming hard sell? Amazement, outrage, confusion? Who's going to stop asking us and start telling us?

What do Coca-Cola, Caterpillar and General Electric have in common? They're just a few of the American companies represented in Moscow at a round of talks on increasing U-S - Soviet trade.

How do writers hatch so many inane question leads? Trick questions no listener could answer, guess at or even care about? If the story's worth telling, tell it.

Did Ponce de Leon ever find the fountain of youth he was seeking in Florida? A Philadelphia man says he ran into the 500-year-old Spanish conquistador back in 1973, and he looked marvelous—not a day over 23.

You don't think I could make that up, do you? Or would want to.

What went wrong? That question tonight confronted doctors after a sharp reversal in the condition of a man being kept alive by the only mechanical heart of its kind.

When a listener hears that question before he knows what has happened, he can't have the slightest idea what the anchor's talking about. Better: "The first man with the so-called Penn State heart has taken a bad turn, and his doctors are trying to find out what went wrong."

Something else wrong with that script: *tonight* should be placed after *doctors*. But is this an honest *tonight*, used because of a development tonight? Or is it a fishy tonight, inserted to try to make a daytime development seem fresh? In any case, the sentence would be improved if the verb in the script's first line—without *today* or *tonight*—were used in its present tense: *confronts*.

Now, what did the United States know during the hijack in progress and when? How did this affect what Egypt ended up doing and what the United States may have been planning to do?

You're asking me?

When did NASA know about problems with the shuttle's rocket boosters, and what did the agency do about it?

Why not skip the questions and go straight to the news? Better: "The commission on the *Challenger* explosion will try to find out today when NASA learned about problems with the shuttle's rocket boosters. And what the agency did about them."

Question: What did the French president and the prime minister know and when did they know it?

Question: Dear anchor, don't you think listeners can recognize a question by the word order and the rising inflection? And without being told they're about to be asked a question? Isn't there a better way to start this story than with a question, a question that echoes one first asked during Watergate, one that through overuse has become waterlogged? Another overusage that has become soggy: "Smith's throwing arm is the big question mark."

> Should a nurse be paid as much as a prison guard? That's the contention of the American Nurses Association. . . .

Should a writer be paid for generating that non sequitur? No one can contend a question.

> Here's a riddle: What totally American art form has been overhauled by some people in Argentina who want to bring it back home to America right after they market-test it in France?

Market-test or test-market? Do you "drive test" a car or "test drive" it? A riddle? That question is no riddle; it's a muddle.

> Of course, they play the same courses, they use basically the same equipment, but how different is women's golf, that is, big-time women's golf, from men's golf? We're going to be putting that question to two of the very best women on the golf tour in just a few minutes.

The opening of course is way off course. That's no way to start a story or an intro. Didn't the anchor consider the peril of a premature pronoun (*they*), one that precedes the subject? In this case, the peril is more pronounced because the anchor never does say who *they* are. As for the opening question in the script, that isn't the way I'd put it—or putt it.

> What looks like a large potato and travels at high speeds?

A promo for "M*A*S*H"? The newscaster's answer to his own half-baked question: Halley's Comet.

> Is it good news or bad news: the falling dollar and the rising yen?

True or false: The newscaster was writing under the influence of Sam Goldwyn. Reportedly the Hollywood producer once said, "For your information, I would like to ask a question."

What's wrong with question leads? When was the last time you started a conversation with a question? (Except for "How are you?") When was the last time you bought a newspaper to read its questions? Or turned on a newscast to catch the latest questions? Who needs rhetorical questions? We turn to newscasts for answers. Any other reasons question leads are objectionable? Yes; question leads can sound like quiz shows or commercials. Question leads don't inform, they trivialize the news, can be hard to deliver and don't go straight to the point. So why do writers persist in whipping up question leads? Is it because they don't know the answers? Or mistakenly think a question is a good hook? Or do they persist because it's easier for them to ask a question than burrow through a jumble of facts and think through good leads?

Question leads can sound like quiz shows or commercials.

Is a question lead ever acceptable? Perhaps, if the anchor isn't playing games with the listener and if the question is one that a listener can answer, almost instantly, or one that provokes thought. But not too much thought, lest the listener lose the thread. In almost every case, answers beat questions. No question about it.

BABBLEDYGOOK

Let's look at a shooting script to examine what can go wrong when you say too much. The television critic Marvin Kitman, a *Newsday* hitman, would probably call all the hash (and rehash) below "babbledygook."

The story: the opener on a television network flagship. The first word of the shooting reached a 9-1-1 operator at 7:21 p.m.—more than three and a half hours before the newscast. The place: New York City. The time of the newscast: 11 p.m.

Good evening. Gangsters and gunfire, a breaking story at this hour.

The co-anchor picks up the intro:

Well, it looks very much like a mob hit tonight outside Lenox Hill Hospital. Police say a member of John Gotti's Gambino crime family was gunned down. He is now inside that hospital as doctors work to save him. Ed Thomas [To protect the guilty, I've changed his name] *is at the scene now with more for us. Tim.*

Ed:

Well [Another *well*? A good, folksy word, but don't go to the well too often]*, it's an incredible story.* [If it's incredible, how can we believe it? But what's so incredible about a shooting? And in the Big Bagel? Instead of wasting our time, go ahead, tell the news. And calm down.] *It's reminiscent of the* [should be a] *Chicago gangland hit circa 1920.* [Mr. Reporter, tell us what the story is all about before telling us what you think it's reminiscent of. Better yet, don't tell us what it's reminiscent of. Especially in another city. Hasn't New York City had enough of its own gangland shootings? And why use a Latin word, *circa*, instead of *around?*]

This is the victim's car behind me. Again, you hear that he is an alleged member of the Gambino crime family. ["You *hear*"? Is it hearsay? In fact, Anchor Number Two had already quoted the police as saying the guy is a Gambino bambino.] ***What we have, police are telling us*** [who's *us?*]***, is that somebody*** [better: *someone*] ***was driving down this street, apparently waiting for the victims to walk out of Lenox Hill Hospital. Driving down the street*** [again?] ***when they saw their intended victims, they pulled their car up, got out of the car and opened fire.***

And perhaps [a weak word for this scene, and I don't mean maybe] ***you can see that the window of this car, several windows of this car, were actually*** [unneeded] ***shot out.*** [Q: What connection did that car have with the shooting? A: The wounded man had been getting into the parked car. Ed should have told us.] ***We have tape shot here shortly after this happened at 7:30 tonight and perhaps*** [again!] ***you can see that Police Commissioner Bratton was one of the first people to arrive and try to figure out exactly what happened here.***

[*One of the first?* One of the first fifty? If the Commish *was* one of the first on the scene, how did he get there so fast? Who cares? The next day, the *New York Times* ran an entire column on the shooting, about 750 words, but didn't mention the Commish at all. A better opening line than the vague and vapid "Gangsters and gunfire": "A Gotti henchman shot on the Upper East Side." Reference to that area classes it up a little.]

Again [*again* again?]***, the person, the victim*** [previously, we were told of *victims*] ***is, we're told, Handsome Jack Giordano*** [In fact, this is the *first* mention of him; better: "Jack Giordano, known as Handsome Jack"; another question: known to *whom* as Handsome Jack? Most such nicknames are bestowed by newsies]***, allegedly a capo in the Gambino crime family.*** [For the Gambino family, that's a threepeat.] ***We also spoke to someone who witnessed*** [better: *saw*] ***it.*** [What's *it?* And what's Giordano's condition? His age? Was he armed? Where does he live? Is he an ex-con? (Yes.)]

Witness:

Just I heard gunshot, just people were running out. [Some witness! That's the entire soundbite. His name and speech suggest he's a foreigner. (This verbatim text was recorded by a commercial transcription service.) Next, we hear from a police captain, four unidentified people, none of them witnesses, then Ed again.]

Police are telling us [better: "Police say"; leave *us* out of it; most information comes from someone's telling us] ***that Giordano and his driver were inside Lenox Hill Hospital visiting someone, and they came out of the hospital, and what you were just looking at was a live picture of bullet holes in the doors in*** [*to* or *of* would be better than two *ins* so close together] ***the emergency room of the hospital, so apparently who was firing, whoever was firing that gun, really*** [unneeded; really!] ***didn't care, about anybody*** [better: *anyone*] ***else*** [no kidding!]***, except hitting his intended victims.*** [*Victims?* Who was targeted besides Giordano?]

Now police are telling us [our ears are telling us that we're hearing too much of that locution] *they have one person in custody. They're not releasing his name at this point.* [Instead of *at this point*, why not *yet?*] *Again* [yet *again*], *this happened at 7:30 at night. There were a lot of people out on the street here on 77th Street.* [*There were* and *there is* are dead phrases. Better: "Many people were on 77th Street." Were they in danger? Did they provide descriptions or spot a license number?]

We [*I?*] *also hear* [from whom? a police official? a hospital official? a busybody?] *that Giordano is in very serious condition, in critical condition, I should say, with three bullet wounds to the neck and to the back.* [Should be "wounds *in* his neck and back."] *We are also told* [by whom?] *it's possible that he has been paralyzed. That's the latest here at* [*on*] *77th Street. I'm Ed Thomas. Bill* [also a pseudonym], *back to you.*

Bill:

All right, Ed, thank you. [Who says that being a reporter is a thankless job? Thank him? Bill oughta spank 'im.]

In defense of the reporter, he might have arrived at the scene late, and he might have been new to reporting and new to our language. And apparently he was so pressed for time he had to ad lib. Whatever the excuses, the explanations and the perhaps, we're left with a news report that's wordy, jumbled, repetitious, uninformative—unsatisfactory.

SOUP OF THE MONTH

One script I read after it was broadcast illustrates several common problems in writing, reporting and editing:

> And, [name of co-anchor], in case you didn't know it, [name of city] Mayor
> _____ _____, has proclaimed January as National Soup
> Month. In honor of the event, the Campbell's Soup Company brought their
> Soupmobile here to_____ _____. One of the three stops they
> made today was here at the Salvation Army. _____ _____ city
> employees as well as some of_____ _____'s needy stood in
> line to warm up. The Soupmobile is making a 10-city tour of the country. It
> will be here for two more days before the chefs on board pack up and move
> on to_____ _____for a three-day stop.

The lead-in and voice-over are riddled with flaws from start to finish: Why should an anchor deliver the news to a co-anchor? And why suggest the co-anchor may be unaware of that item? Why use the mayor's first name? And why not get the company's name right—Campbell, not

Campbell's? (The soup itself is called Campbell's.) Also, *their* Soupmobile should be *its*. And why does an anchor say *here* (unless the Salvation Army is encamped in the studio)? Who cares where the Soupmobile is going next (especially when it'll be hundreds of miles away)? And who cares how long it'll park there?

The biggest problem, though, is the naive (yet souped up) approach. The event has all the earmarks of a press agent stunt—commercialism but with no commercials. A Campbell press agent probably drafted the proclamation and arranged for the mayor to sign it. The script implies that Campbell was responding to the mayor's proclamation, but any reporter who has ever covered mayors or governors knows they sign proclamations at the drop of a hint or a contribution. Or a hint of a contribution. Why would a mayor spontaneously proclaim a National Soup Month? And how could a local official make it *national*? What a crock! No one was hurt, I suppose. And some poor people were helped. Not to mention the press agent (and good press agents seldom want to be mentioned).

In a small town on a slow news day, it may be news when the Campbells are coming. But the news should be written with some savvy. If a writer needs seasoning, then it's up to an editor or producer or anchor or news director to set the writer straight. No matter what size the town or the newsroom, every script should be read by other eyes so another company product doesn't go bad—and another writer doesn't wind up in the soup.

As writers, our goal is to do more than stay out of the soup, even alphabet soup. Our goal is to write better scripts—shorter, sharper, stronger. Writing requires far more than simply putting words down. Writers must think clearly, understand language thoroughly and watch what they say, intently. You can improve your writing skills, but only through writing and writing and, when time permits, rewriting.

Attribution: Says Who?

How to quote people and attribute facts

I've said it before, and I'll say it again: In broadcast newswriting, attribution precedes assertion. In this story you'll see why.

An 11 p.m. newscast on TV in New York City began:

> Good evening. The United States and Iran . . . locked in aerial combat over the Persian Gulf . . . with oil prices skyrocketing and Western economies sagging.

Jolted by this ominous opening, I strained to catch every word as the co-anchor picked it up:

> That's the fear tonight . . . in the wake of a series of air attacks on oil tankers in the Persian Gulf. . . .

What? The newscast starts with a slam-bang lead, boldly describing U.S.-Iranian combat, but retreats from aerial combat by saying it's just a fear. Nowhere in the long package does anyone—other than an anchor—express such a fear.

The script—and I quote from it exactly (including ellipsis points)— goes on to say that at the State Department, concern over the Persian Gulf was evident. But the script doesn't mention how that concern was apparent. Nor how concern became fear. That scary lead alarmed me. Many people, after hearing only the first few seconds of the newscast, might have started talking or shouting to other people about the news of U.S. combat. In the hubbub of the household, they might not have heard the next anchor say it was only a fear. They might not have listened carefully to the rest of the story and realized that fear was expressed only by the anchor. Many listeners—and half-listeners—who caught the mention of fear were probably left worried and confused. Some might have even become fearful themselves. All were misinformed.

What bothers me is the apparent willingness of the anchors, producer(s) and writer(s) of the newscast to ignore one of the basic questions a reporter should ask: "Who says so?" If they had paused to ask, "Who says he fears U.S.-Iranian combat?" they would have realized that their imaginative lead was just that—merely their imagination. If they did ask—and answer—that question and went ahead anyway with the fabrication, they ignored their obligations to their news director and to their public.

They could have tested the validity of their approach by applying a basic rule of broadcast newswriting: Start the lead by identifying the source of the assertion that someone fears the entry of this country into the fighting. Apparently, the information the newsroom had available, probably wire service stories, didn't identify or point to anyone who had expressed such a fear. So by that time they should have concluded that their hard-hitting lead was hollow. And they should have shot it down.

Few leads are as misleading as that one, but I hear many that are unsatisfactory because they make startling, controversial or questionable assertions without first saying who's doing the asserting.

And some leads start with quotations (without first saying who's being quoted). The offense is compounded when the quotation contains a *you* or an *I*, or both, as in this broadcast script:

> "If you don't come here this year when I want you to, I won't go there next year." So says President Reagan to President Mikhail Gorbachev. Reagan doesn't want Gorbachev here in September. He says it's too close to the congressional election in November.

Besides starting with a quotation, this script, reprinted in its entirety, has several problems. It didn't identify the country headed by Gorbachev, who was not the president. Usually, we don't have time for propriety, but I think it's desirable, on second reference, to grant the president of the United States the courtesy title of Mr.

On first hearing that item—and there is no second chance—a listener would wonder who "you" is—or are. And he'd wonder who "I" is. And where "here" is. After the listener hears, "So says President Reagan," the listener has to try to go back in his mind and fit in the pieces in the puzzle and at the same time keep up with the flow of the story. The writer probably intended the *he* in the script to refer to Mr. Reagan, but *he* refers to the last person named, Gorbachev.

When we converse, we naturally put the source first: "He told me. . . .";
"She told him. . . ."; "I told them. . . ." People are attuned to this pattern

of conversation, which is why it makes sense for broadcast newswriters to follow the same pattern and write the way people talk. But writers for print routinely hang attribution at the end of a sentence (frequently with "according to"). Or they tag the tail of a 25-word sentence with "he said."

Broadcaster writers must keep in mind that they're not writing for the eye but for a much different sensor, the ear. But they shouldn't overdo attribution. Not every story, let alone every sentence, needs attribution. When you have a story where the facts are public knowledge and indisputable—say, two cars collided on Main Street—you needn't attribute the story to the police. But if the police say one driver had been drinking, or the police affix blame, you'd better attribute that assertion to the police.

> *Not every story, let alone every sentence, needs attribution.*

When attribution is essential, it should precede the assertion. Experts are seldom unanimous, but they agree on this rule: Attribution precedes assertion. Here's what they've said over the years:

"Attributions must precede quoted material."

Edward Bliss Jr. and James L. Hoyt,
Writing News for Broadcast

"When attribution is needed, name the source at the beginning of the sentence if possible, and never any later than the middle."

E. Joseph Broussard and Jack F. Holgate,
Writing and Reporting Broadcast News

"Attribution precedes statements 90-plus times out of 100, and always before statements of opinion—a criticism, attack, prediction, etc. . . ."

Charles Coates,
Professional's TV News Handbook

"In broadcast news the attribution is placed at the start of the sentence."

David Keith Cohler, Broadcast Newswriting

"Put attribution first."

Carl Hausman,
Crafting News for the Electronic Media

"The attribution should always come at the beginning of the sentence."

Irving E. Fang, Television News, Radio News

"Never lead with a quotation. Always give the source of the information before you give the information."

Daniel E. Garvey and William L. Rivers,
Newswriting for the Electronic Media

"When you name the source of your information at the beginning of a sentence, you give your listeners and viewers a foundation for believing or rejecting it."

Roy Gibson, Radio and Television Reporting

"Because of the characteristics of the broadcast medium, it is confusing for the listener to hear the source for a statement at the end of that statement."

Mark W. Hall, Broadcast Journalism

"Put the attribution high in the story so your audience will not have to wait to figure out where the report came from. And put the attribution at the head of the sentence rather than at the end as is done in newspapers."

Phillip O. Keirstead,
Journalist's Notebook of Live Radio-TV News

"You say who said it before you relate what he said."

Carolyn Diana Lewis, Reporting for Television

"In all cases, attribution precedes the comment."

Peter E. Mayeux, Broadcast News Writing and Reporting

"Begin sentences with a source, with the attribution."

Melvin Mencher, News Reporting and Writing

"Never, under any circumstances, start a sentence with a direct quote and tack the source on the end. . . . This method . . . violates a fundamental rule of good broadcast writing."

1962. The Associated Press Radio-Television News Style Book.

"Attribution always should precede the quotation. . . . Attribution must always precede the indirect quote."

The Missouri Group:
Brian S. Brooks, George Kennedy,
Daryl R. Moen and Don Ranly, News Reporting and Writing

"Put attribution at the top. Although there are occasional exceptions to this, most of the exceptions you hear on the air are examples of a writer opting for effect over responsibility."

Robert A. Papper,
Broadcast News Writing Stylebook

"Place the name of the source you are quoting at the front of the sentence, not at the end."

Frederick Shook,
Television Newswriting: Captivating an Audience

"Broadcast stories usually sound more natural if you name the source at the beginning of the sentence."

Frederick Shook and Dan Lattimore,
The Broadcast News Process

"The best way to avoid . . . confusion is to lead with the source attribution."

G. Paul Smeyak, Broadcast News Writing

"Sentences are clearest when the attribution is placed at the start of the sentence."

Mitchell Stephens, Broadcast News

"In placing the source first, the radio writer again aligns himself with the conversationalist and departs from newspaper style, which in itself was a departure from the earlier oral style."

Carl Warren, Radio News Writing and Editing
(**It came out in 1947—apparently the first year in
which a book was published on broadcast newswriting.**)

"It is best to let the listener-viewers know who is talking before you tell them what is being said. This means the writer begins with an attribution."

J. Clark Weaver,
Broadcast Newswriting as Process

"Attribution in broadcast copy, if used in the lead sentence, is always at the top of the sentence."

Ted White, Broadcast News Writing,
Reporting and Producing

"Name the source at the beginning of a sentence if this can be done without awkwardness. And it generally can be."

Arthur Wimer and Dale Brix,
Workbook for Radio and
TV News Editing and Writing

"We ALWAYS report attribution at the beginning of a sentence, because that's the way we report it in our everyday conversations."

K. Tim Wulfemeyer,
Broadcast Newswriting

"The general rule for broadcast writing is that the attribution comes first."

Steven Zousmer,
TV News Off-Camera

"Getting attribution into your copy early on in the story is a cardinal rule that almost never should be violated."

The Associated
Press Broadcast News Style Book

"The source belongs at the beginning of the sentence."

The United Press International
Broadcast Stylebook (**And yes, the AP and
UPI even had different styles for** stylebook.)

This rule was stated even more forcefully in a book, *Television News Reporting*, by the staff of CBS News, published in 1958. True, no committee ever won a prize for writing, and no one ever erected a statue to a committee, but this book deserves our attention:

> "When writing for television, always say who before you say what someone said or did. . . . The viewer is entitled to know the authority for a statement or action first so that he can gauge what importance to attach to it as the newscaster relates it. . . . Do not make the mistake of leading a story with an interesting quote and then identifying the speaker in the second sentence. Almost inevitably, some viewers will miss the connection and will accept the quote as the newscaster's own opinion."

In other words: Attribution precedes assertion.

QUOTE, UNQUOTE

Quoth a network newscaster:

> Gorbachev delivered his sharpest attack yet against President Reagan's "Star Wars" plan, warning of, quote, "rough times ahead" if President Reagan and his aides, quote, "continue along the perilous path they have laid."

Unquote.

To quote or not to quote? That is the question: whether 'tis nobler in the mind to quote or take another tack to avoid a sea of troubles.

That and other quotidian questions about quotations vex many a writer, so let's see what experts say. And let's start with one of the earliest efforts to quash *quote:*

"Thoughtless use of such hackneyed terms as 'quote' and 'end quote' tend to interrupt the listener's thought. They have a barking, staccato sound no matter how softly they are spoken. They call attention to themselves and detract from the story." The criticism comes from *A Manual of Radio News Writing* by Burton L. Hotaling. It was published in 1947.

Another expert on the same wavelength was the first news director of CBS, Paul W. White. He wrote in *News on the Air,* also published in 1947: "Remember that since the word 'quote' is foreign to the ear as far as ordinary conversation is concerned, it probably always is disturbing to the listener. . . . Please, please don't use 'unquote.'"

"Such phrases as 'and I quote' and 'end quote are . . . shunned by skillful writers," Mitchell V. Charnley said in *News by Radio*, published in 1948. "The need for them can be avoided in most cases by careful use of the more conversational devices." Until 1947, Charnley said, publications on handling radio news were scant: apparently only two mimeographed handbooks printed before World War II and two pamphlets issued by news agencies during the war.

"It is old-fashioned to say 'quote' and 'unquote.'" *Broadcast Writing Style Guide* (1967), U.S. Defense Information School. More often than not, says the 1972 *AP Broadcast News Style Book,* using direct quotations in stories is "lazy writing." The use of these terms is cumbersome and lacks finesse, says Clark Weaver in *Broadcast Newswriting as Process.* R.H. MacDonald says in *A Broadcast News Manual of Style,* the use of *quote* and *unquote* is "a holdover from the ancient days of sending news by telegraph when the sending operator wanted to be certain the receiving end knew the limits of the quoted material."

"These words [*quote* and *unquote*] are jarring to the ear; they are abrupt and interrupt the flow of the story. Rather than clarifying, they may well confuse the listener. Even more stiff and formal are the phrases: 'and I quote' and 'end of quote.'" Roger L. Walters, *Broadcast Writing*.

The same disdain for *quote* and *unquote* is also expressed in more recent books. *Broadcast News*, 3rd ed., published in 1993, says, "This heavy-handed device [*quote*] has become antiquated." The author, Mitchell Stephens, suggests the use of "more subtle and less formal alternatives."

These attributing phrases inform listeners in a conversational way that they're about to hear a direct quotation:

He put it this way. . . .

In her words. . . .

The governor's exact words were. . . .

As he put it. . . .

. . . what she called. . . .

These are the mayor's words. . . .

In other words, there are many other words. Yet some writers use *quote* and *unquote* so often you'd think they're trying to fill a quota. Maybe they need to consider a few more quotations:

"It is awkward and unnecessary to start and end a quotation with the verbal quotation marks *quote* and *unquote*." Edward Bliss Jr. and James L. Hoyt, *Writing News for Broadcast*. (1994)

When should a writer use a direct quotation? "Only when it's neat, compact and the wording is exceptional," says Mitch Stephens. "Otherwise, paraphrase."

In *Crafting the News for Electronic Media*, Carl Hausman says, "You do not read 'quote' and 'close quote' or similar indicators over the air, except when the quote is of such a controversial or bizarre nature that you want to ensure that listeners or viewers completely understand that these are the newsmaker's words and not yours." One such extraordinary remark could be handled this way: "President Nixon said—quote—'I am not a crook'—unquote." If you wrote, "President Nixon says he's not a crook," you'd drain the remark of its tang.

So let's rewrite what the newscaster said in the excerpt at the outset: "Gorbachev made his sharpest attack yet on President Reagan's 'Star Wars' plan. He warned of [here the newscaster can pause or punctuate with his voice] 'rough times ahead' if President Reagan and his aides continue on what he called their 'perilous path.'"

And now if you need help in your newsroom to give *quote-unquote* its quietus, you can quote our quorum.

SOURCES SAY

If someone in your newsroom whispered, "They say you're resigning," wouldn't you ask, "Who are *they*?" And wouldn't you want to know whether *they* is one person or several? And, if only one person, is she the news director? Or an intern? Wouldn't you want to find out who has been bad-mouthing you? Or, worse yet, true-mouthing you? If you can learn who they *is* (or are), perhaps you can gauge the weight of the assertion. Or whether your informant is making it up. Making it up, perhaps, to get your goat, or to make himself seem knowledgeable. And did *they* say *resign* or *re-sign*?

Those questions—and more—come to mind whenever newscasters present news sourced so vaguely it's not sourced at all. So vaguely that listeners are left up in the air.

On a network newscast, a U.S. general in Bosnia commented about a U.S. colonel who was quoted in a newspaper. The colonel had spoken bluntly about the U.S. mission there. The general's on-camera reaction: He said he was disappointed in the colonel's comments and was looking into them.

In the next scene, in a follow-up to the flap, the television correspondent said,

But sources say the U-S government is embarrassed and concerned.

Sources is too vague. All news comes from sources. Was *sources* the general? He knows better than to go on record with that comment. So if he *was* the source, perhaps the correspondent could have attributed the remark to *a high-ranking U.S. officer.* Or if that would put the general on the spot, then perhaps a U.S. officer. But the correspondent said *sources*, plural. Two generals? Other reporters? A high-level U.S. official? A foreign official? A grave-digger?

The remark attributed to *sources* is such an obvious conclusion that you wonder whether it's the correspondent's own assertion, one he decided to pin on the ubiquitous and suspicious *sources.* But putting words in other people's mouths is unhygienic—and unsavory. The remark about the U.S. government sounds plausible. But the best news organizations ban the practice of quoting *sources* and ban the plural sources when a reporter has only one source. "When quoting one person," the *Broadcast News Style Guide* says, "don't manufacture others to make a point." Broadcast News (a part of the Canadian Press news agency), goes on to tell its staff, "After interviewing a fire investigator, for example, it's misleading to write, *Fire officials say. . . .*"

When you attribute a fact or a remark to a *source,* you raise several questions: Was the source a piece of paper or a human? Did someone really say that? And say it like that? If a listener believes you're honest *and* accurate, still another question arises: Is that unidentified someone in a position to know what he's talking about? Is he someone whose word we can take, someone whose opinion is worth listening to?

Another sore spot: using the passive voice to say a news organization *has been told*. This type of nonsourcing is as uninformative as *sources*. A television network script:

> ____News has been told that this is the critical weekend for retired General Colin Powell. Powell [should be *he*] is known to want to run for president, but his family is known to have deep reservations about that. He reportedly will finish weighing all considerations and decide this weekend whether he will or won't run. . . .

____News *has been told*? By whom? Powell? Someone in Powell's camp? Someone in a rival camp who wants to push Powell into declaring himself? A pollster? A consultant? A mischief maker? The reporter himself?

If, for valid reasons, reporters can't identify a source, they should at least give us a sense of who their sources are. But the best sources say *sources say* should go:

The *Wall Street Journal Stylebook* tells the WSJ's staff: "The word *source* itself is usually best avoided. It often conveys the idea of either more or less authority than the person deserves. *Sources say* may suggest to the reader that we are uncertain that we have the facts straight, so we are putting the onus on an unnamed *source*. In other cases, *sources say* carries the connotation of *inside knowledge*. . . .

"If a negative quotation isn't involved and the person's identity isn't confidential, there may seem to be no specific objection to calling a source a source: *a police source, a White House source*. But *spokesman* or *representative* is much preferred if the information is provided on the record."

The *New York Times Manual of Style and Usage* says: "The best news source . . . is the source that is identified by name. But it is also true that a newspaper, to give its readers information vital to them, must sometimes obtain it from sources not in a position to identify themselves.

"The decision to permit anonymity of a source must first of all be justified by the conviction of reporter and editor not only that there is no other way to obtain the information, but also that the information is both factual and important.

"When it is established that anonymity of the source cannot be avoided, the nature of the source must be specified as closely as possible. The bald and meaningless *sources said* will not do, and *reliable sources* is not much better. *United States diplomat* is better than *Western diplomat,* which is better than *diplomat.* And better still is *a United States diplomat who took part in the meeting.*"

Canada's national news service, the Canadian Press, says in its stylebook: "News sources given anonymity should be identified as specifically as possible. *Sources said* is bare bones and lacks credibility. Also don't use the hackneyed or meaningless phrases *political observers* and *senior officials* and adjectives like *key, informed, veteran.*" The Canadian Press also says: "Don't use others' unnamed sources as if they were CPs. Unnamed sources in stories picked up from newspapers or broadcasts should be [tied to the specific] paper or broadcaster. . . ." That means, I take it, that no one at CP should take a story from another news outfit that attributes its info to Joe Geronimo and then run a story CP attributes to Joe Geronimo. So CP's stylebook says CP should identify the paper or broadcast that carried the story lacking a specific source.

And the *Reuters Handbook for Journalists* says, "Avoid the vague *reliable sources, well-informed sources, sources, quarters, circles* or *observers.*"

So be as specific as possible. That way, listeners can consider the source. Feel free to quote me (by name, please): What's a source for the goose isn't always fit for the editor who takes a good gander.

Words, Part I: Put in a Good Word
Find the right word at the write time

W ords without thoughts never to heaven go," said Shakespeare. And scripts without thought, or enough thought, barely get off the ground. So let's look at a few scripts whose writers should have had second thoughts:

A Florida man is in custody tonight . . . charged with threatening President Clinton's life. Ronald Gene Barbour . . . , an unemployed limousine driver from Orlando, was arrested and indicted yesterday.

As soon as we find out he was arrested yesterday, we realize *is in custody tonight* is even weaker than the ordinary *is . . . tonight,* because Barbour has been in custody since last night. The news is, an alleged aspiring assassin has been collared. That script was broadcast in California, so why start by mentioning a place (Florida) all the way across the continent? Also, how does the suspect rate three names? And why do so many broadcast writers commit copycat crimes by using middle names for serial killers and presidential assassins?

Investigators say Barbour planned to kill the president during one of his jogging runs. And he [Barbour?] went to Washington, D-C, in mid-January, staying in this Virginia motel. But during that same period, Mister Clinton was on a nine-day European trip. Police say Barbour returned to Florida without ever getting close to the president.

If the arrest were made public today, it would be better to cut to the catch: "An unemployed limo driver has been charged with threatening the life of President Clinton. Investigators [Secret Service agents?] have arrested Ronald Barbour of Orlando, Florida. He was taken into custody [where?]

yesterday. Barbour allegedly intended to kill the president when he was jogging. So, in mid-January, Barbour went to Washington. But the president was in Europe."

How did investigators learn of the alleged plan? If the writer's source material didn't say why the suspect wanted to kill the president, the writer should have added, "No word yet why the suspect allegedly wanted to kill the president." Which leads to another question: How was the suspect allegedly going to do the job? With a gun? A club? An ax? (Just axing.)

> Police are investigating the death of a young man from Brooklyn killed in a spray of gunfire. A gunman opened fire on 17-year-old Dupree Bennett around 10:30 last night at 14-hundred East New York Avenue.

Police are investigating is one of the weakest leads in creation. You're right; it's not at all creative. If the police do not investigate a fatal shooting (or any shooting), you've got yourself a strong lead. But in this case, the lead is the shooting itself. And if the story is getting a little stale, perhaps: "Police are searching for a (fill in the blank) in the fatal shooting of a Brooklyn man."

Any wrongdoer who *opened fire* is, by definition, a gunman, so you don't want to say *gunman* there, especially so soon after *gunfire.* Instead of *gunman,* perhaps you could insert a few specifics: "a young man" or "a man in his mid-20s." Or whatever the facts justify.

> Bennett was brought [should be *taken*] to Brookdale Hospital suffering from at least four bullet wounds. He died a short time later. [*Suffering from bullet wounds?* Never heard that before. And hope not to hear it again. Better: "He was shot at least four times."]

> An unidentified woman, also injured in the incident, was shot in the leg. [Better: "And a woman was shot in the leg." No need to say she was hurt. If she was shot, she was wounded. People are wounded when they're injured by a weapon—shot, stabbed, hit by shrapnel or stung by a critic.]

> Police are investigating whether the woman knew Bennett or the gunman or whether she was an innocent bystander. Police are still searching for the gunman.

Bystanders, passers-by or victims aren't *innocent.* Describing any of them as innocent is journalese. And no strangers are *perfect.* Why did the shooter shoot? If the writer can't find out, perhaps she can say, "Police say they don't know why the [shooter] fired."

> Louisiana lawmakers have hit a major stumbling block in the effort to redraw the state's congressional districts. His name is State Senator David Cain of Dry Creek, and he . . .

His name is David Cain, not State Senator David Cain. *Major stumbling block?* Ever hear of a *minor* stumbling block (besides this one)?

> Two Illinois men have been charged with transporting over 200 pounds of marijuana after their car was stopped for speeding near Joplin.

How could they transport marijuana *after* being stopped?

> Once again today, the situation in Somalia is capturing the national spotlight.

The national electrician should pull the plug *on the national spotlight.* And cart it to the junkyard for rusty clichés.

> Everyone seems to be talking about Japan at the moment. Correspondent
> _____ _____ reports that the country really isn't ready for the spotlight.

Everyone is a dangerous word. Have *you* been talking about Japan? I know I haven't. Why *at the moment?* How can a nation be in a spotlight—or under a microscope? (Other dangerous words: *always* and *never.*)

> And January's earthquake caused so much damage to a historic Los Angeles church that it went under the wrecking ball today.

Sounds as if the church had been jacked up, moved onto rollers, then pushed along until it passed under a wrecking ball. In any case, *went under a wrecking ball* is vintage journalese. It's akin to saying that a surgery patient *went under the knife.* Better: "And January's earthquake caused so much damage to an old Los Angeles church that today a wrecking crew tore it down."

> A huge winter storm has much of the United States in a frozen grip of ice, snow and sub-zero freezing winds. . . . Some tough New Yorkers bundled up and braved the brutal elements. . . .

The writer deserves an A for alliteration and an I for illiteration. All sub-zero winds are freezing. *Frozen* and *freezing* shouldn't be used in the same sentence, at least not that sentence. *Brutal elements* sounds like journalese. And don't credit people who go out in storms for braving the weather. That's not bravery; it's probably either necessity or stupidity.

A Los Angeles man was shot and killed today in a fight that broke out between two buildings.

That lead from a city news wire could use a few good words. Skyscrappers?

As we see from those examples, a script can easily get on air, yet never to heaven go.

WASTING TIME . . . AND WORDS

Many newscasters fritter away time by talking too much about time. Example: "The space shuttle *Mercury* will be landing later today."

Later is unneeded. As soon as we hear *will be*, we know that the shuttle has not landed yet, is not landing now, but that it *will be* landing. Because it *will be*, the landing will have to take place in the future—and, we hope, not in the pasture. Everything that happens after the anchor or reporter speaks must be *later*. It's inevitable. So if an event will take place *today* after the newscast, there's no need to say *later*.

We hear morning newscasts say the president will meet with his advisers "*later* today." If he's going to be meeting today, it must be *later* (not *later on*). Later, we hear stories telling us he met with advisers "*earlier* today." If he has met with them, the meeting is already past-tensed. Whatever happened before the newscaster spoke *had* to have been *earlier*. So why say *earlier*? Sometimes we hear a story like this:

> The Union Carbide Company says it will resume production of the deadly chemical . . . at its plant in Institute, West Virginia, *some time* today.

If the writer had spent some time thinking, she might have realized that everything occurs at *some time*. Perhaps she wanted to suggest that the time of the resumption is unknown or indefinite. So what? Even if she knew that production would resume at 2 p.m. or 3:30 p.m., she needn't take time—hers and ours—to tell us the precise moment. What's important is that the factory will resume production today. Mention of the time may be essential when a newscaster is reporting an impending community event, like a town meeting. But for 99 stories in 100, it's a waste of time. Are there any exceptions to the advice against writing *earlier today* and *later today*? Yes. Almost every bit of advice or rule is subject to exception. Example: "The president will meet with his cabinet this afternoon and will confer *later today* with his National Security Council." But sooner or later, we have to deal with other words that add nothing to a sentence. And if they don't add, they detract. Here's a Washington correspondent's opening line:

> Well, needless to say, they were not encouraged here by Nabih Berri's comments.

If something is needless to say, there's no need to say it—nor to say it's *needless to say*. And we have no need to hear it. But if the story's worth reporting even though the reporter doesn't think much of it, he shouldn't dismiss it on the air by introducing it with a put-down. And when that correspondent said *here*, did he mean *here in the studio*?

Obviously is another wasted word. If something is obvious, why say so? A fact may be obvious to the reporter. And to some listeners. But not to all. If it's obvious to everyone, there's no need to say so. Of course not. Aha! Another superfluity: *of course.*

Another example from a network newscast:

> Today is Good Friday, of course, the day when Christians around the world
> . . . And, of course, at sundown tonight [*tonight* is not needed] Jews begin
> the celebration of Passover.

The curse of *of course* is that it sounds apologetic and condescending. It sounds as if the newscaster is sorry he has to say something that everyone knows. But on another level, it sounds as if his message is, "You undoubtedly know this already, *of course;* you know you do, but I'm going ahead because not everyone knows as much as you and I do." Or it may sound as if he means, "*I* know this, *of course,* but I'd better inform you." Listeners who didn't know about today's religious holidays might well resent the *of course* because they'd think it implies they should have known.

Often, the information that a writer couples with *of course* is not obvious or widely known. Even when dealing with a widely known fact, a writer should skip the *of course* and tell the story straightaway. Better: "Today is Good Friday, the day when Christians . . ." Or: "Christians are observing Good Friday." The use of the present tense says it's going on at this very moment, so there's no need for *today.*

One way for a writer to deal with a widely known fact that many people may not be mindful of is to mention it only in passing, not as the news itself: "The celebration of Good Friday by Christians today coincides with the start of the Jewish Passover. The two holidays fall on the same day only once every . . ." That way, the coincidence becomes the news. Yet the listener learns—or is reminded—that today is Good Friday and the start of Passover. In my book, but not in the Good Book, the *news* value of both holidays has, through the ages, depreciated.

Of course is a short form for another phrase that popped up in a network story about the airlines' frequent flyer programs:

> But, *as we all know,* you can't get something for nothing forever. The I-R-S
> is now pondering whether frequent flyers should pay income tax on all
> those trips.

Sounds as if the reporter knows she's going to dispense an obvious truth, so she wants to assure the listener that she's no fool, that she knows that what she's about to say is clear to everyone. The truism that you can't get something for nothing is about as profound, informative and newsy as saying, "Nothing lasts forever." Or, as many a Wall Street sage says when a growth stock falters, "No tree grows to the sky." Even the frequent flyer programs don't give away anything; airlines have built the cost of the programs into the price of tickets.

Also a waste of words, not to mention an assault on reason, is the lead that goes like this—and, in fact, went like this:

> Everyone this morning's talking about the big fight last night. . . .

Not everyone was talking about it. I didn't even know there'd been a fight. And not everyone who did know that was still talking about it. Any assertion that brooks no exception or qualification is an assertion that bears scrutiny. Although it's safe to say that everyone is mortal, any sentence that uses *everyone* is risking an implosion.

A network example, this one about the stock market's steady advances early this year:

> Everyone is looking for an even bigger winning streak.

If everyone on Wall Street—and elsewhere—were of one mind, the market might stand stock-still. Everyone doesn't think alike anywhere; unanimity exists only in the graveyard. Another broadcast generalization:

> All of Britain is talking about a royal scandal. . . .

Whatever the scandal, I can't imagine that everyone in Britain was talking about it. Or knew about it. The *royal scandal* dealt with a member of the royal family—through marriage—who had confirmed that her father had been a member of the Nazi S.S. She herself was not a Nazi, and her father was long dead. So who was scandalized? Was *everyone* in Britain talking about it? In a nation with so many subjects?

The flip side of *everyone* is *no one*. One of my favorites—but not everyone's—often appears in stories about escapees: "*No one* knows where he is." *He* knows where he is. And his whereabouts may be known by a friend, a relative, someone harboring him without knowing he's wanted. If the police knew where to find him, he wouldn't be a fugitive. By definition, a fugitive is someone who has fled and whose whereabouts is usually unknown. A fugitive doesn't broadcast his escape or departure. And *needless to say,* he goes without saying.

EMPTY WORDS

Quick. Name anyone in public life who isn't "controversial"—or any subject, from abortion to zip codes, that's not "controversial." If Mother Teresa went on a newscast and said, "God bless America," someone would complain. Listeners complain about every blessed thing.

Almost everything in the news is controversial, which means that almost every item is subject to or marked by controversy. Controversy is "a dispute, especially a lengthy and public one, between sides holding opposing views." And in some minds, *controversial* has come to mean "disapproved of" or "causing criticism." Whatever writers may mean when they insert *controversial,* many writers seem to think it's a flavor enhancer that's bound to spice up a script:

> Senator Edward Kennedy's controversial tour of South Africa has ended on a controversial note.

What made Kennedy's tour *controversial?* Most Americans probably didn't even know about it. And of those who did, probably few cared. At least, not enough to create a controversy. And how did the senator's tour end on a *controversial* note? According to the network newscast, about 100 demonstrators prevented him from making a speech in the black township of Soweto in South Africa. Is the stifling of a speech *controversial?* True, there was a ruckus. But the relatively small group heckling Kennedy hardly caused a controversy; and listeners in the States hadn't even known about the dustup.

In any case, nothing justified that script's use of *controversial* twice in one short sentence. The writer probably used the word because it popped into her head, and she figured it would add punch to the story. Instead, she should have taken the time to construct a strong sentence, relying on nouns and verbs, not mindless hype.

The *New York Times*'s in-house monitor, *Winners & Sinners* (now defunct), said, "*W & S* would be hard pressed to cite a word that tells less, yet appears more often, than *controversial.*" *W & S* also said that during a lull on night rewrite, two reporters tapped the *Times*'s Information Bank computer to see what the staff had been calling "controversial." They found that in two recent weeks, *controversial* had been applied more than 30 times—to Robert S. McNamara, McGeorge Bundy, the suffragist Lucy Stone, a fumble by a football player, pet projects of legislators, a U.S. stamp honoring the memory of St. Francis of Asissi, banks' alliances with brokerages, an endorsement by NOW, a new building in Portland, Oregon, an umpire's home-run call, Linda Ronstadt's "new wave" album, remedies for the rising cost of health care and the NCAA. No wonder *W & S* called *controversial* an empty word. Not only has overuse drained it of meaning, but *controversial* has also become a sort of cliché, constantly on call to try to prop up a story. But its emptiness leaves it impotent.

Listeners are showered by hollow words, the latest outpouring inspired by the presidential inauguration. Take *pomp and circumstance.* Please. In his *Dictionary of Clichés,* Eric Partridge defines "p. and c." as "splendour of the whole and magnificence of the details." But the average listener doesn't know what *circumstance* means, even circumstantially.

Here's an example of its use on a newscast:

> Soviet Defense Minister Dmitri Ustinov is being buried in Moscow's Red Square today with the full pomp and circumstance that his motherland can offer.

What does *circumstance* add to that sentence? Color? Detail? For me, it adds only pomposity. And prolixity. When I hear *pomp and circumstance,* I think of Sir Edward Elgar's march, composed in 1901. Shakespeareans might think of the line from *Othello:* "pride, pomp and circumstance of glorious war." In the 17th century, *circumstance* meant any formal show or ceremony. But now the *Dictionary of Word and Phrase Origins* by William and Mary Morris says that meaning is archaic.

The sentence about Ustinov's burial has another problem: *"the full p. and c. that his motherland can offer"* should be *"all the p. and c. his motherland offered."* Ustinov received all the p. and c. Moscow *did* offer, not all that Moscow *could* have offered.

Editors should also rule out old sayings served up as fresh dressing for what's supposed to be news. Here's how a network anchor began a story:

> Haste makes waste, as the saying goes. . . .

Haste does make waste; it also makes for reliance on clichés. Centuries ago, that line was good, so good it became a proverb. And its popularity has turned it into a cliché. Air time is too valuable to waste; as the saying goes, *"Time is money."*

But the writer who relied on "Haste makes waste" might not regard it as a cliché. Opinions vary. What constitutes a cliché is the subject of a verse printed by Roy Copperud in his *American Usage and Style:*

> If you scorn what is trite
>
> I warn you, go slow
>
> For one man's cliché
>
> Is another's bon mot.

With the approach of April 15, dedicated wordwatchers should keep a sharp watch for clichés that tax us all. One that's recycled annually is T. S. Eliot's line from *The Waste Land:* "April is the cruelest month." Even as you read this advisory from WordWatching Central, a newscaster some-where is probably delivering that line as if it were newly born. Instead, after a life of overemployment since its birth in 1922, the line deserves retirement. So do most variations: "For the Chicago Cubs, September has become the cruelest month."

Another Eliot inspiration that deserves a long rest is *not with a bang but a whimper.*

Also certain with the advent of April is that many newscasters will work into a story or a lead-in Benjamin Franklin's wrinkled adage: "Nothing is certain but death and taxes." And clichés.

But the cartoonist John Caldwell has managed to turn clichés inside out and upside down: "The early dog gets the worms," "There is no free brunch" and "What goes up must calm down."

As Prof. Ted Peterson of the University of Illinois said, "If you must perpetrate a cliché, rework it for freshness. For instance: When a veterinar-ian removed the bladder from a cat, he remarked, 'Just a case of letting the bag out of the cat.' Get the idea?"

Got it.

USING SALUTATIONS: MS. GUIDANCE

At the risk of being *exCommunicatored,* at least from this issue on women and minorities, I want to say I'm a Ms.ogynyst: I don't like *Ms.* No, I don't mean I personally dislike Mss. or whatever they call themselves. I just dislike the courtesy title "Ms." I don't hear it, I don't say it, I don't write it. Network newscasters rarely use it, perhaps because of misgivings over the buzz-saw sound: *Miz.* But in workshops and classrooms I'm often asked about *Ms.* In reply, I can't do any better than quote Trevor Fishlock, who wrote about *Ms.* in the *Times* of London:

"It is artificial, ugly, silly, means nothing and is rotten English. It is a faddish, middle-class plaything and far from disguising the marital status of women, as is claimed, it draws attention to it. It is a vanity." Fishlock ended his 1980 essay by saying, "There is an important battle to be fought for all women, not just a tiny elite." But, he said, "Ms. is one of the excesses of the revolution and should be junked." The *Times* did junk it. And many U.S. publications also junked it. Which prompted the author Willard R. Espy to observe that "Ms." will probably last longer in junk mail than any-where else.

According to a 1985 survey of copy chiefs of the top U.S. newspapers and magazines, *Ms.* was on its way out, at least in print. Three years earlier, the annual survey found that *Ms.* was acceptable to 57.3 percent of those surveyed. But the new survey said only 28.4 percent of the 200 respondents would let it stand in copy; 76.1 percent would change or omit it. The survey, conducted by Richard L. Tobin, who taught journalism at Indiana University, was published in the April 1985 issue of *Quill*.

The 1996 AP stylebook advises using *Ms.* for an unmarried woman only if she prefers it. The *New York Times Manual of Style and Usage*, published in 1976, was more restrictive: "As an honorific, use it only in quoted matter, in letters to the editor and, in news articles, in passages discussing the term itself." But 10 years later, the *Times* reversed itself. An Editors' Note in mid-1986 said, "Beginning today, The New York Times will use 'Ms.' as an honorific in its news and editorial columns. Until now, 'Ms.' had not been used because of the belief that it had not passed sufficiently into the language to be accepted as common usage. The Times now believes that 'Ms.' has become a part of the language and is changing its policy. The Times will continue to use 'Miss' or 'Mrs.' when it knows the marital status of a woman in the news, unless she prefers 'Ms.' 'Ms.' will also be used when a woman's marital status is not known, or when a married woman wishes to use it with her prior name in professional or private life." That prompted Gloria Steinem to express gratitude that she would no longer be referred to as "Miss Steinem of *Ms.* magazine."

And the *Times* of London also changed its stance. Its *Guide to English Style and Usage*, revised in 1992, tells the paper's staff to use *Ms.* on subsequent mentions for unmarried women only when they express a wish for that appellation (as the *Times* terms it). "In stories originating in America, however," says the stylebook, "use Ms. in preference to Miss, unless requested otherwise."

Whatever the policy of publications, few people use *Ms.* as a spoken form of address. Or say it at all. Some of the copy chiefs who replied to the survey quoted in *Quill* said their newsrooms had dropped all courtesy titles, including "Mr.," "Mrs." and "Miss," except for certain types of stories, like obits and engagements.

In writing for broadcast, I use "Mister" in a second or subsequent reference to the U.S. president. I was taught that at CBS News. In a second mention of a woman in a story, I use her title, if any, or I refer to her as "Miss" or "Mrs." When a newscaster refers to a woman only by her last name, I sometimes wonder whether he's referring to her or to her husband. For example, in the Patty Hearst case, hearing "Hearst" made me think of her father or grandfather. Newscasters would have dispelled confusion about the cast of characters in that case by using a simple "Miss" before her name. In any case, if you abandon *Ms.,* you won't be amiss. (As for how to deal with other disputed words in the debate over sexist and alleged sexist language—including *snowman, statesman, fisherman, manhole, maiden voyage* and *motherland—* that's a whole other book. A mankiller.)

Arguably also confuses me. It's a word I've been seeing and hearing more and more. When the trial of Claus von Bülow on the charge of attempted murder was moved to Providence, Rhode Island, a network correspondent said,

Newport has lost what is arguably the socialite trial of the century.

Arguably is so mushy that even dictionaries disagree on a definition. *Webster's New World* gives only one definition for *arguably:* "as can be supported by argument." My favorite desk dictionary, *American Heritage,* defines *arguable* as "open to argument."

In *Power Language,* Jeffrey McQuain classifies *arguably* as a Janus word, named for the Roman god of doors, who was represented by two faces looking in opposite directions. McQuain—research associate for William Safire's weekly *New York Times Magazine* column, "On Language"—says *arguably* can mean "easily argued for" *or* "easily argued against." In a *New Yorker* humor piece about clichés, Roger Angell wrote that *arguably* "allows me to say something and then partly take it back." And the *Wall Street Journal's* in-house bulletin (Sept. 5, 1996) said, "One could argue that *arguably* is the most overworked adverb extant."

The network correspondent who used "arguably in Rhode Island" might have thought, "I want this story to sound important. This may be 'the' trial of the century; I can't say so with certainty, though I can try." But that's an assertion not susceptible of proof. No one can pin it down. For casual listeners, the newsman *was* calling it the trial of the century. Few people notice *arguably;* fewer still realize it's being used as an escape hatch. Which is why the journalism educator Mel Mencher says *arguably* means "Don't hold me responsible if I'm wrong."

Another argument with that script: Was the von Bülow trial "bigger" than the sensational trial of Harry K. Thaw, the socialite who murdered architect Stanford White because of his affair with Thaw's wife, Evelyn Nesbitt Thaw (made into a movie, *Girl in the Red Velvet Swing*)? "Bigger" than Gloria Vanderbilt's scandalous custody trial? "Bigger" than the stock fraud trial of socialite Richard Whitney, the president of the New York Stock Exchange who was sent to Sing Sing? "Bigger" than the trial of Miss Hearst? Even if the von Bülow trial isn't the "biggest," it's big enough. Anyway, what does "biggest" trial mean? Whatever *socialite trial of the century* might mean, if it means anything at all, the correspondent needn't have embroidered his script.

As Einstein put it, "If you are out to describe the truth, leave elegance to the tailor."

REDUNDANCIES: ONCE IS ENOUGH

Ever hear a newscaster speak of an *acute crisis*? Or a *new* record, a *controversial* issue or a *final* outcome? If so, you've heard a redundancy—something said superfluously. Using too many words to express an idea or repeating needlessly is objectionable—unless you're talking about Pago Pago, Walla Walla or Sirhan Sirhan.

> *Redundancies waste time, blur meaning and lessen impact.*

In newscasts, economy in language is not merely desirable, it's essential. Redundancies waste time, blur meaning and lessen impact. The fewer words used to tell a broadcast news story, the clearer and more forceful the communication. Flab weakens communication and crowds out other news. With leaner stories, you can fit more stories into a newscast and make your newscast newsier.

I was nudged into writing about redundancies by a suggestion from a wordwatcher, Mike Berriochoa of central Washington. He passed along a few redundancies he had come across: a forest fire that's *fully surrounded,* a burning home that's *completely engulfed,* then *totally destroyed.* Other redunduncies we need to guard against:

all-time record	*head* honcho	first *and foremost*
new bride	*state of* Ohio	bouquet *of flowers*
new baby	capital *city*	*foreign* imports
new recruit	*sworn* affidavit	*root* cause
build a *new* jail	funeral *service*	disappeared *from view*
circle *around*	*self-*confessed	invisible *to the eye*
square-*shaped*	asphyxiated *to death*	*major* breakthrough
green-*colored*	smothered *to death*	*major* milestone
large-*size*	strangled *to death*	*mental* attitude
friendly *in nature*	suffocated *to death*	*value* judgment
short *in stature*	*originally* established	judgment *call*
few *in number*	*first* began	*temporary* reprieve
wide variety	*first* discovered	*temporary* suspension

while *at the same time*

widow *of the late*

advance planning

positively identify

grocery *store*

invited guests

fall *down*

lose *out*

pay *out*

cancel *out*

continue *on*

lift *up*

up above

down below

exact same

necessary requirements

serious danger

old adage/proverb

grateful thanks

basic fundamentals

usual custom

customary practice

still remains

component parts

appointed *to the position of*

commute *to and from*

shuttle *back and forth*

join *together*

eliminate *entirely*

so *consequently*

cirrhosis *of the liver*

death by *lethal injection*

strictly prohibited

surrounding circumstances

depreciate *in value*

opening gambit

undergraduate *student*

fellow classmate

doctor *by profession*

true facts

over-exaggerate

exact address

violent explosion

vitally necessary

nodded *her head*

shrugged *her shoulders*

winked *an eye*

a smile *on her face*

Easter *Sunday*

Christmas *Day*

legal contract

personal opinion

as a *general* rule

general public

general consensus

consensus *of opinion*

repeat *again*

total extinction

total monopoly

totally annihilate

totally destroy

flaming inferno

passing fad

ten acres *of land*

a distance of five miles

seems *to be*

appeared *on the scene*

they're *both* alike

definite decision

ever since

awkward predicament

hired mercenary

pair of twins

grand jury indictment

county coroner

at the corner of Oak and Polk

for *the purpose of*

future outlook

future prospects

minor quibble	*past* history	intents *and* purposes
may *possibly*	*past* record	*ways and* means
short *space of* time	puppy *dog*	*early* pioneer
in *a period of* 90 days	glance *briefly*	*compromise* solution
in three months' *time*	reason *why*	*eye*witness
it's raining *outside*	each *and every*	*ultimate* outcome
joint cooperation	*completely* full	*end* result
mutual agreement	*patently* obvious	*final* climax
previous police record	*close* proximity	*final* completion
previous experience	*close* scrutiny	*complete* stop

Some redundancies show up in ads, repeatedly: *advance* reservations, *pre*reserved seating, *free* gift, *full* quart, *hot water* heater, *new* innovation, *extra* bonus and kills bugs *dead*. When we're chatting, we tend to be casual and sometimes even careless in our use of English. As the language expert Bergen Evans observed, "A man who never said an unnecessary word would say very little during a long life and would not be pleasant company." But when reporters and anchors are on the air, they should be correct and concise.

I used to order a *tuna fish* sandwich. No more. Since a friend pointed out my offense, I've cut back to just *tuna*—and hold the *fish*. But an anchor who says *tuna fish* shouldn't be canned. (Some people say *tuna fish* refers to canned tuna.) Yes, we should guard against wasting words. Air time is precious. The battle cry of Strunk and White in their *Elements of Style:* "Omit needless words."

Strunk and White also say, "Avoid foreign languages. . . . Write in English." When the crew of the space shuttle *Discovery* went aboard for the second time after its first liftoff was postponed, a newscaster said the astronauts must have "a feeling of déjà vu. . . ." What he meant, I suppose, was that they felt a sense of having endured a pre-launch wait before. But that common use of *déjà vu* is wrong: déjà vu is the *illusion* of having already experienced something that is, in fact, being experienced for the first time.

Often, when newscasters use a foreign word, they misuse it or mispronounce it. Even when listeners hear it right, many (most?) misunderstand it or don't get it. After all, how many listeners are familiar with French idioms? Even if a newscaster knows how to use "déjà vu" correctly, he shouldn't use it on the air. Next time you hear the phrase, and you will, remember what Yogi Berra said (or is said to have said): "It's déjà vu all over again."

More important than knowing a few foreign words, writers should know the meaning of English words and how to use them correctly. We often hear mistakes that writers could have caught merely by checking a dictionary. I heard a newsman report on the murder of a Denver talk show host:

Someone fired a salvo of bullets from a high-caliber gun.

According to the *Naval Terms Dictionary,* a *salvo* is one or more shots fired simultaneously by the same battery (set of big guns) at the same target. So one gunman using one gun could not have fired a salvo, no matter what his caliber.

In another misfire, a network *correspondent* said,

So what's Hollywood been up to in the year since Bob Dole fired his barrage of criticism?

A barrage is a heavy curtain of artillery fire, or a rapid, concentrated, discharge of missiles. So one man, even a machine gunner, can't fire a barrage.

While discussing gunfire, let's target newscasters who overdo the word *war.* Let's save *war* for armed conflict between nations, even gangs. When listeners keep hearing of the *war against scofflaws,* the *war against jaywalkers,* the *war against crabgrass,* they get *war*-weary. What prompts me to start a campaign (no, I don't declare *war*) is the misuse I keep hearing. A newscaster said the president's chief economic adviser had often "warred" with the administration. Not *disagreed with, argued with* or *stood up to,* but *warred.* Now that's overkill.

Just as bad, sometimes, is underkill. For example, the first sentence in a story on a network newscast:

There were no surprises at Wimbledon today.

Reminds me of an imaginary newspaper banner: "No One Hurt in No Plane Crash." The tennis lead has several faults: It starts with *There were* and says nothing. Although the tennis results may come as no surprise to the newscaster, the average listener would regard it as news. Better: "The tennis star Martina Navratilova was favored to win at Wimbledon today—and she did. She won her fifth singles title there, her third straight." A network evening newscast:

To no one's surprise, Ross Perot says he's in.

A common fault with those last two broadcast leads: they're negative. Strunk and White urge, "Put statements in positive form. Make definite assertions. Avoid tame, colorless, hesitating, noncommittal language. . . .

Consciously or unconsciously, the reader is dissatisfied with being told what is not; he wishes to be told what is."

> A post-convention boomlet is not unexpected and certainly not unwelcome for the vacationing Mondale. . . .

That construction, expressing an affirmative by negating its opposite, is hard for a listener to sort out. And two double negatives in a row, as in that sentence, leave me out of sorts. And might well leave Orwell unwell as well.

Writers in broadcast newsrooms often work in a din and under pressure. So they sometimes turn in copy that's not so strong as it could be. For example, here's a lead sentence I heard on a network newscast:

> A prominent international bridge player told today how she was threatened with death by kidnappers in Washington, D-C.

That could be strengthened by building up to the strongest words, *threatened with death,* instead of burying them in the middle of the sentence. Also, it's undesirable to put the place name last. Better: "A prominent International bridge player told today how kidnappers in Washington, D-C, threatened her with death."

If the writer of the first version had reread his script just once more, perhaps he would have spotted those weaknesses before he heard them on the air. I ought to know. I was the writer—and still am. Or am I being redundant?

WORDS NOT TO LIVE BY

What's the best way to start a script? Hard to say. It varies from script to script. But it's easy to point out several ways not to start. Let's look at two of the most common wrong ways.

THERE IS/THERE ARE: NONSTARTERS. There is a quick, easy way to start a story or a column: "There is_____." Which is why so many writers start their scripts that way:

"There's a big fire near City Hall."

"There's a shooting at the courthouse."

"There is a train collision near Dullsville."

Now let's toss out the wordy, murky *there is* (or *there's*) and go straight to the news with a vigorous verb:

"A fire has broken out near City Hall."

"A lawyer has been shot in the courthouse."

"Two trains have collided near Dullsville."

These revised sentences are much stronger than the originals because they do away with *there is*, which is indefinite, indirect and indolent. The new leads start with what should be the subject of the sentence. Instead of relying on the static *is*, they move the action along with energetic verbs. As David Lambuth says, "If you have a nail to hit, hit it on the head."

A simple explanation for the weakness of *there is* is offered by Lambuth in *The Golden Book on Writing:* "The habit of beginning statements with the impersonal and usually vague *there is* or *there are* shoves the really significant verb into subordinate place instead of letting it stand vigorously on its own feet. In place of saying *A brick house stands on the corrner,* you find yourself lazily falling into *There is a brick house which stands on the corner.*" Lambuth goes on to say that in that last sentence, your attention is first drawn to *there is*, and from that to *stands*, which should have the whole emphasis, because it's the one definite statement in the sentence. (Lambuth's book, now in paperback, was first published in 1923. That may explain why *house* is followed by *which* instead of the now-preferred *that.*)

"Both [*there is* and *there are*] are dead phrases and should be used as a last resort," says John R. Trimble in *Writing with Style.* "Eliminating them through recasting," he suggests, "usually results in sentences that are more vivid, concrete and terse. There are many exceptions, though, and this sentence is one of them."

"There itself is not bad," says Theodore-A. Rees Cheney, "it's the company it keeps that gets it in trouble. *There* usually hangs out innocently on the corner with other idlers, verbs like *is, was, are, have been, had been,* and other weak verbs of being." In *Getting the Words Right: How to Revise, Edit and Rewrite,* he says, "These colorless verbs merely indicate that something exists, nothing about how it exists, how it behaves . . . nothing to pique our interest."

Equally wasteful in starting a story—or sentence—is *It is.* So experts advise against it. (To be precise, against *it is;* usually, it's also a good idea not to start with an indefinite pronoun like *it.*)

When *there* is used with *is* or any form of *to be* to introduce a sentence, *there* is called an expletive. So is *it* when coupled with a form of *to be,* as in *it is.* The wordiness—and unworthiness—of this kind of beginning can be seen in the Latin origin of *expletive:* "added merely to fill up." So the best rule for newswriters is, Make sure your scripts have their expletives deleted. There are exceptions. So I wouldn't say, "Never start a script with *there is.*"

Newswriters should also be alert to other weaknesses in their scripts. "Be especially ready to revise a sentence," Frederick Crews writes in *The Random House Handbook*, "if you notice that its main assertion:

▸ has as its verb a form of the colorless, inert *to be* (*is, are, was, were, had been*, etc.);

▸ conveys action through a noun rather than a verb (*there was a meeting* instead of they *met*);

▸ has its verb in the passive voice;

▸ begins with one of the delaying formulas—*it is, it was*, etc.;

▸ contains one or more *that* or *what* clauses, suggesting a displacement of your main idea to a grammatically minor part of the assertion; or

▸ seems to go on and on without interruption, requiring an effort of memory to keep it together." (His example: "It is what she recalled from childhood about the begonia gardens that were cultivated in Capitola that drew her to return to that part of the coastline one summer after another.")

Of those six danger signals, Crews says, the last one always calls for revision. The other five are just warning flags: "When you have made an indistinct assertion, it will probably show more than one of the features we have named; and you can make your assertion more distinct simply by replacing those features."

BRING AND TAKE. What do you think of this lead by a networker?

> An American airlift advance team has arrived to help bring food to millions of Ethiopians dying from famine.

Please don't say it's strictly from hunger. But surely it needs help. First, people die *of* an ailment, not *from*. Second, *famine* is not something that anyone dies of. People die *in* a famine. Further, the sentence confuses *bring* and *take*. *Bring* (like *come*) implies movement toward the speaker; *take* (like *go*) implies movement away from the speaker. You ask someone to *take* your letter to the post office; you ask him to *bring* back stamps. A reporter at the airfield where the advance team landed would have been justified in using *bring*, but the newscaster in New York City should have used *take* or *deliver*.

In the impromptu give-and-take between co-anchors or between an anchor and a reporter, there are far more chances for lapses than in a written script. That's why written words are, with exceptions, preferred. An anchor ad-libbed about some new electronic devices:

> Actually, I have heard that some of our correspondents actually will carry these on stories.

One sentence, 15 words, two of them *actually*. When you delete *actually*, you'll see that the sentence means the same thing without *actually*. In 95 cases in 100, *actually* adds nothing. Usually, it detracts. Used twice in one sentence, it distracts.

A good rule to bear in mind is one that writers can apply to every word in a sentence: If it's not necessary to put it in, it is necessary to keep it out.

TODAY/TONIGHT. It's a daily irritant for writers who wonder where in a story to insert *today* and whether to use it at all. It also annoys listeners who dislike having *today, today, today* tapping a tattoo on their eardrums.

"In the broadcasting business," Allan Jackson of CBS News once wrote, "the customers (your listeners) assume you're talking about what happened today; in fact, by the very nature of the medium, they assume you're talking about what is happening not only today but, to a large extent, right now." Allan died about 20 years ago, but his advice is timeless.

The first editor of the "CBS Evening News with Walter Cronkite," Ed Bliss, told me that his chief chore in scrutinizing the scripts of the three writers was deleting *today*. Although Ed was jesting, he made it clear that the overuse of *today* is nothing to wink at. Using *today* in the first story of a newscast seems reasonable, maybe in the first two stories. But in his *Writing News for Broadcast,* Ed advises, "Avoid a succession of leads containing the word *today*, especially in news summaries when repetition of the word becomes painful."

"It is a mark of the amateur to use *today* in every story you write," according to another textbook, *Broadcast News Writing, Reporting and Production* by Ted White, Adrian J. Meppen and Steve Young. "Your listeners," they write, "assume that your stories deal with events that are taking place today without your reminding them every 20 seconds."

On evening newscasts, *this evening* or *tonight* in a story may make a script seem newsier. But some stations, in an effort to make their late newscasts seem different from their evening news and more up-to-the-minute, put *tonight* in every story. So even if a story is fresh or has a new angle, this approach palls.

For example, an anchor on a late newscast reported, "A British researcher said tonight . . ." That was the first time I ever heard of a researcher who made public his findings just before dawn, as it was in Britain—unless he held a news conference at 3 a.m.

When we talk about the time and *today* and *tonight*, we should use our local time. Occasionally, a writer will see a story from Moscow that says the Kremlin said something *tonight*. The time in Moscow when the Kremlin spoke might have been 7 p.m. But in Washington, D.C., that's mid-morning. Yet, a few U.S. newscasters will go on the air at 6 p.m. or later and say, "Moscow said tonight . . ." I'd say the person who writes it that way is either thoughtless or careless with the truth.

A careful writer would make his script read, "Moscow said today . . ." But in most cases, the writer could skip the time element and use the present tense: "Moscow *says* . . ." The illogic of using any but local time is apparent in this imaginary lead: "A top Russian official said *tomorrow* . . ." Only infrequently is it necessary to say that it's tomorrow in Moscow and that something occurred at dawn there.

Unfortunately, some newscasters say a story broke *tonight* even though it broke hours or a day earlier.

If a story—or a producer—does cry out for a *today* or a *tonight*, where in a sentence do we put that adverb? If you use *today* or *tonight* in the first sentence, use it *after* the verb. It makes no sense to use *today* before the verb, before we even tell listeners what the action is.

We hear stories that start, "The White House today said . . ." The use of *today* near the top delays listeners from learning why they should keep listening. If you must use *today* in a story like that, you can make it, "The White House said today . . ." *Today* is one of those words so commonplace in newscasts that they induce yawns, according to Mitchell Stephens in *Broadcast News*. "They are best kept out of the lead," he writes, "or at least out of the first few words of the lead—what might be called the 'lead's lead.' News is what is special about a story, not what is common to every story."

Avoid putting *today* at the end of the first sentence unless it's especially short. Putting *today* at the end can be awkward and make the story wrong. Yet I heard this on a network newscast:

> Another Lebanese died of injuries received in that terrorist bombing of the U-S embassy today.

Sounds like the bomb went off today; but no, the Lebanese died today.

As for starting a story with *today* or *tonight*, don't, unless it's intended as a transition from a closely related story with a different time element. Another possible exception: to draw a sharp contrast, perhaps something like this: "Today, Mayor Meyer passed a tough physical. Tonight, he dropped dead." But I'd probably write it this way: "Mayor Meyer is dead. He died tonight of . . ."

Another angle on *today* comes from the newsman Jerry Bohnen, who says he tries to avoid *today.* He says *today* is too broad and covers too great a time span. Instead, he prefers to "narrow the time frame" for the listener. Rather than say, "A judge will decide *today,*" Jerry favors saying, "A judge will decide this afternoon." Although that's longer than a simple *today,* it is more specific and more immediate. If you have time, his approach may occasionally be appropriate. On an evening newscast, though, I wouldn't say that something happened this morning. That's too long ago, too long to say and immaterial. Nor, on an evening newscast, would I say that something happened this afternoon. It's wordy and immaterial. *Today* would suffice.

In most cases, it's unimportant whether the mayor said something at 10:30 a.m. or 4:30 p.m. But if the story just broke and the news is significant, I might consider featuring the time element: "Mayor Trumbull says he's resigning. A few minutes ago, he said his doctor advised him to move promptly to a warmer climate." Or: "Mayor Trumbull is planning to resign *within the hour.*" Or: "Mayor Trumbull and Governor Graham are meeting now." I think those words, where appropriate, heighten the now-ness of news.

Unless you're writing for an early morning newscast, using *yesterday* or *last night* in a lead is undesirable: listeners want to know what went on today and, if possible (and pertinent), what's going on right now. If you're dealing with a *yesterday* story, write a second-day lead, starting with the *today* angle. If it's a *yesterday* story that has just come to light, focus on today's disclosure or use the present perfect tense: "A man *has been* shot dead. . . ." If you must use *yesterday* or *last night* to avoid misleading listeners, use it in the second or third sentence.

Whatever you do, don't put two time elements in the same sentence. This network example offers the worst of times:

> The Chinese Air Force pilot who crash-landed his twin-engine bomber in South Korea last night today asked for political asylum in Taiwan.

The writer was trying to say the pilot landed last night, and asked for asylum today.

Better: "The Chinese Air Force pilot who landed his bomber in South Korea has asked for political asylum in Taiwan." Or: "is now asking for . . ."

Another lead that causes a listener's mind to swivel:

> And in the news *this morning,* in New York City, four men armed with handguns last night made off with a Wells Fargo truck containing 50-million dollars.

There's no need to say *in the news* in a newscast. And there was no need to say *this morning;* listeners who have windows or alarm clocks can be expected to know that. And the writer can get to the heart of the story sooner by not using the company's name in the first sentence. The story is about the robbery; whether it was Brinks or Purolator or Wells Fargo is secondary. Better: "Gunmen in New York City have stolen an armored truck with 50-million dollars."

Speaking of Brinks, here's a network lead:

> Correspondent _____ _____ begins our coverage of President Reagan on the brink of the summit.

Brink of the summit? Surely they weren't practicing brinkmanship. A brink is the edge at the top of a steep or vertical slope. A canyon or a chasm has a brink or two. And brink can also be used figuratively to mean "verge": "on the brink of bankruptcy," "brink of tears," "brink of war," "brink of day." But "brink of the summit" is faulty—logically and geologically.

The launching of a space shuttle reminds me of another problem: a reliance on clichés by some newscasters. They describe launchings as "picture perfect," "letter perfect," or "textbook perfect." For most of us, a simple "perfect" is sufficiently perfect. And when a shuttle is aloft, some newscasters say the crew has "a mixed bag" of assignments, or "a laundry list" of tasks, or "a shopping list."

Even when writers string clichés together like beads, I can usually figure out what they're trying to say. But this lead left me dazed:

> Like the sailing ship she is named after, the new shuttle *Discovery* will begin its first mission of exploration tomorrow.

Did the writer mean that Henry Hudson's ship, for which the shuttle was named, would also be sailing into space? Don't look for an answer in this space.

When a U.S. balloonist reached Europe, a network newscaster reported he had crossed the Atlantic successfully. That's like the news item we've heard—more than once—that someone has swum the English Channel successfully. But have you ever heard of someone who has swum the Channel unsuccessfully?

TONIGHT. A new blight is blanketing the land: "Tonight" shows, featuring *tonight: tonight* this, *tonight* that, *tonight* the world. Night after night, newscasters start stories with *tonight* and pepper story after story with *tonight*. So many *tonights* are sprinkled in newscasts you'd think some stations were plugging a new product named Tonite. Intended as a stimulant, it's now a depressant.

The writers' intentions may be good: They want to make their late newscasts differ from their early 'casts. To do that, some take the trouble to try to find out what's new—if anything. Some merely reword the early scripts. But many who update early stories think the best way to go is to insert *tonight*. Some go through such contortions to stress *tonight* they twist their sentences out of shape. And when writers inject *tonight* into certain stories, they also twist the truth.

Let's look at several broadcast examples:

> Two top school officials in Du Page County tonight are pleading not guilty to charges they used school funds to pay for activities at sex clubs.

Where are they pleading, in night court? They almost certainly entered their plea that day, not at night. So the use of the present progressive tense, *are pleading*, which stresses the continuity of the action, is suspect. Further, the adverb *tonight* (or *today*) is best placed after the verb. The script would have been strengthened by making it "*their* activities." I assume they're charged with spending the school's money on their own activities.

> In Chicago politics tonight, the mayor and his City Council opponents are locking horns once again. Aldermen from the council's majority bloc forced adjournment of today's council meeting, just 23 minutes after it began.

In the first place, the "in" lead is weak, the word *politics* a waste. (Who'd ever start a story about the president by saying, "In national government tonight"?) In the second place, if the meeting broke up hours ago, during the day, how could they still be locking horns *tonight*? If you keep seasoning your scripts with contrived *tonights,* how do you point up the freshness of a genuinely new story that did break tonight?

And *locking horns* should be consigned to the cliché closet, unless you're writing about trombonists at a jam session. Or about moose or elk. As for that unnatural *tonight,* let's respect our listeners' intelligence and not try to hornswoggle them.

> In DeKalb County tonight, just outside the town of Somonauk, the search goes on tonight for a seven-year-old girl.

This was the lead story, so one *tonight* might be all right, but two in one sentence? After all, listeners know that *are still searching* has to be *now, right now,* at this very moment, and they also know that when it's 10 p.m. and dark outside, they're engulfed by night. So they don't need to be reminded repeatedly.

The first four words of the script hold no attraction for listeners. Starting with *in* is pointless. And there's no reason to turn a good verb like *search* into a noun. And no need for *the town of*. Also, outside can be reduced to *near*. Better: "Police and volunteers in DeKalb County are still searching near Somonauk for a seven-year-old girl."

> Actor Stacy Keach is a free man tonight. Keach was released from a prison in England this morning after serving six months of a nine-month sentence for smuggling cocaine.

On a 10 p.m. or 11 p.m. newscast, why mention *this morning* unless the time element is significant?

If you're trying to avoid *today* in the first sentence of a script in the belief that *today* sounds too long ago, use the present perfect tense. It shows an action has been perfected, or completed, at the time of writing or speaking but is still pertinent; it can also show that an action is continuing into the present. Use of the present perfect tense also enables you to avoid that dirty word *yesterday* in the lead.

It's true that Keach "is free tonight," but *is* is weak. Let's make use of the present perfect to improve that script: "The actor Stacy Keach has been freed from prison. He was released in England today after serving six months for smuggling cocaine." The length of his sentence is immaterial unless you can say why he didn't serve the full term. Maybe the facts warrant your writing, "Because of good behavior, Keach was freed 'three months early.'" That way, you're doing the math for the listener and simplifying the sentence—yours.

> Tonight, all is right in the world. The swallows have returned to San Juan Capistrano.

After the first sentence, listeners may wonder whether all's right with their hearing. They've been hearing a steady stream of what's wrong in the world, so that sentence may throw them. The anchor's delivery might make it acceptable. But if the writer's going to use that line, he probably should use it the way it's most widely known: "All's right *with* the world." There's nothing wrong with saying "All is right *in* the world," but listeners familiar with Browning's line might think the anchor is misquoting it. The broadcast script works if the writer reverses the order of the two sentences and says: "The swallows have returned to San Juan Capistrano, and all's right with the world." The swallows have been returning there for more than 200 years, so you might wonder what makes this story news, what makes it different tonight? The probable answer: video—today's.

UPS AND DOWNS: USUALLY UNNECESSARY. A network correspondent reported that a nationally known candidate was *mired down*. But the newsman mucked it up. Someone who's mired *is* already down—stuck or sunk in mud. Although the use of a superfluous adverb, such as *down,* isn't on the up and up, it seems to be popping up more and more.

So a watchword for wordwatchers is, Tighten copy. (If you tighten it *up,* you may not wind up a titan.) Some verbs—occasionally called *merged verbs*—do take an adverb or preposition: cave *in,* look *over,* sound *off,* and perhaps what that correspondent had in mind, *bog down.*

We often hear newscasters talk about factories that have been closed *down* or opened *up,* and in those cases, *down* and *up* should be offed. In *The Careful Writer,* Theodore M. Bernstein calls these adverbs and prepositions "verb tails." He puts them in three categories: necessary (bottle *up,* break *in,* burn *down*); usually unnecessary (check *over,* head *up,* hide *out*); and unnecessary but idiomatic (slow *down,* hurry *up,* visit *with*). When a reporter is unsure whether a certain verb needs a tail, she can look it up in a good dictionary.

No newsroom should be without a good dictionary. Better: Every newsroom should have a good dictionary. The second sentence is easier to understand and more emphatic. (Not for nothing do Strunk and White stress that writers should put their sentences in a positive form.)

Sometimes, I hear a story open in slo-mo, then slip into no-mo:

> A package of military aid for El Salvador has been the subject of much debate in Congress lately. Today is no exception. House Speaker Thomas O'Neill predicts. . . .

The first sentence isn't news. Someone might try to justify it by calling it background, but it shouldn't be thrust into the foreground. At least, not with that flimsy construction. The first verb, *has been,* is a form of *to be;* like other linking verbs, it's anemic. It links but doesn't move. And the script's second sentence says feebly, "Today is no exception."

Unfortunately, we often have to write stories about the unexceptional, but we don't ballyhoo their banality. Instead, without exaggerating, distorting or misrepresenting, we're required sometimes to pump life into stories that are dead, dying or dormant. If we put aside that lead's dubious news value, we could improve it and yet follow the writer's pattern: "Congress has been debating military aid for El Salvador, and today House Speaker Thomas O'Neill predicted . . ." (We're not in the business of predicting, but the Speaker of the House isn't bound by our journalistic standards. Even so, a prediction is not a fact.)

Whenever possible, it's important to start a story by telling listeners something they don't already know. Using only the facts available in that script, we can strengthen the lead by starting with a today angle: "Congress resumed debate today on military aid for El Salvador."

Another broadcast item began wimpishly:

The diplomatic chill continues between the superpowers.

That's not news; it's olds. If something continues, it has been going on and it still goes on. So it is not new or news.

News generally reflects change. Except for a siege, a strike, a fast, a drought or other long-running story, no change means no news. So *continues* is static. It doesn't advance the story—if there's any story at all. And it doesn't arrest or engage the listener. Even if a newscaster is dealing with a story that changes only by millimeters, like that of hijackers holding a plane on a runway, he should search for a new angle or a new approach. And he should use vigorous verbs. *Continues*, as I say continually, is as colorless and spineless as a jellyfish. These comments are inspired by another broadcast lead I heard:

Power and influence win their magic in many different ways.

I wasn't sure whether the newscaster had said "*win* their magic" or "*wend* their magic," but both would have been wrong. If only someone in the newsroom assembly line had wondered about "*win* [or *wend*] their magic" and wended his way to a dictionary, the newscaster might have been able to work his magic.

Having a good dictionary in a newsroom isn't enough. Writers should be encouraged to consult it. One way to arouse their interest may be to post a sign at the dictionary stand that warns: Don't Open This Book! My experience in newsrooms—broadcast and print, network and local—is that the best writers consult dictionaries most. And writers most in need of dictionaries go to the dictionary least, if at all. Another writer who should have checked his dictionary (but not at the door) said that at the national convention in Dallas (I won't identify the political party or the offending party), *the crescendo rose*. A crescendo is a gradual increase in the volume of sound. So it's the nature of crescendos to rise. And of diminuendos to fall.

A more common error was committed at the convention by a correspondent who said,

But they come to Dallas . . . to bake in the 106-degree heat. . . .

Whatever they might have been cooking up, they didn't go to Dallas to bake. They did bake, but their goal was to stay cool.

One last note: Some newswriters have too many ironies in their fire. In fact, they often have no ironies at all, but they're quick to describe various occurrences as ironic. Perhaps William S. Gilbert was poking fun at a predecessor of theirs when he wrote of "an unlettered man of letters, attracted, like a magnet, to irony." *Irony* is the use of words to convey the opposite of their literal meaning; an irony is also an incongruity between what might be expected and what does occur. The *BBC Style Guide* says of *ironically:* "Overused. Irony is a subtle concept: it is not the same as *paradox* and it does not mean *coincidence.* It's probably a word to avoid."

Here's what a reporter broadcast after an Amtrak train jumped the tracks:

> More than half those on Train Number 60 were from a group ironically called Adventures Unlimited.

Apparently, the members of that group were looking for a new adventure, and they found one. Their name is not ironic, and their being thrown by an iron horse is not ironic. After all, they were seeking adventure, and they found it.

I thought I was rolling on the right track until I received a card from Ridge Shannon of Shawnee Mission, Kansas. He said my use of "refer back" in a column was redundant. He's right, and I'm contrite.

Out of Abounds. If there's anything some writers never run out of, it's *out of:*

"A story out of the White House tonight that. . . ."

"A report out of London today. . . ."

"News out of Hollywood. . . ."

Out of? News comes *from* somewhere. I've never heard anyone else use *out of* that way, except sheriffs in Westerns: "The word outta Fort Dodge is that them varmints is up to no good."

Although some newswriters have made *out of* common, that doesn't make it acceptable. As the columnist William Safire says, "Common usage excuses; good usage demands."

But even with the substitution of *from,* those leads need to be rewritten. Instead of telling the news, they start by saying they're *going* to be *telling the news. People* tune in to newscasts expecting to hear newscasters deliver the news, so an anchor shouldn't start by talking *about* the news but start *with* the news.

Newscasts consist of stories, so there's no need to start with the word *story.* And the lead that tells of a "report out of . . ." has another flaw. The noun *report* can mean a rumor or a factual account. So when we hear of a *report* from somewhere, we have no idea whether it's well grounded or unfounded. We also hear sportscasters describe an athlete as "*out of* Peoria."

Peoria is not something you run out of. And certainly nothing you can run out and get more of, like beer. No matter where you're *from.*

More writing that needs righting:

> Qaddafi also denied that Palestinian terrorist Abu Nidal lives and operates out of Libya.

That sentence has a past-tense denial of present-tense action. So it makes more sense to start with the present tense: "Qaddafi also *denies* . . ." Also: The writer meant "lives in Libya and operates out of Libya." This use of *out of*—after a verb like *operates*—is standard, but *from* is faster.

> The Census Bureau is out tonight with word of a baby boomlet gone bust. . . .

Is out with seems to be getting into more newscasts. But it's blander than bean curd. Like other forms of *to be, is* conveys no motion, no action. It's inert. Better: "The Census Bureau says the baby boomlet has gone bust." Not good, but better. Let's take up a new battle cry: "Out, out, damned *out with!*"

> Police said the exact number and extent of their injuries was not immediately available.

That sentence has what an ad for zippers used to call "gaposis." The gap can be filled by rewriting: "Police said the number of *injured* was not. . . ." But even after closing the gap, we still have a sentence that lacks zip. Better: "Police say they don't know how many people were hurt—or how badly."

> People came from as far as Chicago and Oregon to catch one furtive, far-away glimpse of the future queen.

Furtive = stealthy. The correspondent should have sneaked a look in a dictionary. The people he spoke of didn't travel that far to catch a *glimpse,* which is *a brief, incomplete view;* they traveled that far to get a good look, but they wound up far away. The people who traveled to Springfield, Virginia, from Oregon came from a lot farther than Chicago, so the correspondent had no need to mention an intermediate place— like Chicago. Also, cities and states shouldn't be mixed. If it had been desirable to mention a halfway place, he should have changed "Chicago" to "Illinois."

The faulty construction in that excerpt is heard often: "She returned home *to* find her husband dead." Should be, "She returned home *and* found her husband dead."

The script was also wrong to refer to the Princess of Wales as "the future queen." Wrong in 1986, even wronger today. In my column of June 1986, I wrote, "She may or may not become queen—and definitely not '*the* queen.' If Diana were to die while Elizabeth is still queen, or if Prince Charles dies, Diana won't become queen. And if they're divorced, or if he renounces the throne, she won't become queen."

Later, John McFadyen of Toronto told me that if Charles did become king, Diana would not necessarily become queen. So I wrote, "She would become queen only if Charles exercised his royal prerogative to have her named queen. His mother, Queen Elizabeth, whose royal birth makes her *the* queen, has not chosen to have her husband, Prince Philip, elevated to king. So calling Diana 'the future queen' is presumptuous."

Although Diana and Charles have been O.B.E.—Overtaken by Events (not the Order of the British Empire)—it's useful to retain that paragraph because it still carries a lesson: Make sure you know what you're talking about. And focus on what has happened and what is happening, not on what might happen over the horizon.

> A murder today is sending shock waves through a quiet Abington neighborhood. The body of a woman was discovered at about three-thirty this afternoon in the basement of her home in the 21-hundred block of Rush Road. Police say 44-year-old Marge McAndrews was stabbed to death. Her body was found by her 18-year-old daughter. Police aren't sure what happened, but it appears that the woman surprised a burglar. The search is on for her killer.

Like so many first-day leads, this one focuses on reaction instead of action. The writer should zero in on the murder, not on "shock waves"—whatever they are. If the writer had wanted listeners to know of the recency, he could have said *this afternoon* or *in mid-afternoon*. Or *within the past 90 minutes,* or *a short time ago.* The hour and minute add nothing; everything happens at one time or another. Who was the victim? Occupation? Family? Was it one of her kitchen knives? Rather than write, "Police aren't sure," I'd write, "Police say they think Mrs. McAndrews surprised a burglar." The script's last sentence, about the search for the killer, isn't news. Searching for a killer isn't unusual. It's customary. When a Boy Scout helps an old woman cross the street, that's not news. But if he trips her, that's news. So if police *refuse* to search for the killer, that's news.

> The Soviet Union shot two astronauts into space. . . .

Moscow calls them cosmonauts. So do we. *Shot two astronauts into space?* Was it a shoot-'em-up?

GOING OVERBOARD. We often write too fast, think too slow or know too little. How else could some of these snippets find their way onto the air?

> He's a Soviet seaman who twice jumped ship near New Orleans.

In fact, he jumped overboard, so the best way to put it is, "He jumped *off* his ship." *Jump ship* is slang for "desert"; it also means to go ashore without permission. But some sailors do go ashore with permission and then *jump ship*.

Ridge Shannon of Shawnee Mission, Kansas, tells me he heard a news report that the Soviet seaman had "*literally* jumped ship." In almost all cases, *literally* adds nothing to a sentence—except length. And *literally* should not be confused with *figuratively*. For instance: "He *literally* hit the ceiling." He hit it *figuratively*, unless you're writing about Michael Jordan or Michelangelo.

How about *virtually*? Ridge asks. Many people use *virtually* to mean *almost*. But most careful writers use *virtually* to mean "in effect although not in fact." An assistant news director filling in for his boss, who's on indefinite leave, is *virtually* the N.D.

> The American Museum of Folk Art is actually holding a contest for the best quilt in America. . . .

The sentence means the same without *actually*.

> The devastation was so widespread and communications so bad that only tonight did it become clear that this is a very major disaster. . . .

"*Very* major" is a solecism—an ungrammatical combination of words; an intensifier (*very*) can't be used with a comparative. Writers should use modifiers—reinforcing terms like *very, absolutely, certainly, definitely, quite*—seldom. If you choose the right nouns and verbs, you probably won't need modifiers. *Disaster* means large-scale destruction and death. Is there ever a minor disaster?

In *The Penguin Dictionary of Troublesome Words*, Bill Bryson says the *New York Times* was reporting a *major* initiative, a *major* undertaking, a *major* speech, two *major* changes, a *major* operation and a *major* cause on the same day the *Times* of London was reporting a *major* scandal, a *major* change, two *major* improvements, two *major* steps, a *major* proposal, a *major* source of profits and a *major* refurbishment. Not to mention Prime Minister John Major.

Bryson, a former *Times* of London editor—born and educated in Iowa—says, "*Major*, it seems, has become a major word. Generally imprecise, frequently fatuous and always grossly overworked, it is in almost every instance better replaced by a more expressive term." As far as I'm concerned, and I *am* concerned, that's a major pronouncement. A network evening newscast:

> Tonight's _____ looks at the major overhaul of welfare signed into law today and the major questions it raises for recipients.

Major is a major player in too many scripts. Remember: Where everything is major, nothing is major.

> It is only possible to understand the enormity of what happened here by taking one case—one heartbreaking case—at a time.

The writer was talking about an earthquake, but *enormity* = great wickedness. He meant *enormousness.* Better: *immensity.*

> Hospitals were filled to capacity.

A redundancy. Fortunately, the writer didn't say some patients were "in guarded condition." *Guarded* = cautious; only a doctor's prognosis can be *guarded.* A patient can be in guarded condition only when he's a suspect under guard.

Another term we shouldn't borrow, one used by police reporters after an accident: "The two boys were *treated and released.*" If they'd been kept in the hospital, we'd say they were *hospitalized.* Ever hear of anyone who has been "treated and hospitalized"? If you say the two boys were *treated,* that implies they were *released.* (The comedian George Carlin complained that whenever he was treated, he was detained.)

> *The final completion* of I-95 to the airport is a major step in making Philadelphia a modern city.

Do you think the perpetrator of that redundancy should *be finalized*? And does a stretch of road make a city *modern*?

> The three armed gunmen who have been holding court officials as hostages left the building and are at a nearby airport.

Gunmen are men with guns, so those *armed gunmen* should be *disarmed.*

> The F-B-I says that he's been given a safe haven in Cuba, along with a part of the stolen loot.

A *haven* is a place of safety, so *safe* is unnecessary. *Loot* = stolen goods, so *stolen loot,* too, is redundant.

A keen wordwatcher, the former CBS News executive Emerson Stone, recalls another odd redundancy, a superfluous suffix: A computer expert said her company had simplified its computer's keyboard. And she added,

"We wanted to eliminate jargonese." No *jargonese*, if you please. *Jargon* alone does the job.

> The stock market's been flying higher for months, breaking one new record after another and racking up profits for investors big and small of 201 billion dollars.

New record is an old redundancy. The total value of all Big Board stocks traded that year was 970 billion dollars, but there's no way of determining what the aggregate profits were. Only the individual investor knows whether the sale of her stock was profitable. If she sold for less than she paid, she wasn't racking up profits. The value of her stock might have increased, but if she didn't sell, she couldn't make a profit. The reporter didn't specify how many days it took to reach that "201 billion," a sum that strikes me as bogus.

> He said his personal secretary and her cohorts have left the Rajneesh organization 55 million dollars in debt.

A *cohort* is not a crony, a consort or a colleague; a cohort, originally a large unit of Roman soldiers, is used to describe a group with the same characteristic(s), such as the cohort of people born in 1965.

> After months of wrangling over which oxes should be gored on the horns of tax reform, the House Ways and Means Committee, after voting down a G-O-P alternative, approved a Democratic rewrite of the nation's tax code.

Oxes should be *oxen*, and they should be gored no more, especially by *the horns of tax reform*—whatever that is, or they are.

> Each player admitted that Strong was not the only source of their drugs and that their cocaine use had been extensive.

Someone can admit his own use of drugs, but he can't *admit* anyone else's. *Each* is singular, so *their* should be changed to *his*.

> A devastating fire early this morning swept through a stable at the famed Belmont race track. . . .

The story isn't about the celebrity or obscurity of Belmont. It's about the 45 horses killed in the fire. And scratch *famed*. It's not a conversational word. *Famous* is conversational but a good word to avoid in newswriting. *Famous* means *widely known*. And if a place is widely known, it needn't be called *famous*. Besides, if a listener never heard of a place, calling it *famous* won't help him or the story.

> Something of a royal sendoff today for Prince Charles and Princess Diana as they left swanky Palm Beach, Florida, for London.

Something in me not fond of an incomplete sentence like that one. Something in me not fond of *something of a*. Something else: please, no *swanky*-panky. *Swanky* smacks of gushy gossip columnists. In the same breathless bag: *posh, pricey, ritzy, glitzy, glittery* and *glammy*. Also *chi-chi* (sounds like a panda). A Canadian newsie, John McFadyen, told me, with a wink (I think), that Americans should use *royal sendoff* only when writing about the Boston Tea Party or the American Revolution.

> Police in New York City are looking for a trio of thieves who robbed a subway token booth early this morning.

They were not a *trio,* even though they did act in concert.

> A pair of U-S warships is on patrol in the Gulf of Oman, monitoring radio frequencies, ready to escort any cargo vessel that calls for help.

Ships don't come in pairs. Shoes do.

> Last week in Congress, a surprise upset for President Reagan.

Sometimes an incomplete sentence or sentence fragment works—but that one doesn't. *Surprise upset* is redundant; an upset is a surprise. Did the president score an upset or did someone upset him? The meaning would have been unambiguous if the writer had said "an upset *by,*" instead of "an upset *for.*"

> Almost 500 alleged Mafioso are on trial.

The plural is *Mafiosi.* Contrariwise, don't use the plural *graffiti* when you mean only one *graffito.* Or the plural *paparazzi* when you mean one *paparazzo.* And remember that *kudos* exists only in that form. But don't use *kudos* in a script—and never *kudo,* kiddo.

> And in Great Britain, the media takes the unofficial holiday quite seriously.

Media is the plural of *medium,* and as far as I'm concerned, no matter who says *media is,* and no matter how many say it, it's wrong. The media *are,* data *are,* criteria *are* and phenomena *are.* That's the way it is.

THE *ING* THING (AND OTHER WRONG THINGS)

When I wrote regularly for *Communicator,* a reader once wrote to me asking this question: "A question about a trend I find disturbing in news-writing. I'd like your opinion. I hear more and more stories leading with something like the next couple of examples:

> "President Clinton and Russian President Yeltsin signing an important trade deal today. The President saying it's a good deal for the U-S and Russia. . . ."

> "British Prime Minister John Major deciding to talk to the I-R-A. Opposition leaders calling the move a disaster."

The reader, Cameron Knowles of WSGW-AM, Saginaw, Michigan, went on to say, "I think the writers are trying to eliminate the use of the conjugated form of the verb 'to be'—is, are, etc. I think the use is grammatically incorrect. What's the word, Mr. Block?"

Ungrammatical. Not only ungrammatical, but also unnatural, unconversational, unjournalistic and unjustifiable. Literate adults don't talk like that. Literate children don't, either. But toddlers learning to talk do talk like that: "Mommy going out?" And Mommy or Daddy might reply, "Yes, Mommy is going out." Without thinking about it, a grownup speaks correctly by inserting *is*. Unless that grownup lapses into baby-talk.

When you take the subway in New York City, you can hear people *ing*-ing in the train: "My brother going to that game." When people speak that way, you figure they're new to English.

Literate speakers of English aren't always able to recite the rules of grammar, or parse a sentence (let alone diagram one), or explain why they say what they say the way they say it. But they know, almost instinctively, from speaking English all their lives, from hearing it spoken, from going to school and from reading books, magazines and newspapers, they know that those examples offered by Cameron are wrong.

In the first example, *signing,* a participle with no helping verb (like *is*) in front of it is an adjective. A verb has three basic tenses: past, present and future. Tense tells us whether an action has already taken place, is now taking place or will be taking place. If the first example had used *signed,* or *is signing,* or *will sign,* it would help clue in the listener.

A participle is called a *verbal,* but it's not a verb. So the sentence fragments in Cameron's examples lack the one element that has the power to drive a sentence: a verb. No one can make a sentence go without a verb. No one. Not Hercules, not Houdini, not even Hillary.

Some listeners would assume *signing* in the example is the start of an adjectival phrase set off by commas, and they'd wait for the sentence to be completed by what grammarians call the predicate—and what Prof. Paul Niwa of Emerson College calls the meat and potatoes. The way that example is written, listeners haven't the slightest clue whether the two presidents have already signed, are signing this very moment or will be signing.

So let's supply verbs and convert those examples into sentences that make sense: "President Clinton and Russian President Yeltsin signed an important trade deal today. Mister Clinton says it's a good deal for the United States and Russia." We should be aware that we need a *where* soon and insert the name of the place where the signing occurred. But at least we've translated that example from *Ing*lish into English. Now let's do the same for the second example: "British Prime Minister John Major has decided to talk to the IRA. But opposition leaders call the move a disaster."

The spread of the *ing* thing is what the grammarian H.W. Fowler might have called the survival of the unfittest. What impels writers to *ing* it? Probably a feeling that it makes news sound more newsy, more streamlined, more even-as-I-speak. But as we can see and hear (from the *ing*ing in our ears), *Ing*lish is the wrong thing.

ING SPOTS

If you keep hearing an *ing*ing in your ears, it may be because some newscasts carry more *Ing*s than buses in Beijing. (Ng, a common Chinese name, is usually pronounced by Americans as *Ing*.)

> *Raising* clenched fists and singing freedom songs, 20-thousand blacks are gathering for a mass funeral in a segregated South African township. Police are out in force, but there has been no trouble. 29 victims of racial unrest are being buried. . . .

Instead of telling us at the outset who or what the story is about, the writer starts with a participial phrase and slides in low gear to another participle. Those preliminary participles conceal the subject and leave us baffled. The weakness of that first sentence is compounded by the lack of a verb with a tense.

The second sentence is weak because it rests on *are* and *has been;* both are linking verbs and forms of *to be. Are* is in the active voice but expresses no action, so it's static. The use of *but* is incorrect; it implies that what is to follow changes course or is contrary to what might be expected. If police are plentiful, I don't expect trouble. It seems more logical to write, "Police are out in force, so there has been no trouble." But we can't use *so* because we can't know for sure the reason there has been no trouble. So instead of *so* there, let's say *and.*

The third sentence of the story says *victims of racial unrest* are *being buried*—as if it's being done now. Yet the first sentence said people were *raising* fists, *singing* songs and *gathering* for the funeral. Could all four of those activities be going on simultaneously?

Let's assume the victims were "*going* to be buried" and rewrite the opening: "A mass funeral in South Africa has drawn a crowd of 20 thousand blacks. As they gathered for the burial of 29 blacks, killed in riots, the mourners sang freedom songs and raised their fists."

Let's look at another network weakling: It bounces from *ing* to *ing* like the cartoon character Gerald McBoing-Boing:

> A U-S Supreme Court *ruling* today that could affect millions of workers nationwide, a *ruling* that states may force employers to provide particular kinds of benefits in their company insurance plans, for instance, *requiring* mental health, alcohol or drug abuse services.

The subject is a ruling that could affect millions. An incomplete sentence works occasionally, but that sentence, which is the entire item, is too long and confusing. And it needs more than downsizing.

When you were reading *a ruling that states,* didn't you think—for an instant—that *states* was a verb? In that script, the first two *ing* words are nouns, the third is a participle. But whether an *ing* word is a participle (an adjectival form derived from a verb), a gerund (a noun-like form) or a noun, some writers often use them in threes and fours. Here's a script from the Midwest:

> U-S Agriculture Secretary Richard Lyng spent the *morning* in Buffalo County, *eating* breakfast in Gibbon and *talking* with community leaders there and *visiting* two Buffalo County farms.

Is there something in a writer's first *ing* that triggers a mechanism that sends a stream of *ings* cascading into his copy? Just asking. This script comes from elsewhere:

> President Reagan and his wife, Nancy, are *continuing* their August vacation in Southern California, but correspondent _____ _____ is *saying* the president and his wife are *taking* a break from the routine of the presidential ranch near Santa Barbara.

News reflects change, so *continues* or *continuing* is an unsatisfactory word to use in a lead because it tells the listener that whatever has been going on is still going on.

That lead-in implies that the correspondent is going around saying something. And saying it and saying it. And in the next lead-in, the same writer keeps doing it:

> Big-city mayors from across the country are *meeting* in New York City *talking* about drug trafficking. And correspondent _____ _____ is *saying* a great deal of attention is *being* paid to the latest drug fad, the *smoking* of crack.

One possible explanation for writers' *ing*ing is that they want to tell listeners that events are going on at this very moment, even as we're speaking, and they think *ing* imparts immediacy: An occasional *ing* may add zing, but a cluster cloys. And can make a story soft, ungrammatical, illogical or false.

One of the most disagreeable of all *ings* is the mistaken use of a participle as the main verb in a sentence, as in this network lead-in:

> Japan's transport minister today ordering inspections of all Boeing 747s now in use in the country. . . .

On the same newscast, another leaden lead-in:

> Pope John Paul *continuing* his visit to Africa with a stopover in Zaire.

Writers who lean on *ing* may not be *Ing*bats, but they ought to ditch that feeble *Ing*lish.

Words, Part II:
No Journalese, Please
How to write plainly and clearly for stronger scripts

rong words weaken many a script, so we all need to watch our words. Exhibit A comes from a New York City radio station:

> In the Bronx this morning, a guilty conviction.

Wordwatcher's verdict: Guilty of aggravated redundancy. When you say someone has been found guilty, he has been convicted. Other exhibits from elsewhere:

> This fellow . . . did the exact same work in the exact same shop. . . .

Verdict: Guilty on two counts of aggravated redundancy.

> Police say the fireman was knocked from an aerial ladder by a hose when he fell to the ground.

Huh?

> Pan Am will continue to service its other routes.

Correct: "Pan Am will still serve its other routes." A mechanic *services* a plane; a boar *services* a sow.

Reporting from Geneva on the arms control talks several hours after the death of Soviet President Konstantin Chernenko, a correspondent said,

> The new negotiations are expected to last for years. In any event, Chernenko would have been unlikely to live to see the end.

Do negotiations *last*? Or do they *drag on*? An ice cream bar lasts. Chernenko *unlikely* to live? He didn't even live until that newscast. At least, the newsman didn't say Chernenko's death was a turning point in his life.

> Communist forces entered the city from six different directions.

All directions are different, so *different* is superfluous. In another newscast:

> They make speeches in seven different languages.

Same problem. And this:

> Four explosions in three different parts of Belgium . . .

No different.

> For the second time in the past four days, federal authorities are landing a knockout blow on a local outlaw motorcycle gang.

If the first blow had been a knockout, there would have been no need for a second knockout. Also, the opening phrase—"For the second time in the past four days"—delayed the action and diminished its newsiness. If the writer had had room, he could have gone on to say, "It was the second raid in four days." He did go on to mention

> four separate indictments.

At least, he didn't say the feds arrested "13 separate people."

> The rock group Wham! [has started] their history-making tour of China.

The collective noun *group* takes the singular, so *their* should be *its*. Newswriters don't determine who *makes history;* historians do. No one, not even Wham!, enters history books by whim. I don't want to slam Wham!, but I doubt that it will make even a footnote. Except in a history of hype or a history of histrionics.

> [Edgar Degas] will be 150 years old this year.

No matter what the anchor meant to say (in 1985), that sentence would have made the French painter more than an old master: the oldest master. The anchor was wrong on two counts. Degas was born in 1834, so this was the 151st anniversary of his birth. And he died in 1917, so he stopped at age 83. That means he wasn't able to reach 84, let alone 150—or 151.

> There was even a new American record established in Potsdam today.

A record set today *is* new, so *new record* is redundant.

> Firemen tonight called to the scene of . . .

By omitting *were* before *called,* this incomplete sentence sounds as if firemen responded to the fire by phone. When they go to a fire by fire truck, firemen go straight to the fire; they don't bother with *the scene of* the fire.

> It's May 29th, if you're just getting up.

And if I were up already, it's still May 29.

> A 44-year-old mother and nurse was found stabbed to death by her daughter.

Did the daughter commit the crime? Or did she discover it? Sharp-eyed Emerson Stone has found another ambiguity (*tribiguity?*) in *by*, which means *next to;* he asks whether the writer meant the mother and daughter were found side by side. In fact, the daughter found the body.

> *The only place so awash in emotion is Clichéville.*

The lead should not have compounded the confusion by identifying the victim as both mother and nurse. And the victim's age should not have preceded what happened to her. Age isn't more important than everything else in the story. In fact, age isn't exciting; everyone has an age. I'd use the victim's age—but later in the script. Better: "A nurse has been found stabbed to death in her home. Her daughter found the body. . . ."

> Emotions run so high in these games, where hopes soar one minute and are dashed the next, _____ _____ has been on this emotional roller coaster with the Villanova fans. What's the mood in Lexington, _____, or need I ask?

The only place so awash in emotion is Clichéville. Never let emotions run high. And never let them on a roller coaster.

A story about the arrest of a suspect in a fire that killed seven persons:

> His name is 18-year-old Walter Craig.

Imagine squeezing *18-year-old Walter Craig* onto a nameplate.

> It happened last night at 13th and Locust in City Center, Philadelphia. A fight between a pair of transvestites ended in death for one and arrest for the other.

Transvestites may pair up, but they don't come in pairs. (Socks, gloves and bookends do come in pairs.) Also, the lead is weak. Avoid starting a story with the indefinite pronoun *it*. I'm not saying *never*. (Almost never do I say *never*.) And I wouldn't use *last night* or *yesterday* in a first sentence. Another problem: The only verb in the second sentence is *ended*, a poor choice in reporting a killing.

A transvestite is someone who dresses in the garb of the opposite sex; in a story like that, the sex should be specified. Better: "Two male transvestites started quarreling in City Center, Philadelphia, and one was stabbed to death. The other one has been charged with murder. The fight occurred last night at 13th and Locust. . . ."

In a story about the president's impending visit to Bitburg, West Germany, a newscaster said a certain development had

reawakened the furor.

For all we listeners could tell, he might have spelled it "Fuhrer" (as the German dictator Hitler was called). If the writer had read his copy aloud carefully before he broadcast it, he could have caught that unfortunate ambiguity. Another newsman referred to a high-powered broadcaster as a "broadcasting magnate." Which made me think of a magnet used in a speaker.

These cases of hearing something other than what the newscaster meant should remind us of the risk in using homophones: words that sound the same but whose meanings differ. Other words to watch out for—and listen for—when we read our scripts softly to ourselves before turning them in:

accord/a chord	faint/feint
aides/aids/AIDS	farewell/fare well
attacks on/a tax on	formally/formerly
breadth/breath	half/halve/have
censer/censor/censure/sensor	hear/here
cite/sight/site	heroin/heroine
complement/compliment	malicious/militias
council/consul/counsel	passed/past
cymbal/symbol	pedal/peddle/petal
deceased/diseased	rain/reign/rein
defuse/diffuse	raise/raze
sects/sex	to/too/two/tutu
soar/sore	where/ware/wear
their/there/they're	wholly/holey/holy
threw/through	

Yes, we do need to use most of those words. But we need to make sure they're not combined with other words that lead to ambiguity or hilarity.

The homophones in that list are just a few of the many lurking in our keyboards, but enough are included in the list to remind us of all the double meanings we must guard against. We should keep in mind that what makes sense to the eye can cause double trouble for the ear. An amusing example of the confusion caused by homophones occurs in a skit by the comic Benny Hill. Two workmen drag sacks of telephones into a room and put them on a table. Hill snaps peevishly, "I told you, two saxophones!"

LEGALESE

Let's look at the following examples of journalese straying into the land of legalese.

> Until and unless this citizen is proven guilty, he is, of course, presumed innocent.

You can't call *until* and *unless* a cliché because the writer has it backward. The correct cliché (if a cliché can be correct) is *unless and until.* But either word alone works. A cousin of *unless and until* is *if, as* and *when.* And that, too, is a cliché. Both phrases are legalese.

Lawyers like to use a string of synonyms or near-synonyms in doublets: *null and void, do and perform.* Or triplets: *cancel, annul and set aside; give, devise and bequeath; possession, custody and control.* Lawyers use these phrases to be emphatic, to cover all bases and to sound lawyerly. But newswriters should keep from, abstain from and refrain from chewing their cabbage thrice. Even twice.

The word *citizen* in the excerpt is too fancy. Why not call him a man? Also, *proven* should be *proved.* And *of course* is best avoided. For listeners who know of the long-standing legal presumption of innocence, *of course* doesn't help. And for listeners who don't know, *of course* doesn't help at all. Of course not.

> Alcoa was the point-size gainer in the Dow Jones Industrial Average today, rising two and three-eighths after several days of losses after being downgraded and having its earnings estimates cut.

After, after! Twice in one sentence is enough to cause *aftershock.* And that sentence in the script is too long, too lumpy, too loopy. What's a *point-size gainer*? That lingo is a loser. More to the point, who cut Alcoa's earnings estimates? Management? A newsletter? A brokerage house? "*Having* its earnings estimates cut" sounds as if Alcoa *arranged* to have the estimates cut.

Better: "The biggest gainer among the Dow Jones Industrials today was Alcoa, up two and three-eighths. Recently, earnings estimates for Alcoa were cut—and the stock was downgraded. So Alcoa started slipping—until today." Original: 28 words; rewrite: 31 words. Slightly longer, but clearer.

> Since last Tuesday, New Yorkers have been riveted over the fate of a woman brutally attacked in Central Park. As the woman fights for her life in the hospital and the search for her assailant continues, the story has sent shock waves across the country.

The script was broadcast on a Sunday, five days after the crime, so there was no need to say "*last* Tuesday." Instead of "Since last Tuesday," make it "for five days." Undoubtedly, the attack upset people, but I doubt that shock waves, whatever they are, spread across the country.

"Riveted *over*"! You can be riveted *by* someone's story. Or riveted *to* a spot. Or riveted *at* the sight of a horror. But not riveted *over* anything. If you don't think it over, you may be raked *over* the coals.

Fights for her life is journalese. And *continues* is a weak verb for a lead or lead-in. Better (if you would retain that lead-in's structure—and I wouldn't): "and the police search for her attacker. . . ." Yes, *attacker*, not *assailant*. At least, the writer didn't call it a *senseless* attack—in contrast to a *sensible* attack.

The correspondent went on to echo the anchor and say the victim was "brutally beaten." The beating *was* brutal, more brutal than most beatings. But one *brutally* is enough. I heard you the first time. More network work that needs work:

> Right after Buddy Lazier took the checkered flag to win the 80th running of the Indy 500, three other cars were involved in a spectacular crash just before the finish line. In Brooklyn, Michigan, for a running of the U-S 500, they were delayed by a spectacular crash before the race even got under way. It continues outside of [delete *of*] Detroit.

The first sentence in that excerpt raises several questions. *Involved* is a fuzzy word. Did poor driving by one of the three cars cause the other two to crash? Or what? And what does *just before the finish line* mean? Two *spectacular* crashes? *Spectacular* is a much-overused word. Twice a year it may be bearable, but not in two straight sentences. Or even in two ovals. (Perhaps the writer needs a crash course.)

Got under way = began. Also, the last sentences of that excerpt need straightening out. Those sentences suggest the race was moved from Brooklyn to a track *outside Detroit.* (And better than the two-syllable word *outside* is *near.*) But no, the writer was merely slipping in a geographical clue to tell us where Brooklyn is.

Another network excerpt:

> Now a published report says that to save money the cut-rate airline is offering voluntary unpaid leaves to many of its four-thousand employees.

What's a *published report*? A thoroughly sourced article in a reliable newspaper? A rumor in a gossip column? (We don't report rumors or gossip, except in highly unusual circumstances.) Why not identify the source? Also: no need for *voluntary*. If the leaves were involuntary, they'd have been *imposed*, not *offered*.

And another network sourcing problem:

> _____ News has learned the Medicare trustees will report tomorrow that by the year 2001, the Medicare Part A Trust Fund—the part that covers hospital costs—will be 16-billion dollars in the red, according to sources close to the trustees.

The best sources in the art of writing for the ear agree that one rule in broadcast newswriting is inviolable: Attribution precedes assertion. So never hang *according to* or *he said* on the end of a sentence. But that script opened by crediting the network with *learning* something, then, at the end of the long sentence, tagging on a vague attribution. That means the network has learned something according to *sources*. Absurd! Where were those newsroom eyes that are supposed to eyeball—and, if necessary, blackball—scripts?

Network, too:

> Later, behind the scenes at Sotheby's for the famous Jackie Kennedy Onassis auction . . .

Famous is generally as useless as feathers on a snake. So please don't call the former First Lady or the auction *famous*. If a listener has heard of her—and breathes there a soul with mind so dead who hasn't—*famous* is silly. As for listeners who don't know the name, *famous* can't fill the void.

No wonder Steve Martin says a writer's best friend is sometimes the delete key.

CLICHÉS: THE WRONG STUFF

Some writers work so hard trying to reach listeners they must think a metaphor is something you shout through. Occasionally, a figure of speech, like a metaphor or simile, can bring copy to life, but only if it's fresh or at least not stale. Too often, though, writers fall back on a device so worn-out its fizz has fizzled.

No central registry keeps track of every use of a metaphor (an implied comparison) or simile (explicit comparison). Yet even half-listeners can sense that *war of words* is overworked by newscasters. A word doctor would pronounce it dead. If it is dead, it needs burial. If it's only overworked, it needs a rest. Yet a network anchor said someone had *triggered* a war of words.

The first use of *war of words* is attributed to Alexander Pope (not to be confused with Pope Alexander). According to the *Oxford English Dictionary,* the English poet used *war of words* in 1725. So that metaphor is more than 280 years old. Not even the comedian Milton Berle—known as the Thief of Bad Gags—would take material that old, not even from a Youngman. (Yes, Henny Youngman.) As for *trigger,* that word is so misused and overused, I'd avoid it unless I were writing about Roy Rogers' horse.

Metaphor comes from the Greek word for transference. And Pope has been praised for his ability to transfer the fury of fighting to speech. And for the first recorded use of *war of words,* he certainly deserves credit. So does the first wordwatcher who recognized Pope's imaginative phrase and used it himself (with or without credit). But by now, it has become a lame warhorse, trotted out so often by so many writers that it's ready for the glueworks.

Instead of striving for originality and shunning clichés, unthinking writers turn every clothesline quarrel, as we used to call a backyard shouting match, into a "war of words." These overkillers should be reminded of Strunk and White's advice in their *Elements of Style:* "Use figures of speech sparingly." Orwell, as we know, put it more sternly: "Never use a metaphor, simile or other figure of speech which you are used to seeing in print."

THE CLICHÉ HIT LIST

Below is a list of more than 250 clichés that hurt broadcast copy. I've assembled this list from several sources, including *Newsman's English* by Harold Evans, *Interpretative Reporting* by Curtis D. MacDougall, *The Associated Press Guide to News Writing, Words into Type* and *The Written Word.* The editorial consultant Albert Toner has listed hundreds of once-bright words and phrases that have lost their luster and become clichés. "How many of these tranquilizers," he asks, "do you mistake for stimulants?"

64,000-dollar question	back to basics . . . or square one	beginning of the end
a shot rang out	back-to-back	bewildering variety
agonizing reappraisal	back to the drawing board	beyond the shadow of a doubt
agree to disagree	battled furiously	bit the dust
aired their grievances	beat a hasty retreat	bitter end
as a matter of fact	beautiful people	blazing inferno
as luck would have it	beauty and the beast	blessed event
ax to grind		blessing in disguise

blissful ignorance

brave the elements

bright and early

brutal reminder

brutally murdered

built-in safeguard

bull in a china shop

burning issue

by the same token

calm before the storm

can of worms

can't see the forest for the trees

caught red-handed

chalked up a victory

charged with emotion

charity toss

checkered career

cherished belief

city fathers

clear as crystal

close encounters of any kind

clutches of the law

collision course

colorful scene

comparing apples and oranges

conspicuous by its absence

conventional wisdom

cool as a cucumber

couldn't agree more/ care less

coveted trophy

crying need

cutting edge

cutting room floor

Dan Cupid

daring daylight robbery

deadly earnest

deafening crash

death car

different drummer

doctors fought

doing something right

doomed to disappointment

down the tubes

dramatic new move

dreaded disease

drop in the bucket

dull thud

easier said than done

extra mile

eyeball to eyeball

failed to dampen spirits

fall on deaf ears

fast lane

fat city

father figure

Father Time

feelings ran high

few and far between

finishing touches

fly in the ointment

foregone conclusion

forget it

fusillade of bullets

GI Joe

game of inches

game plan

garbage in, garbage out

give the green light

glaring omission

glutton for punishment

go over the top

goes with the territory

Grim Reaper

grind to a halt

gruesome find

hail of bullets

handwriting on the wall

hard ball

hearts and minds

Herculean efforts

hit the ground running

hit the nail on the head

hit the spot

hook or by crook

hue and cry

hurriedly retraced his steps

if the truth be told

ill-fated

in full swing

in no uncertain terms

in the limelight

in the nick of time

in the shadow of their own goal posts

infuriated mob

interestingly enough

iron out the difficulty

irony of fate

it stands to reason

Jack Frost

John Q. Public

keep options open

Lady Luck

land-office business

lashed out

last but not least

leaps and bounds

leave no stone unturned

leaves much to be desired

left up in the air

lend a helping hand

like gangbusters

limp into port

long-felt need

looking for all the world like

man in the street

masterpiece of understatement

matter of life and death

method to his madness

mind-boggling

miraculous escape

moment of truth

Mother Nature

move into high gear

Mr. Average Citizen

mystery surrounds

name of the game

nation that can go to the moon

not to be outdone

on cloud nine

one-on-one

only game in town

Operation Whatever

over and above

paint a grim picture

part and parcel

pay the supreme penalty

pecking order

picture of health

pigskin

pitched battle

point with pride

police combing the city

police dragnets

pool of blood

powers that be

pre-dawn darkness

Project Anything

pros and cons

proud heritage

proud parents

proud possessor

psychic income

psychological moment

radiant bride

rain cats and dogs

red faces

red-letter day

reign of terror

reinventing the wheel

rifled the ball

ripe old age

rubber chicken circuit

rushed to the scene

says it all

scintilla of evidence

separate the men from
the boys

separate the sheep
from the goats

shot in the arm

shrouded in mystery

sick and tired

silver lining in the
cloud

since sliced bread

single most

sleuths

slippery slope

slow as molasses

smart money

smoking gun

spearheading the
campaign

speculation was rife

spirited debate

spotlessly clean

spotlight the need

sprawling base

stagger the
imagination

state of the art

storm of protest

superhuman effort

supreme sacrifice

sweet smell of success

swoop down

take a dim view of

tangle with

tell it like it is

tender mercies

that's for sure

threw a monkey
wrench into

tip of the iceberg

trail of death and
destruction

truth is stranger than
fiction

uncharted seas

understatement of the

_____

unprecedented
situation

untiring efforts

up for grabs

upset the apple cart

vanish into thin air

venture a suggestion

very private person

view with alarm

voice the sentiments

voice approval

walking encyclopedia

wall-to-wall

watery grave

wealth of information

what with one thing or
another

when all is said and
done

where it's at

wide-open spaces

won't fly

worked like Trojans

wrapped in mystery

you can say that again

you win some, you
lose some

you're damned if you
do, you're damned
if you don't

young hopeful

your guess is as good
as _____

If we use these phrases in casual conversation, no one is going to get his nose out of joint. But if we use those phrases in news scripts, we risk being written off as hacks. "They [clichés] are so smooth from wear," says *The Written Word*, "that they slip off the tongue or pen with great ease, and that can be the undoing of an unwary writer or speaker. . . . The temptation [to use them] is great merely because many of the expressions in question are catchy (or once were), and to an untrained user of language their surface appeal and never-ending appearance may seem a recommendation in itself. . . . *Do one's thing, bite the bullet* and *keep a low profile* suggest that such expressions seem to age very fast through relentless use."

Now that we've disposed of that "mixed bag of leftovers," a term minted by a newscaster (a mixed metaphor like that is what Theodore Bernstein calls a "mixaphor"), let's look at another case of wrongdoing, one that was broadcast:

> New York City detectives today will pick up self-admitted subway vigilante Bernhard Goetz, who waived extradition at a court appearance in Concord, New Hampshire.

Obviously—except to the writer who wrote the copy, the editor who edited it, the producer who produced it and the anchor who delivered it—no one can admit to wrongdoing but oneself. So self-admitted is tautological. A logical thought would have prompted someone to delete *self*; it should have been self-evident.

After a second look at that broadcast excerpt, I'd rewrite it and try to place *today* (as I always do if I use it) after the verb: "New York City police are going to bring back the so-called subway vigilante, Bernhard Goetz, today from New Hampshire. He waived extradition at a hearing in Concord." I substituted *police* for *detectives;* it's shorter. Besides, they didn't have to do any detecting.

A network newscaster reported that indictments against a mess of mobsters had been handed down. Rub out *down* and make it *up*. A grand jury hands *up* indictments to a judge; a judge hands *down* rulings. That's today's final decision.

POLITICAL CLICHÉS: THE WRONG STUFF

As an old city editor of mine is reputed—or disreputed—to have said, "We need some new clichés." Or we need to try harder to resist the first cliché that comes to mind. Clichés spring to mind because we've heard them so often they've saturated our consciousness, ready for instant retrieval. But we should be on guard against them precisely because of their instantaneity and ubiquity.

Here are some of the political clichés that ricochet and re-echo through our minds, clichés that we should not use at the drop of a hat in the ring:

FRONT-RUNNER. Put it on the back-burner. Who knows for sure which candidate—or non-candidate—is ahead until all the delegates or voters have cast ballots? As an article in the *Washington Journalism Review* said, "Hart's New Hampshire surprise did not show that reporters need better ways to pinpoint the leader; it showed the error of trying to do so at all." When Sen. Gary Hart dropped out of the race for the presidency in 1988, it was called a Hart-breaker. We also heard *Hart attack, Hartstopper, Hart failure.* Bypass 'em. Puns on people's names age rapidly. And most people whose names lend themselves to puns have heard them all—many times. Just don't "Kick that Block!"

THE LAST HURRAH. When Edwin O'Connor wrote *The Last Hurrah* in 1956, the phrase was fresh. But it has long since gone stale. Like *It's all over but the shouting,* it deserves its own bye-bye.

AN IDEA WHOSE TIME HAS COME. When Victor Hugo (or his translator) wrote, "Greater than the tread of mighty armies is an idea whose time has come," he expressed an idea with originality. But his line has been trampled by his followers' footsteps. Even the variations since it was written in 1852 have become tiresome: "an idea whose time has come again," "an idea whose time has come and gone," "an idea whose time will never come." For all of them, original and variations, time has run out.

THE RIGHT STUFF. Clichés don't have it.

ON THE CAMPAIGN TRAIL. Too tired for *the comeback trail.* Why not merely say the candidate is campaigning?

ON THE HUSTINGS. It's an outdated and wordy way of saying someone is on the road campaigning. What are the hustings? And where are the hustings? (Not to be confused with the Battle of Hustings or Hustings-on-Hudson.)

ON THE STUMP. Worn to the stump.

A real horse race. Fits the definition of a cliché by Eric Partridge: "So hackneyed as to be knock-kneed and spavined." When tempted to use it, just say neigh.

Political warhorse. Ready for pasture.

Neck and neck. Ditto.

Won his spurs. Pack it away with the buggy whip.

Homestretch. Save it for Hialeah.

Beauty contest. Save it for the Miss America Pageant.

Dark horse. Has been ridden into the ground, but because it packs a lot of meaning in two short words, still good for more outings. (Didja hear the one about the dark horse that won a beauty contest? A chestnut came in second. That, of course, is a color of another horse.)

Political animal. A bone-weary critter ready for the glue factory.

Stormy petrel. Out of petrol.

Crossed the Rubicon. Next time it crosses your mind, ask the first five passers-by what the phrase means.

Stemwinder. That word may still be a favorite of politicians and political reporters. But I've never heard anyone else say it—or understand it. Its time has passed.

_____is expected to win. Expected by whom? As Confucius should have said, "Man who lives by crystal ball ends up eating glass."

Warts and all. See a dermatologist. Better yet, a dictionary or a thesaurus. What's wrong with calling an appraisal "frank" or "blunt"?
Has worn two hats, *kept a high profile* **and** *kept the political pot boiling.* They're all burned out.

Political litmus test. How many listeners know what a litmus test is? It fails the acid test.

CURRENT INCUMBENT. A redundancy. An incumbent is the current occupant of an office.

MARGIN. It's not a cliché, but it is a word that reporters covering elections and polls often misuse. If Clyde gets 500,000 votes and Merrill gets 400,000, some reporters would say, "Clyde won by a five-to-four margin." Wrong. He won by a five-to-four *ratio.* A margin is the difference between two sums (100,000 in that case); a ratio is a proportion.

OPEN SECRET. If it's open, it's no longer secret.

TOPIC A. Passé.

FLUSHED WITH SUCCESS. Use it only if you're writing about a prosperous plumber.

Bandwagon, for example, is a cliché I wouldn't retire (even if it needs new tires). It works: it's not wordy; it saves many words. It presents a clear, colorful picture. And it's a lot shorter and faster than this definition of *bandwagon* (from William Safire's *Political Dictionary*): "a movement appealing to the herd instinct of politicians and voters to be on the winning side in any contest."

WORD CHAMPS

Let's mark the end of this chapter by awarding No-bell Prizes. These prize-winning scripts were broadcast by networks as *news*—not parody.

The first non-bellringer takes the prize for misleading lead-in:

> Japan's drive to be number one, the excellent Japanese education system, teenage suicides, schoolyard bullying and extortion at school. Some or all of these elements are in tonight's report from Tokyo by _____ _____.

After the anchor broadcast that item, I wondered whether the writer would be emboldened to write a lead-in like this for a shootout: "Sex. Drugs. Greed. Violence. Sudden death. Some or all those elements figure in the story from . . ." *Some or all* sounds like the legalistic language of a contract. In fact, the correspondent said nothing about "Japan's drive to be number one."

Even if the writer had written the lead-in accurately, he would have done it incorrectly. Starting with a list and then telling listeners why is like giving a recipe and finally telling what it's for.

Prize for startling comeback:

> At least three people were dead tonight and three more missing as . . .

Were dead but no longer dead? Those who were killed *are* dead; the dead were oil workers. Even if the writer had lined up his tenses correctly, he got off to a weak start because he began with numbers and backed into the action.

Prize for resistible lead:

> In the "what-else-is-new?" department, the U-S dollar rose again today.

Prize for negating the positive:

> The chairman of the P-L-O, Yasir Arafat, had no kind words for President Reagan today.

No kind words is negative. Be positive. The lead would be far stronger this way: "The chairman of the P-L-O, Yasir Arafat, denounced President Reagan today as 'a robot and a parrot.'"

Prize for superfluous use of prepositions:

> European space scientists phoned NASA today for emergency help in fixing their . . . space probe that's meeting up with Halley's comet. . . .

Anyone who says *meet up with* is going to collide with me.

Prize for ambiguity:

> For the first time since 19-62, it appears that a woman will be executed next month.

Sounds as if the newscaster is a forecaster.

Prize for poise in the heat of battle:

> The lobby of the Commodore Hotel became a battleground as Terry Waite held a news conference with the foreign press about the fate of four American hostages. . . . It was a classic Beirut scene—Waite trying to be calm as Druse and Amal militiamen fought an intense street battle outside.

Was the battle in the street or the lobby?

Prize for quick-change artistry:

> What was a tragic accident on Sunday has now become a possible murder investigation.

It's a strange world, but how does an accident become an investigation? And is that a possible murder or a possible investigation?

Prize for absurd word:

> That's an embarrassment, a pozzible—a puzzle and a possible future trouble spot for . . .

That ran on a network? *Impozzible.*
Prize for sensitive opening line:

> We had hoped not to have to report it, but an Ohio doctor said today, "There were just too many strikes against him." He was speaking about that little boy. . . .

Prize for wordiness:

> Hundreds of worried parents stood face to face with armed soldiers outside a Soweto police station.

Armed soldiers? Are they comrades-in-arms of *armed* gunmen?
Prize for impossible questions put to listeners in a lead-in:

> What's cutting into the steelhead trout population in the ship canal? Some deadly disease? Or is it only Herschel and his friends? Only Herschel?

Why ask *us?*
Prize for gratuitous explanation:

> Now, we didn't lead with this next story because, frankly, we feel strongly about not raising any false expectations.

When I hear someone say *frankly,* I wonder whether he's saying that because he's usually not frank.
Prize for mangling syntax—consumer reporters' division:

> Well, first I want to tell you these are not new products. These are when you borrow it from somebody else.

Prize for mangling syntax—anchors:

> Foreigners found themselves jeered at, spat at and had their cars overturned.

Did the foreigners arrange to have their cars overturned to collect insurance?
Prize for most informative first sentence:

> Winter kills and snow is dangerous. Yet another reminder has happened in a small town along the coast of the Japan Sea. . . .

Reminders don't *happen.* And a sea does not have a coast; a country does.
Japan Sea? Is that anywhere near the Sea of Japan?

Prize for hype and tripe:

> By the rules, what goes up must come down, but that was before the rule-breaking, record delay-breaking bloops [sic], foul-ups and bleepers mission of space shuttle *Columbia*.

By staying in space longer than planned, *Columbia* didn't break any rules. No rule says an object in space must return to Earth—and when.

Prize for iffiness:

> And if you love the ancient canal city of Venice, good news this morning.

But how's the news for people who *don't* love Venice?

Prize for clear thinking:

> For many Americans, the biggest problem with having babies is not having babies.

Such a problem is inconceivable. But so are all those network scripts.

After Math
How to deal with numbers

Getting the words right is hard. But getting the numbers right can be still harder. Let's look at an excerpt from a network newsmagazine. A correspondent:

> He [an economist] says the average French citizen hands over fully 46 percent of all his income to the government in all kinds of taxes. The average American, he says, hands over just 30 percent. That's more than 15 percent less.

Whoa! More than 15 percent less? The *more* and *less* are baffling, more or less. And woe unto those who trip over simple numbers. What Americans pay is 16 percentage points less.

According to the script's basic figures on taxation, the French payment exceeds the American payment by 53 percent. To calculate how much more the French pay, subtract the American payment (30 percent) from the French (46 percent) and divide the result (16) by the first number (30). When you divide 16 by 30, you get .5333. That's 53/100. Voila: 53 percent.

How much less is the American payment? Divide 16 by 46. The answer: 35 percent.

But the numbers in that script aren't the only problem. The words need work, too. The correspondent said the average American hands the government just 30 percent of his income. Just 30 percent? Just or unjust, leave out *just;* let the number speak for itself: *30 percent* will do. As for the French, who hand over *fully 46 percent*, that number doesn't need a modifier either.

The correspondent also reports that the director of a French orchestra says the government provides *a full 20 percent* of his budget. If the correspondent calls 20 percent full, what would he call 100 percent? I don't want to fulminate about *full* and *fully*, but they suggest that the writer is huffing and puffing.

Another faux pas: The correspondent calls the Champs-Elysees noisy and fume-filled. Noisy it is. But *fume-filled* isn't conversational. Filled with fumes is conversational, but as far as an observer can see—and smell—not true.

The correspondent goes on to say that a French actress in the 60 percent tax category must pay an extra wealth tax that boosts her tax rate to 70 percent. He calls the jump to 70 percent from 60 percent an increase of "10 percent." Wrong again. It's an increase of 10 percentage points. When we follow the formula for figuring percentages, we subtract the smaller number (60) from the larger (70) and divide the result (10) by the first number (60). The result: an increase of .1666—16 percent.

If you, too, are an innumerate, welcome to the club. Many of us need to review a high school textbook that deals with percentages. And we all need to keep in mind some advice in the newsletter *Copy Editor*. It offers five rules from Edward MacNeal, author of *Mathsemantics: Making Numbers Talk Sense.* He advises:

▸ Mistrust all percentages over 100.

▸ Don't use the word *times* with comparative modifiers, such as *more, larger, better, less, fewer, smaller* and *worse.* [The *Wall Street Journal's* in-house gazette, *Style & Substance,* says, *Three times greater* than is the same as *four times as great as,* but the latter is less confusing. The WSJ also says we should write *times as high* or *times as fast* or whatever, to avoid the ambiguity of *times higher* or *times faster.*]

▸ Double-check comparisons containing words like *tripling* and *threefold.*

▸ Avoid mixing fractions, percentages and decimals . . . and never mix them within a single comparison.

▸ Mistrust percentages added to other percentages.

Copy Editor also passes along a passel of other tips on percentages. Two of them:

1. A tripling is an increase of 200 percent, not 300 percent. An increase of 300 percent is a quadrupling. [Doubling is a 100 percent increase.]

2. A phrase like "six times fewer than" is absurd.

To see that your math doesn't do a number on you, ask someone in your newsroom who's good at figures to check your math. (No, it isn't called aftermath.)

Some writers are so taken with numbers that they plug them into scripts in the belief that numbers make scripts impressive. But they don't. Let's listen to this network anchor lead-in:

> It took the six-man, six-woman jury just over eight hours to reach and deliver today's verdict in the trial of John Salvi. The defense said Salvi was insane when he stormed two abortion clinics and pumped out deadly rifle fire. Correspondent _____ _____ reports what the jury said.

When a jury returns a verdict, our first question is, Guilty or not guilty? We don't ask, "How many men on the jury?" "How many women?" After all, or before all, we knew the composition of the jury from the outset, so it's not news. The length of the jury's deliberations may be worth mentioning, but it's not more important than the verdict. Nothing is. Just over eight hours? We round off numbers, so if we needed to use that number, we'd say merely "eight hours."

And *pumped out deadly rifle fire* doesn't sound like anything that should be said on a newscast. Or anywhere. People don't talk that way. What Salvi did was, he shot two people dead. After the anchor's lead-in, the correspondent said,

> John Salvi stood without emotion as a visibly shaken jury delivered its verdict.

As for Salvi's showing no emotion, people's emotions are often not discernible. *Visibly shaken* is journalese. The next words on the air came when the forewoman of the jury spoke, and we learned that the defendant had been found guilty—of murder. No matter what arguments someone might advance for delaying the news—Salvi found guilty—it's not sound journalism. If it makes sense to delay the news to hold the audience, why not tease the verdict and save the story for the last item in the newscast? But no longer would it be a newscast.

Another network newsmagazine has been found guilty (by me) of committing first-degree attempted thought control:

> Finally tonight, a look ahead to a story you'll be talking about this week: a comet that hasn't passed this way in, oh, about 10-thousand years. Could be the brightest in decades. . . .

We don't know what's in anyone else's mind, and often not even in our own, so how can an anchor tell us what we're going to be talking about? Did you go around talking about that comet? Or was your conversation like mine: comet-free—even comatose?

They say more listeners can name the Three Stooges than can name three Justices on the U.S. Supreme Court. As if to confirm that assertion, an anchor in the Midwest broadcast this tease about the remake of the $100 bill:

> Coming up, a facelift for former President Ben Franklin.

Former president? We don't refer to a person long dead as a former president, especially when he was never president.

More bits and bites from broadcasts:

> Indeed, Europe is said to have larger banks but fewer of them. We have more banks but they are smaller than those in Europe.

That second sentence is a funhouse mirror of the first, which indicates a lack of reflection. The item is reminiscent of a parody of T. S. Eliot: "As we get older, we do not get any younger."

And when I hear a newscaster use *we*, I wonder whether he's referring to himself, his station or his nation. According to Mark Twain, the only people entitled to use *we* are presidents, editors and people with tapeworms. (And perhaps pregnant women.)

> Twenty-seven people are dead, 43 injured, the result of a bus accident in Mexico. Police say the crowded bus blew a tire and went spinning off a highway 150 miles west of Mexico City. The bus crashed at the bottom of a gorge.

Stories that start with numbers leave me numb. My mind needs a warm-up before I hear the final score. Any form of *to be* is weak, so saying people *are* dead is lifeless. The accident was dramatic. But *are,* the only verb in the first sentence of that script, lacks ardor. Also, by putting the place name last in that first sentence, the writer keeps the listener wondering whether the accident occurred in her town or even in her country; she doesn't find out until the sentence ends. And that's too late.

Another drawback: after the newscaster gave us the outcome in his first breath, the sentence rolled downhill. A writer can create a strong sentence by building up to the high point, not down from it. Better: "A bus in Mexico blew a tire, spun off a highway and plunged into a gorge. Twenty-seven people were killed. Forty-three were hurt." Or the jiffy version: "A bus accident in Mexico has killed 27 people."

> More than 40 people were injured today when a couple of bombs exploded aboard a truck transporting military explosives through Oklahoma. reports it could have been much worse.

Like the previous story, this anchor lead-in starts with a number and proceeds in reverse chronological order. *Then* it tells us what caused the casualties and where. Also regrettable: The script talks about *explosives* that *exploded.* And the story would have more impact by starting with the most vivid aspect and using a vigorous verb: "A truck carrying military explosives in Oklahoma blew up today, and more than 40 people were hurt."

The newscaster's intro to the correspondent says *it could have been much worse,* which is inane. After just about any accident, someone can say it might have been much worse. Or can say, "It didn't have to happen."

Here's how another newscaster reported the story:

> There's now a crater 30 feet wide and 18 feet deep on a highway near the town of Checotah in eastern Oklahoma. It was created today when a car going the wrong way on an entrance ramp hit a military truck carrying 10 bombs. Some of them detonated. . . .

Detonated? Why use a four-syllable Latin-root word when *blew up* does the job? Almost any lead that starts with *there is* or *it is* should be changed. The writer backed into that story. His script could have been worse (but not much worse).

> According to court documents, Whitworth relayed his information to Walker in Hong Kong when the carrier pulled in for a port visit.

The most important element in the sentence is the circumstances of the alleged transfer. But buried in the middle of the sentence, *Hong Kong* is passed over quickly, so it lacks importance. The key facts in the news item could have been highlighted by progressing chronologically and building up to the main idea: "Court documents say Whitworth gave Walker the information when the carrier visited Hong Kong." (With Walker convicted of running a spy ring for Moscow, could he be labeled *Johnnie Walker Red?*)

> There's new concern this week about an old air safety problem, near-misses in the sky.

If two planes nearly miss but don't miss, they collide. If they nearly collide, they have a near-collision, not a *near-miss.* Isn't a *near-miss* a bride who was almost jilted?

If you write that two planes collided over Grand Canyon, the *over* conveys the idea that the collision occurred in the air instead of on the ground. So steer clear of near-miss and midair collision. Also avoid "near-panic" and "near-riot." The law says a riot is a violent disturbance by three or more persons. So is a "near-riot" a ruckus caused by *two* persons?

Bad News

Characterizing news is bad—and tips for sports and weather scripts

We start with some bad news,

the anchor said somberly on his network newscast. I was only half-listening, but that grim opening hit me like a brick. The news sounded grave. Was it an assassination? A terrorist bombing? A disaster? The anchor went on to report that an actor had died.

I wondered, for whom was that news bad? Presumably, family, friends and fans. But the death of one person, even a personage, is generally accepted by listeners as just another news item; we've become accustomed to a cascade of calamities, catastrophes and cataclysms. By the time the actor, James Mason, died, he was no longer a big name on moviegoers' mental marquees. Opening the newscast with a story on his death would have been all right if the newscaster had reported it straight—without telegraphing us that he was going to deliver *bad news.*

Whenever I had to write an obituary or, for that matter, any story, I was guided by a rule I learned in school: Don't label the news as good or bad. What's bad for some listeners is good for others. Heavy rain can be bad for pedestrians, motorists and sunbathers; but it can be good for farmers, taxi drivers and umbrella vendors.

"Good news" abounds on broadcasts when the prime interest rate drops. But for listeners, a drop in the prime has both positive and negative sides. Anyone who takes out a home improvement loan will benefit right away. And if other borrowing costs start to fall again, consumers could save interest on adjustable-rate home mortgages and similar borrowings. But for many listeners, lower rates are "bad news." Many consumers like high interest rates because it enables them to earn strong returns on their investments, such as money market funds and U.S. government securities.

I was also taught not to tell an audience that a story is distressing, or amazing, or amusing; stick to the facts and just tell the news. If the "good news" or "bad news" is tied to a specific person or group, characterizing the news may be valid. For example: "Mayor Murphy received good news today from his doctor." Or: "The I-R-S has bad news for taxpayers." Otherwise, a newscaster should let listeners decide whether it's good or bad. But how many listeners do you think are sitting out there with clipboards checking off each story as "good" for them, "bad" for them or "indeterminable"?

Anchors should also avoid "good news–bad news" leads, such as "Governor Graham has good news and bad news for farmers. The good news is . . ." The "good news–bad news" approach is suitable for a comedian. But some newscasters have used it so much and for so long that it has lost whatever appeal it had—and has simply become bad news.

A network newscaster said diplomats had worked out an agreement and had "initialized" it. *Initialized?* The suffix *ize* has long been fused onto nouns and adjectives to turn them into verbs: *apologize, burglarize, computerize, hospitalize, jeopardize, legalize, pasteurize, polarize, synthesize,* even *decriminalize.* I won't itemize them, but writers should realize they can't slap on an *ize* indiscriminately, especially if an existing verb does the job. *Initialize* is not needed because an established verb, *to initial,* already means "to sign one's initials."

A community newspaper in St. Louis told of someone who had been *funeralized.* And a local newscaster spoke of *unionized* teachers. This usage seems strange; it made me think of teachers who had been processed in some way.

Another misbegotten verb is *finalize.* It has the ring, or thud, of bureaucratic jargon, and we already have ways to convey the action intended by *finalize:* "end," "make final," "put in final form," "finish," "complete," "wrap up." Under *finalize,* the *American Heritage Dictionary* (1992) says the verb "is frequently associated with the language of bureaucracy and so is objected to by many writers." And the *AHD* says *finalize* was unacceptable to 71 percent of its Usage Panel. But the 1969 *AHD* reported *finalize* was found unacceptable by 90 percent of the panel; so opposition to *finalize* has slipped about one percentage point a year. The final word isn't in yet, so let's wait till the fat lady croaks.

Another problem I don't sympathize with or temporize about: what some grammarians call *stacking.* That's the practice of piling adjectives and nouns-as-adjectives in front of nouns. One of the most horrendous examples was uncorked by a network newscaster who spoke of

a new and improved revised downward federal budget deficit forecast.

Rather than punctuate that, I'll puncture it. When the anchor reaches the first noun, *budget,* the average listener probably thinks that's the subject of the sentence. But it's quickly followed by another noun, *deficit,* so he realigns his train of thought, if he can, and surmises that the story is about a budget deficit. Wrong. All those adjectives and nouns modify what it's really all about: a *forecast.*

A listener can catch a couple of adjectives before a noun, but seven adjectives are far too many, especially those seven. What makes it even tougher to untangle is that two of them (*budget, deficit*) are nouns pressed into service as adjectives. The sentence should be rewritten—and the writer sentenced.

A newspaper reader might be able to thread his way through that terrible thicket of words because he'd first see the headline, read the sentence at his own pace, reread whatever isn't clear and then perhaps rip it out of the paper for another read-through. Any script written that heavy-handedly ought to be ripped out—and up. But a *listener* who wanted to figure out that sentence as it was spoken would have had to be a Champollion (the French Egyptologist who deciphered the Rosetta stone). Or have total recall—with instant replay.

The problem with that kind of overwriting is that a listener can't grasp it instantly. The problem with that writer was not that he wasn't trying. He was trying too hard. Maybe he wanted to make himself heard by hammering out a punchy sentence, one that would put a dent in the listener's mind. But no one will ever remember it, and children will never recite it. And that's *my* forecast.

WORLD'S BIGGEST SNOW CONE?

Some newspapers run children's pages with a picture puzzle that asks, "How many mistakes can you find?" So I'm going to challenge grownups with a word picture: How many mistakes can *you* find?

> Five years ago today, with unprecedented fury, Mount Saint Helens erupted, decimating 150 square miles of lush green forest.

That's the lead of a story broadcast by a TV network reporter. Although she didn't sign a consent card for this autopsy, she should be gratified that she's contributing to the advancement of newswriting. We can't tell from her lead whether she meant that the fury was unprecedented for Mount St. Helens or for all volcanoes everywhere. In either case, she was wrong.

The most destructive eruption in modern times was that of Krakatau in 1883. The volcano, in Indonesia, generated tidal waves that killed 36,000 people.

The *Encyclopedia Britannica* says, "The enormous discharge threw into the air nearly five cubic miles of rock fragments, and the fine dust [caused] spectacular red sunsets all over the world through the following year."

But the *biggest* blowup in modern times was that of Tambora, also in Indonesia. According to the U.S. Geological Survey, Tambora's eruption in 1815 disgorged more than seven cubic miles of material. Mount St. Helens spewed less than one cubic mile. And, more important, the USGS says the 1980 eruption wasn't even Mount St. Helens' biggest blowup.

That network reporter would have been on safe ground if she had just told her story without straining, if she hadn't tried to punch it up with *unprecedented*. When an editor sees *unprecedented,* his mental alarm should go off. Other absolutes and superlatives should also set off his alarm: *only, unique, first, fastest, fattest, foulest* and other *est* words. An editor should ask, How do we know this is the world's *biggest* snow cone? Even if we're satisfied it is, does that make it worth reporting? If we can't confirm it on our own, are we attributing it properly? How do we know this is the world's *thickest* waffle? Or that it's the *first* time anyone has hijacked a bandwagon? Is there a central registry that keeps track of everything everywhere for-ever—accurately? (An exception: sports, where statistics are part of the game, and statisticians seem to record even the cap size of batboys.)

A reporter on the scene of the Mount St. Helens eruption couldn't know or easily obtain the history of volcanoes (unless she's a closet volcanologist). Even the people I spoke with at the Geological Survey had to dig out the information and call me back. But a prudent reporter doesn't trot out *unique, unparalleled, unprecedented, unsurpassed* or any other such word without knowing that it's correct—*and* worth mentioning. Another problem with the reporter's lead: She misused *decimate*. Originally, it meant to kill every 10th person. But now it's sometimes used to mean the destruction of a large part of a group. Yet, even a volcano can't *decimate* trees, only people. The reporter might have meant *devastate,* meaning *destroy* or *lay waste*. (I've also heard a newscaster tell of a building in Beirut that had been *decimated* and a network correspondent speak of an effort in Washington to *decimate* a plan.)

By starting the volcano story with "Five years ago today," the reporter deprived the anchor of the anniversary angle for the lead-in. Ordinarily, a correspondent in the field (or forest) should start with what will become the second sentence of the story. She does that by picking up from—or playing off—the anchor's lead-in. That's quite a trick, because the anchor's lead-in is usually written after the correspondent's piece has been put into the lineup.

Another point: The first sentence in the script can be improved by changing the participle to a verb with a tense. And by using only one adjective:

"The volcano blew up with great fury—and destroyed [not *decimated*] 150 square miles of forest." That's shorter, sharper, stronger.

My suggested anchor lead-in—based on hearing the whole story: "Mount Saint Helens erupted five years ago today, but nearby residents are, in a sense, still feeling after-shocks. Jane Jones has the story in Washington State."

One way to make sure that the lead-in and the script dovetail, says a former CBS News producer, Norman Glubok, is for the correspondent to submit, with her script, a proposed anchor lead-in. Once the correspondent thinks through what her story is all about, she'll know how to write the lead-in, and that'll give her a head start on writing her script. If the story is about a volcano, a correspondent can expect the anchor to identify the volcano in the lead-in. So the correspondent can start her script with "the volcano," skipping the name. But she should make sure that she leaves the anchor a strong fact or two for the lead-in. In most cases, she should omit those facts from her script. Otherwise, when the piece is broadcast, she'll be the one who'll sound repetitious.

Speaking of blowups (and if you like that transition, you'd better raise your standards), a news director, Dick Nelson, asked me about my reference to a story on the blowup by the so-called subway vigilante Bernhard Goetz. Dick wants to know whether it's permissible to call Goetz a vigilante.

Vigilante was first used more than 140 years ago to refer to a member of a "vigilance committee." The committees were formed, mostly in the South and West, to see that criminals were punished. Often, punishment was inflicted by members themselves, occasionally on suspects who were blameless. One case of frontier justice administered by vigilantes was reported in Denver's *Rocky Mountain News* on May 31, 1862: "The vigys pointed to an empty saddle and gave him just 10 minutes to skedaddle." *A Dictionary of Americanisms* by Mitford M. Mathews also offers examples showing *vigilante* was used even in the 20th century. And in recent years it has been widely used to describe people who take the law into their hands.

I'm not keen about writing *subway vigilante* (when I used it in a column, I was quoting someone else), but I think it's acceptable—at least in this case. The term has been so widely applied to Goetz, people know in an instant who he is and what he did. It's not as if we were declaring him guilty; he acknowledges being a vigilante. But I'd precede that label with *so-called* to remind listeners we hadn't declared Goetz guilty, that we're merely using a standard label.

By using the shorthand device *subway vigilante,* we capture an event that would otherwise take many words to describe. Let's try it without the shortcut: "The man who shot four teenagers in a New York City subway train, Bernhard Goetz, was arraigned today and pleaded not guilty." Now, using our shorthand, let's set the scene swiftly: "The so-called subway vigilante, Bernhard Goetz, has pleaded not guilty."

I, too, can be insufficiently vigilant. The newsman Alan Cohn pointed out my incorrect reference to Claus von Bülow's "murder trial." Von Bülow was tried for *attempted* murder. I plead guilty.

WRITERS UNDER THE WEATHER

"Don't knock the weather; nine-tenths of the people couldn't start a conversation if it didn't change once in a while."

Frank McKinney (Kin) Hubbard

Start a *conversation*? If it weren't for the weather, I couldn't even start this examination. That's why I don't knock the weather. So that leaves me with a few extra knocks for weathercasters and newscasters. But Ed Bliss says an editor should be hard on copy, not on people. So I'll edit myself and say the knocks are for weather *copy*.

> *He who overwrites undermines.*

The worse the weather, the worse the copy. Instead of telling a dramatic story in a simple, sober style, many writers shift their typewriters into overwrite. But he who overwrites undermines. Read the simple yet powerful account of the biggest story ever. Here's how a Hebrew rewrite man handled the lead: "In the beginning, God created the heaven and the earth." Period. Big event, simple words, short sentence, great impact.

One of the most objectionable aspects of much weather coverage is what the 19th-century British critic John Ruskin called the "pathetic fallacy": When a writer ascribes human behavior, motivation or characteristics to inanimate objects, animals or natural phenomena, he commits a "pathetic fallacy." Some poets have made this approach, known as "anthropomorphism," work—the *cruel sea, smiling skies, laughing waters*—but in broadcast scripts, it's usually overdone or inappropriate. Here are some broadcast examples:

> Residents are also waiting, waiting for the fickle but dangerous Hurricane Elena to make up her mind.

Fickle? Make up her mind? Nonsense. No storm has a mind to make up, so it can't be fickle. Also: in *fickle but dangerous,* the word *but* is wrong; Elena's "fickleness" helps make the storm dangerous. So *but* should be *and*—and *fickle* should be cast to the winds.

The stylebooks of leading newspapers say that for references to a hurricane, writers should use *it*, not *he* or *she*. And the Associated Press stylebook advises, "Do not use the presence of a woman's name as an excuse to attribute sexist images of women's behavior to a storm."

Hurricane Nele has apparently decided not to visit Hawaii.

If that Nele had any sense, it would have decided to reserve space between a pineapple plantation and a macadamia grove.

Hurricane Gloria is still 550 miles out in the Atlantic, but already it's drawing a bead on the Outer Banks of North Carolina.

Drawing a bead? Hurricanes can't aim. They're aimless (but not blameless). Another script:

Hurricane Gloria first dropped anchor and came ashore overnight across the unprotected Outer Bank islands of North Carolina, almost a worst-possible-case scenario.

Trying to visualize that scene almost blew me away. When a ship drops anchor, it can't go anywhere. Not unless it weighs anchor. So how can a storm drop anchor and come ashore? How can a storm drop anchor at all? *Worst-possible-case scenario* seems to be an effort to pump up "worst-case scenario," which is bureaucratic jargon. But the sly *almost* says it's not the worst. And the weather-beaten word *scenario* is best left for Hollywood.

Hurricane Diana is on a collision course with the coast of North Carolina.

A car can hit a tree, but a car and a tree can't collide. Only moving objects collide. For objects to collide or to be on a collision course, they must both be moving. And to make that script correct, North Carolina would have to be coasting.

A mammoth hurricane in size and scope, but not the killer hurricane forecasters feared it might become.

Mammoth describes its size, so *size* adds nothing. If the writer used *scope* to mean "the area covered by an activity," as the dictionary defines it, then *mammoth* does the job alone. Better: "The hurricane is mammoth but not so mighty as forecasters had feared."

Her threat was more menacing than her power.

Threat = menace, so the sentence is windy double-talk.

This heavy-with-water hurricane dumped as much as 20 inches of rain on Puerto Rico.

Heavy-with-water hurricane? No one else would say it, and no one should write it. *Dumped rain* is journalese. And that's no compliment. So dump it.

Dolly is packing top winds of about 75 miles per [should be *an*] hour.

Packing winds is termed by the UPI stylebook as "low-grade journalese."

Those killer tornadoes, reminders that just because records are set doesn't mean the news is good.

Who needs reminding that a record might relate to bad news? But that writer does need reminding that there's no such thing as a *killer tornado*. Or a *killer cyclone* (though sci-fi does have "killer clones"). Storms have the means to kill, but no mind, no motive. Storms don't set out with a hit list or malice aforethought. Storms can kill, but that doesn't make them *killer storms*. Likewise, there is no such thing as a killer wind, killer hurricane, killer typhoon or, as a network newscaster said, a killer volcano. But there are killjoys, killer whales and Kilkenny cats.

Vice President Bush will visit the strickened area to let the people of this state know the administration's concern for their plight.

Strickened? The writer meant *stricken.*

Officials along the Mississippi and Alabama coasts are trying to convince residents in the danger area to leave their homes.

The writer has mistaken *convince* for *persuade.* You *convince* someone *that* he should leave or *convince* him of the need to leave. But you *persuade* him *to* leave.

As we said earlier, many people, thousands, have been evacuated, and, as we said earlier, the hotels also have been closed down. Now this is the first time in the history of Atlantic City that something like that has happened. Many schools are closed today, and, as we said . . .

If you've already said it, why repeat it and also say you've said it? And why keep saying you've said it? Why, why, why? In the second sentence of the script, *now* is meaningless. Also in the second sentence: What does *this is the first time* refer to—the hotel closings? The extent of the evacuation? The magnitude of the storm? The script reminds me of what Abraham Lincoln said about a long-winded politician: "That blower can compress the most words in the fewest ideas of any man I ever knew."

The path that it's taking now is reminiscent of the storms that go way back in time to 19-38 or so, the one that would affect central Long Island and southern New England. If it had gone maybe farther east, it would have missed some of those areas. But it's just hugging the coast now until it does that.

That's what the man said, but what *did* he say?

Those kind of rains can be moving all the way up to northern New England.

Make it *kinds.* And instead of *can,* make it *may.* We know the rains *can—* that they have the ability. But *may* indicates a possibility.

DROP-KICKING SPORTS METAPHORS

Some sportswriters seem to think that writing in simple English might cause them to be benched, so they do their double-barreled damnedest. They say a batter has *belted a four-bagger, clouted one for the circuit, poked one out of the park* or hit *a roundtripper, a tater, a goner, a dinger, a grand slam,* even *a grand salami.* (I never sausage a thing.) They'll go to any lengths—*even the length of two football fields*—to sidestep simplicity.

The ESPN sports producer Willie Weinbaum also tells me of a few more old standbys that sportscasters rely on to avoid that dreaded word *homer: You can hang a star on that baby, It's see ya later time* and *That dog will hunt.* Intent on grandstanding, they ignore the easiest—and best—way to say it: *He hit a home run.* Or *He homered.* After some of the offenders condescend to write *hit,* I recommend they learn to use *win*—as a verb. I keep hearing about teams that *triumphed, grabbed a win, rolled up a victory* or *handed a defeat to.* I'd like to hear more about teams that just *won.* And teams that simply scored runs, goals, baskets and touchdowns. "When sportscasters try to be too cute," Weinbaum says, "they come across as clowns." And imitators come across as clones.

Warning. Reader discretion advised: adult content, adult language and excessive violence—to good taste and good writing. Let's go right to the script:

Barry Switzer, that emotional, errogant [the sportscaster probably meant "arrogant," not "error-prone"] idiot who coaches the Dallas Cowboys, has done it again.

Voice-over:

Yes, that's the man I'm talking about. He blew today's game with the Philadelphia Eagles. We pick it up with game tied at 17 on a 4th and one, and Switzer goes for it, and Emmitt Smith is stopped. . . .

A super identified Switzer as "Bonehead Coach." Yes, *bonehead.* And "idiot" is what the man said. Not in a bar. Not in a car. But *over the air.* In a major market. (If the questionable play had worked, Joe Durso Jr. asks, would the sportscaster have called Switzer a genius? And Prof. Durso, of the University of Montana, also wonders whether the sportscaster would have used the same words if he'd been broadcasting in Dallas.)

Sportscasters *are* allowed considerable latitude—and attitude. But the writer of that script went out of bounds. There are certain norms we don't overstep. We don't insult people. And we don't call people nasty names. Especially in front of the whole world—or whatever share we have.

If Oscar Wilde had been watching that sports segment, he might have said, as he once did, "There is much to be said in favor of modern journalism. By giving us the opinions of the uneducated, it keeps us in touch with the ignorance of the community."

The sportscaster who wrote that script may not be uneducated (or undereducated), just untrained—and unrestrained. In any case, he's not the person responsible for letting that script go on the air. The person at fault is the editor (if any). Or the producer. But, ultimately, the news director.

The writer might have been doing the best he knows how. But supervisors must supervise. And impose norms: norms of fairness, impartiality and civility. And even broadcasters allowed to express opinions on the air shouldn't abuse that privilege by name-calling. Ben Bradlee, the former executive editor of the *Washington Post,* urges reporters and editors to ask themselves at the end of every story, "Have I been as fair as I can be?"

"Good sports writing," says *The Associated Press Stylebook and Libel Manual,* "depends on the same writing and reporting tools as any other story. A stylebook . . . is an aid in reaching that goal."

For style *and* class, we also might look to *The Economist.* It, too, looks down on that sportscaster's kind of name-calling. And every other kind. The style guide of the British newsweekly cautions, "Do not be hectoring or arrogant. Those who disagree with you are not necessarily stupid or insane. Nobody needs to be described as silly: let your analysis prove that he is."

While we're at it, let's look at some more good advice in *The Economist Style Guide:* "Do not be too pleased with yourself. Don't boast of your own cleverness by telling readers that you correctly predicted something or that you have a scoop. You are more likely to bore or irritate them than to impress them. So keep references to *The Economist* to a minimum, particularly those of the we-told-you-so variety. References to 'this correspondent' or 'your correspondent' are always self-conscious and often self-congratulatory."

Another script:

> We all know by now that Saint Ignatius is going for football championship number five! And on the other side of the field, Brunswick is looking to be the spoiler! _____ _____'s got a preview of tomorrow's big matchup [delete *matchup*, make it *game*], coming up next!

Delete *coming up next; next* says what's needed.

All those exclamation points, one after each sentence, exceed the quota good writers impose on themselves for a whole year. Viewers can't see the bangs, of course, but they can *hear* them. And that story isn't worth shouting about. In fact, no story is. If it's big, you don't need to raise your voice. What you need to do is write it right—tight and bright. And we should all know that we never start a story by saying, *We all know.* Because we *don't* all know.

As for *looking to be* in the second sentence of that script, that's not English, even in Sportsville. It's substandard. Remember, we must maintain our norms. (No, not Norm Crosby, Norman Bates or Norman Oklahoma.)

Next up to bat, another sports story that also was broadcast in a major market:

> A former high school baseball star was arrested for stealing a uniform worn by Babe Ruth, plus 200-thousand dollars' worth of baseball cards.
>
> William W_____ the Third stole the uniform Ruth wore in the 19-42 movie "Pride of the Yankees."
>
> The uniform was first stolen from a Hollywood costume company in 19-52, another owner was killed in a mob hit, and it spent much of the early 19-90s in a police property room. Ruth's uniform was size 44 pants and size 50 shirt.

That script tosses out far more questions than it even takes a swing at: Where was the uniform stolen? How? When? Did the Babe ever wear it in a game? Or did he wear it only in a movie? Were the uniform and the baseball cards stolen from the same place? How many cards? Were they in a display case? A vault? A closet?

Was any of the loot recovered? When the latest thief stole it, was it already stolen property? Was it in the police property room when it was stolen? Where? Who was the owner killed in a mob hit? (Was he a heavy hitter?) Where was the arrest made? How? Was the alleged thief trying to fence the stuff? Pawn it?

The script's second sentence says "William W_____" *stole* the uniform. Excuuuse me: Was he *convicted* of stealing it? Where? What's his sentence? And who cares what sizes Ruth wore? Except his tailor, his biographer and baseball fans who cherish stats.

Even if we could get answers to all those questions, we couldn't—and wouldn't, and shouldn't—use them. But if we had answers to just a few, we could do a better job.

All in all, all those sports scripts should have been sent to the shredders and the writers to the showers. Not so incidentally, Barry Switzer's team, the Dallas Cowboys, went on to win the Super Bowl. Not bad for a *bonehead.* So the sportscaster who maligned him violated several rules, including a basic rule in broadcasting: "Never kick a man when he's up."

Even more tiresome is the use of sports jargon in non-sports news. So resist the lingo of the jargonauts, where all the world's a game and all the men and women merely players.

WANTED: NEWS, NOT VIEWS

More and more, newscasts tell us less and less. That's not true of all newscasts, but it's too true of too many. The problem is newscasters who misspend time by telling us what they think. Or what they think *we* think. Or, even worse, how to think. Here are some network excerpts to think about.

> Good evening. We begin tonight with news that millions of people throughout the world will think is long overdue.

Whatever that is, it's not news. Much of what we hear on newscasts may strike millions of people as long overdue. But the population of the world exceeds five billion, so those *millions* (whether two million or 200 million) are only a small fraction of the total. If it makes sense to describe the expected reaction to news not yet reported, why not use even bigger numbers to beef up a script: "Billions of people in the world will be indifferent to this news. Or will think it premature. Or right on time. Or somewhat overdue."

The news is the action, not the presumed reaction.

What *is* long overdue in that script is the delivery of news. It's best to just tell what happened today, the *facts.* Don't speculate on what people *will think.* Or how they might react. The news is the action, not the presumed reaction. Also, the anchor needn't announce that he's beginning. As soon as he says, "Good evening," we know he has begun.

Same newscast:

> Here's a sad piece of news from overseas about health. At a meeting in Malawi, in Africa today, the news for Africa's senior defense officials must have been devastating. International health officials have told [why not the simple past tense *told?*] them that in some African armies one of every two soldiers is infected with the AIDS virus.

Much of the news we hear is sad, but an anchor shouldn't tell us a story is sad. We can figure that out for ourselves. We don't have to be cued. The script said the news *must have been devastating,* a tense you might call the past-presumptive. But who needs speculation? Or devastation?

Or characterization of news? What we need is news—unadorned, unadul-
terated, unadumbrated. (Of that last word, Emily Dickinson might have
said, "Now, there's a word you can tip your hat to!")

Next in the newscast came this:

> In California, the horror caused by children. An attack so brutal that authori-
> ties are groping for an explanation.

No light. Just fright. And *authorities*? Authorities in child behavior? Medical
authorities? Police?

In his lead-in, the anchor told of

> an infant victim and the suspects who are not much older . . .

Not much older? The correspondent went on to say the victim was one
month old and the suspects in his beating were three boys—one 6 years old
and two 8 years old. Figure it out: the 6-year-old was 72 times as old as the
victim, and the 8-year-olds were 96 times as old.

The correspondent said the boys had walked into a home to steal a
bicycle. Did the boys break in? Or did they find the door unlocked? And *did*
they steal a bicycle?

The next night, the newscast carried another piece on the beating but
for the second time didn't mention that the two 8-year-olds were brothers.
Twins. The anchor tagged the piece:

> Violence and sadness in California.

That's a big help for listeners who don't realize that the beating of an infant
is both violent and sad.

Another network's evening newscast introduced a package:

> This is not the kind of story the world wants to see or hear, but it is important.

Don't worry; the *world* won't see or hear it—just the audience. But why tell
listeners it's not what they want? And why call the story important? Aren't
all network stories important? Shouldn't they be? Our job is to report the
news, not to tell folks that they don't want to hear what we're going to tell
them.

Nor is there any point in telling people they may not know what they're
about to be told. Yet one network correspondent said,

> You may not know this, but a brave new world of medical records is upon us.

You could begin most news stories, "You may not know this. . . ." But you
should know enough not to. Unfortunately, the correspondent's assertion—
about patients' medical records not being so confidential—has been widely

known for a long time. Further, his tired allusion to the 1932 novel *Brave New World* has gone flat.

And a third network's newsmagazine on another subject:

> When we come back, new discoveries about what really happened that night. And what we found out, many doctors and hospitals may not want you to see.

Sounds like one of those ads for an insider's newsletter: "What your dentist doesn't want you to know." Or: "Bagels! What's *really* in them."

Some network scripts have other holes:

> Then the doctor gave her the terrible news, but at first, she didn't understand his meaning.

She didn't understand his meaning? That passeth all understanding. Perhaps the anchor meant "She didn't understand what the doctor told her."

> For companies, domestic violence also hits the bottom line hard, up to five billion dollars lost annually. . . .

That *up to* makes the total as elastic as a bungee cord. How was that sum arrived at? In fact, it's an *unk-unk:* unknown and unknowable.

> On Capitol Hill, it's now a six-pack of Senate Democrats calling it quits for re-election—six and counting.

A six-pack? Would you say the people who put that on the air were a sick pack?

> Captain Tony, who ran for mayor here as a self-confessed gambler, adulterer and gun smuggler and won, says a clean, orderly themed Key West is no Key West at all.

Self-confessed? Who can confess for you but you? So *self* should go on the shelf. Also, many lawyers consider a confession a *written* instrument. In any case, that excerpt needs rehabilitation: "Captain Tony ran for mayor in Key West as a gambler, smuggler and adulterer—and won. He says a clean, orderly theme-park Key West is not Key West."

> For travelers trying to get home for the holidays, it's been nothing short of frustrating.

If it's *nothing short of frustrating,* it's frustrating.

> The accused in this case is a Georgia man named Ellis Wayne Felker, who was to have died [better: *was to have been executed*] last month for the murder 15 years ago of Evelyn Ludlum.

An inmate on death row is not referred to as *the accused*. Right after the crime, when he's considered the *culprit*, we refer to him as a *suspect*, later *the accused*. But when the accusation is proved in court and he's found guilty, he's no longer merely *the accused*.

Also: Why give the murderer a middle name—but not the victim? Broadcast style calls for the elimination of middle names, except when there's a possibility of confusion with someone else. Or when someone of substance has long been identified with a middle name: Harriet Beecher Stowe, Henry Wadsworth Longfellow, George Washington Carver. All of them made their name in a more leisurely time. But nowadays we have less time and can't afford to misspend time—while telling listeners less.

When a young beauty told the comedian Phil Silvers she'd do *anything* to get into television, he replied, "It's not that easy." Nor is it easy to write a think-piece—or any piece. Let's listen to this network think-piece and see what *we* think:

> **Summer is supposed to be a season of escape and renewal.** [Tell me something I don't know.] **This year, summer has turned into the season of sorrow.** [For whom? Not for everyone. Not for most. Not even for one-tenth of one percent.] **Fear and mourning have suddenly become our new national pastimes.** [Nonsense.]
>
> **The vast majority of us don't know any of the people killed in this summer's tragedies, yet we hang on the coverage of these horrid events because the people who were harmed were innocents.** [We followed those events because they were so unusual and so many people were killed—not because the *harmed* were innocents (whatever that means).] **They never had a chance.** [A maudlin cliché.]
>
> **From the barracks bombing in Saudi Arabia, where Americans were slaughtered** [better: *killed;* animals are slaughtered, people are *massacred*] **as they slept, we learned that our military is never safe anywhere, even in a country not at war, even in a place where opposition is practically illegal.** [We've long known that military people are never safe anywhere in peacetime, not even aboard warships and warplanes. *Especially* aboard warships and warplanes.] **From the crash of TWA Flight 800, we're afraid we'll learn that a determined terrorist can strike virtually at will, that what happened overseas in places like Lockerbie can happen here, too.** [We've also long known that terrorists can strike anywhere at any time: Terrorists tried to assassinate President Truman in 1950. And in 1954 they shot five congressmen.] **And from the attack at the Olympics in Atlanta, we learn that the place that was said to be the most secure place was not.** [Who ever said Centennial Olympic Park was the *most* secure place? And what's to learn?] **It's what makes terrorism so sinister: Everyone is a target.** [*Everyone* is not a target. But anyone might be.] **Sometimes we take for granted that which is most important.** [Platitude: "a flat, dull or trite remark, especially one uttered as if it

were fresh or profound."] ***Freedom is a good example. Until a week or two ago, who of us gave a second thought to the basic privileges we enjoy every day, our comings and goings?*** [Our *comings and goings* are basic *rights*, not *privileges*.] ***Freedom, it turns out, is fragile. A blow against it anywhere injures us all.*** [More banalities imparted as profundities.]

During this summer of sorrow, most of us will try to maintain a demeanor of normalcy, but underneath the facade of everyday life, we share fear. [Our everyday life is not a *facade*. And polls tell us the dominant fear is of crime. Besides, we share much more than fear.] ***Terrorism is what we talk about now.*** [We talk about everything under the sun.] ***Terrorism is what we don't want our kids to look at on TV.*** [How about not wanting them to watch criminality? Barbarity? Obscenity? Vulgarity? Vacuity?] ***Terrorism is what hangs in the air like the heat of a hot summer's day that no breeze can blow away.*** [More hot air.]

That's it, folks, word for word: a plenitude of platitudes. Nothing new, insightful, engaging, original or interesting. When you think about it, what's missing from that so-called think-piece is thinking. Please don't accuse me of textual harassment, but that think-piece was more than twice as long as Washington's second inaugural address.

Next, another network correspondent:

> **Today, Hurricane Bertha focused its fury on the fragile Bahamas island chain.** [Storms can't focus on anything.] **Storm-force winds raked Nassau early this afternoon.** [*Storm-force winds?* Try "windstorms."] . . . **Not a single cruise ship remained in port. All left early to escape the potentially treacherous seas.** [Delete the *potentially*. And instead of *treacherous*, try *rough*.]

The next correspondent on that newscast reported from Savannah, Georgia, that 50,000 people had been told to leave the Outer Banks:

> **And, in fact** [delete *in fact*], **the U-S Navy has taken some extra** [delete *some extra*] **precautions as well, ordering its sailors to remove 45 ships and submarines to safer ground.**

Safer ground? Sailors can't move ships ashore—or to *safer ground*. (If a warship runs aground, the captain will land in hot water, boiling hot.) When Navy ships are in port—anchored, or moored to buoys, or tied up to a pier—and a big storm is approaching, the ships usually sail away lickety-split—to take less of a licking.

Another network storm:

> **The reason why so much rain fell here in Puerto Rico was because the storm was moving at only six miles an hour.**

A multiple redundancy: *reason why* and *reason . . . was because.*

More net's work:

> **An incredible scene in Quebec. Take a look at this.** [Please, don't tell viewers to view—or listeners to listen.] **Rivers armed** [*armed* rivers?] **with nearly a foot of rain over the weekend turned into an invasion force.** [That military metaphor should be scuttled.] **Floodwaters took over the streets, sent thousands of people running for their lives and wrecked many of their houses. . . .**

A family buys a *house*, then turns it into a *home.* Better: "wrecked many homes."

A network non-storm:

> **Spiver Gordon is the leading civil rights leader in Alabama who believes this racial division is fueling the fires of hate.**

A leading leader? Whoever let that get by was not a leading reader. *Fueling the fires of hate* is journalese. Don't fuel fears, fuel controversy, or fuel speculation. In short: Don't fuel around.

Another network nugget:

> **And so the senator leaves the place he has loved with the most fulsome praise ringing in his ears. . . .**

Fulsome does not mean abundant. It means excessive or insincere. The anchor went on to ask the senator,

> **You will miss it** [the Senate], **won't you?**

That short question violated two basic rules of interviewing: Don't suggest an answer. And (with few exceptions) don't ask a yes-or-no question. Instead, let's hear the interviewee think and speak for himself.

And let's see more proof that writers, reporters, editors, producers and anchors are thinking.

Noosepapers (and When They Eat Their Words)

On the dangers of fishing for a fast fact in a print story

Do you ever fish frantically for a fast fact to plug a hole in your script? If you fish in newspapers or magazines, you fish in hazardous waters. Though many publications do a remarkable job of gathering, writing and printing tens of thousands of facts in each edition, they do make mistakes. Real whoppers. Which leaves us fishermen not knowing whether a detail in an article is a firm fact, or a fishy fact—or a false fact, which is, in fact, a non-fact. If you use just one assumed fact that turns out to be a non-fact, you may be heading for deep discomfort—or dismissal.

You get an idea of how risky fishing for facts can be by looking at some mistakes newspapers have owned up to. The *New York Times,* for instance, ran this Editor's Note on Feb. 17, 1995:

> "A front-page article on Feb. 5 about drinking on college campuses included a description of a University of Virginia student, Brett Sanders, who was quoted as saying he had moderated his drinking after a trespassing conviction involving alcohol.
>
> "In fact, Mr. Sanders was not convicted, nor was he ever involved in such an incident. The account came from a member of Mr. Sanders's campus fraternity who identified himself to a reporter as Mr. Sanders, whom he otherwise described accurately. The reporter visited the campus again yesterday and verified that Mr. Sanders was not the student he had interviewed."

That sobering correction came from one of newspaperdom's best. The *Times* also stumbled in another front-page article on Sept. 25, 1994.

It said the treasurer of Sandusky County, Ohio, had placed $6.5 billion in an interest-rate investment. The correct amount was $6.5 million—a difference of $6.4935 billion. The paper also acknowledged misplacing Portage County, Ohio. It's east of Akron, not near Toledo. Similarly, on Nov. 24, 1991, a *Times* travel column placed Biloxi and Gulfport in Louisiana instead of Mississippi. Imagine if you had borrowed bum dope from that Ohio story in the *Times:* you might have been dismissed, deported and doomed to gather guano on Guam. Or to sell seashells in the Seychelles.

But *Smart Money* topped the *Times'* $6.5 billion error. The monthly magazine, co-published by Hearst and Dow Jones, acknowledged in June 1996 that it had said franchising accounts for $800 million in annual U.S. sales—but that "the figure is actually $800 billion," an error of $799,200,000,000.

Most corrections seem minor, except for the people affected—including broadcasters who misappropriate a fact that's not a fact. Errors even creep into long-settled historical facts. The *Times* said (Aug. 10, 1993) Benjamin Franklin watched the first American balloon flight in 1793. That would have been an out-of-grave experience; Franklin died in 1790.

Some newspaper mistakes can be toxic: The *Times* acknowledged (Aug. 6, 1996), "An article on Sunday about endangered plants in Hawaii described castor beans erroneously. While castor beans are used to produce an oil that functions as a laxative, the beans themselves contain a protein, ricin, that is highly poisonous. They are not 'edible.'"

Time magazine even misplaced Elvis Presley. It reported (Feb. 12, 1996), that he was in "permanent residence" at Forest Hill Cemetery, Memphis. But a reader pointed out that Elvis had been moved to the grounds of Graceland Mansion in 1977. And *Time* also acknowledged (Jan. 27, 1997) an erroneous time shift: "In our review of Walter Mosley's *Gone Fishin'*, the original in his series featuring black hero Easy Rawlins [Books, Jan. 20], we said the publication of Mosley's *Devil in a Blue Dress* had been aided by the commercial success of Terry McMillan's novel *Waiting to Exhale. Waiting to Exhale* was published in 1992, two years after *Devil in a Blue Dress* appeared."

They say doctors bury their mistakes; so do newsweeklies. *Time*'s correction about Mosley's book ran at the end of its Letters section. And *Newsweek* ran this correction (Jan. 27, 1997) at the end of its Letters section: "Our article 'The Trials of Silicone' (Society, Dec. 16) reported that Dow Coming's 1996 sales were $250 billion. In fact, its sales were projected at $2.5 billion. *Newsweek* regrets the error." *The Economist* often runs letters as corrections (Jan. 25, 1997): "You say that the Caribbean hurricane season begins in September. Actually, it officially begins on June 1st and ends

November 30th." But *The Economist* usually runs corrections in tiny type at the bottom of a column. On Feb. 1, 1997: "Our piece on gambling last week incorrectly stated that the industry earned $44.4 billion in profits in 1995. This figure was for revenues. Our apologies to all those who have scrambled to set up or invest in casinos since our story appeared."

If a reporter or writer doesn't make a mistake in an article, an editor can. The *Washington Monthly* conceded (November 1994): "Someone must have spiked our water cooler the night we edited Chalmers Roberts' review of Doris Kearns Goodwin's *No Ordinary Time* [September 1994]. (1) Joseph Lash, not Eleanor Roosevelt, was the author of six books. (2) It was Missy LeHand's suffering a stroke, not FDR, that prompted the president to change his will to leave her half his estate. (3) FDR depended on two of his unmarried cousins, not married cousins, for company. (4) FDR's mistress and longtime friend is Lucy Rutherfurd [*is*? she died in 1948], not Lucy Rutherford. These errors were ours, not Roberts'. . . ."

In another mix-up, the playwright Edward Albee was wronged. The author of "Who's Afraid of Virginia Woolf?" wrote to the *Washington Post,* which printed his letter Dec. 11, 1996, under the head "Distressing Mistake": "While I was delighted that *The Post* photographed me at the Kennedy Center, I was shocked that the newspaper had given me a wife, and that her name is Percy ["Star-Studded Praise for Hard-Earned Achievements," Style, Dec. 9]. This kind of sloppy journalism is deeply distressing, for two people are with me in the photograph: Mrs. John Steinbeck—widow of the Nobel laureate, who is a dear friend, though to whom I am not married, and whose name is not Percy—and Mr. Jonathan Thomas, with whom I have been living happily for 27 years."

Even a journal published by the Smithsonian Institution, *Wilson Quarterly,* can slip. In spring 1991, for example, it said Aristotle had refined a theory first proposed by the Greek anatomist Galen. The next *WQ* admitted, "The review should have stated the opposite; Aristotle died in 322 B.C., some 450 years before Galen was born."

A *Chicago Sun-Times* columnist wrote (Dec. 17, 1992), "Scoopsville. It's a done deal. Bill Daley, brother of Mayor Daley is President-elect Bill Clinton's ABSOLUTE DEFINITE [her emphasis] pick to become the next transportation secretary." Wrong. Four years later, the columnist said (Dec. 6, 1996) Bill Daley was "expected" to be appointed U.S. Secretary of Transportation. One week later, Daley was appointed Secretary of Commerce.

In 1992, that *Sun-Times* columnist also said she deserved "the dumber-than-a-crate-of-tombstones award for wishing happy birthday Wednesday to actress Colleen Dewhurst. Wish you were still here, Colleen." Miss Dewhurst had died in 1988.

The *New York Observer* reported (Aug. 12, 1996) that a young couple had bought an apartment in a Manhattan condominium where "they will now have as neighbors Fran Warren, a singer from the big-band era, and comedian-actor Ted (*The Mary Tyler Moore Show, Caddyshack*) Knight." That's not such a pleasant prospect when you consider that Ted Knight had died in 1986.

A magazine that covers the newspaper industry, *Editor & Publisher,* admitted (Nov. 2, 1996) what it called "an honest blunder": *E&P* had run an obituary of a journalism professor, Terry Clark, but it was Dr. Clark who wrote the obit (of a colleague). In its editing process, *E&P* said, "the writer mistakenly became the subject."

USA Today acknowledged (Dec. 13, 1996) another kind of mistake: "Cardinal John O'Connor did not ask the pope to excommunicate Madonna from the Catholic Church. A story Wednesday in *USA Today* was incorrect."

The *New York Daily News* ran this correction Jan. 18, 1995: "A profile of retiring Patrolmen's Benevolent Association president Phil Caruso on Jan. 11 should have made clear that a statement about his 1988 grand jury testimony regarding a PBA escrow fund was based on a story in another newspaper and had not been verified independently by the *News.* Caruso denies authorizing a withdrawal from the fund." *Not verified independently!*

Corrections, too, sometimes need correction. The *New Republic* admitted once, "The correction we ran in this spot one week ago was itself incorrect. . . ."

The *New York Times* occasionally runs a quarter-page ad that says "to err is human." The head over the ad reads, "We Mean to Be Right. But Sometimes We're Wrong." ("What one reads in the newspaper," Bismarck said, "can also be true.")

Don't rely on a newspaper or magazine for correct spelling you use in a super. Misspellings crop up in print often. On its cover for May/June 1996, *Ms.* magazine misspelled "feminism" as "feminisim." A founding editor of *Ms.,* Gloria Steinem, has said, "Writing . . . keeps me from believing everything I read."

We all make mistakes. Who needs to borrow mistakes from other people? Mistakes to the left of us, mistakes to the right of us, mistakes in front of us, printed and perpetuated. (Tennyson, anyone?)

When we want to borrow something from the *Times*—or any other publication—how do we know whether what we're appropriating is 100 percent accurate? Which word or words, which assertion, which implication, may be wrong? And which word may be terribly (but not noticeably) wrong? The best course is to follow these guidelines:

1. Don't steal stories from newspapers, even if it's only petty larceny. Use papers only as tip sheets.

2. Don't accept everything you read as fact. No matter how respected the paper, or how prominent the byline, or how well written the story, newspapers are bedeviled by mistakes. (I hope you don't find any of mine—or too many of mine.)

3. Proceed with extreme caution.

4. If you don't have the time or resources to confirm a story, go ahead: rewrite it. But be sure to credit the newspaper (in broadcast style). One prudent reason: you won't be sticking your neck out; you'll be sharing—or shifting—responsibility. When the *Daily Herald* says the mayor told it something or other, and you need that story, write it warily: "The *Daily Herald* quoted Mayor Mole-hill as saying. . . ." That way, you're protecting yourself because you don't know whether the newspaper quoted the mayor accurately, or whether anyone at the paper even talked to him.

A writer who lifts a word or a story from a newspaper without determining whether it's correct risks trouble. So the best policy in a newsroom is to use newspapers merely as tip sheets, not as the truth, the whole truth and nothing but the truth, so help me FCC. As the Italian proverb has it, "To trust is good; not to trust is better."

> *Don't steal stories from newspapers, even if it's only petty larceny.*

The English writer Samuel Butler has put the problem of print's plausibility into perspective: "The most important service rendered by the press is that of educating people to approach printed matter with distrust."

So keep your nose in the news but your neck out of the noose.

PART III

BEST PRACTICES

12

Rewriting
If you find time, rewrite

The art of writing—as an editor somewhere says every seven seconds—lies in rewriting what you've already rewritten. True, broadcast writers barely have time to write, let alone rewrite. But when they do have time, or can make time, rewriting usually improves their scripts. Which is why the text for today's sermon is itself a rewrite: "Writers of the world: Repent and rewrite."

How can writers find time to rewrite? One way is to start writing earlier. Or curtail or rearrange other activities. Another way is to avoid dawdling.

Before we rewrite, we should examine our scripts for signs of sloppy—and sleepy—writing. In the pressure cooker atmosphere of a newsroom, we often put down the first words that come to mind and lapse into constructions and locutions that are weak and wordy. But if we read—and reread and rethink—our scripts carefully, we can see the soft spots. Some need to be cut out, others need to be fixed. Before we turn in copy, we should ask ourselves at least three questions, according to René J. Cappon, author of *The Word:*

1. Have I said what I meant to say?

2. Have I put it as concisely as possible?

3. Have I put things as simply as possible?

One of the most common problems in scripts is wordiness. In a medium where time is precious and scripts should be brief and brisk, a good writer makes every word count. Generally, the fewer words a writer

> *One of the most common problems in scripts is wordiness.*

uses to tell a story, the stronger the impact. Suppose you discover a fire and shout, "A conflagration is consuming the premises." If no one responds, make it short and simple: Try "Fire!" That'll get action.

The first words to look for when you review a script are words that don't count—except in adding to the word count. "Stretchers" is what Sheridan Baker calls them. "*To be*, itself," he says, "frequently ought not to be." In *The Complete Stylist and Handbook,* Prof. Baker offers examples of sentences where *to be* should be deleted: "He seems [to be] upset about something," "She considers him [to be] perfect," "This appears [to be] difficult."

"Above all," he writes, "keep your sentences awake by not putting them into these favorite stretchers of the passivists, *There is . . . which, It is . . . that,* and the like." And he advises that if you can, cut every *it* not referring to something. Some *it*s and *there*s are immutably idiomatic: It is raining, There is nothing to do.

And Baker says, "Next to activating your passive verbs, and cutting the passive *there is*'s and *it is*'s, perhaps nothing so improves your prose as to go through it systematically, also deleting every *to be*, every *which, that, who,* and *whom* not needed for utter clarity or for spacing out a thought. All your sentences will feel better." And sound better.

Also watch out for signs of what Baker calls "the of-and-which disease": "The passive sentence also breaks out in a rash of *of*'s and *which*'s, and even the active sentence can suffer. Diagnosis: something like sleeping sickness. *With*'s, *in*'s, *to*'s and *by*'s also inflamed. Surgery imperative."

The skills of a surgeon—or a rewriter—were needed on a network newscast that was slowed and sapped by a slew of stretchers, several in one segment:

> Elsewhere in the country, in Clinton County, Missouri, today, there was a violent protest against the forced sale of a family farm. About 300 people from an agriculture protest group . . . tried to keep officials from carrying out the sale. They failed. The sale went on. There were a few arrests, and there were no injuries.

Let's take a look: no need to start a story with *Elsewhere* or *Elsewhere in the country.* Almost every story comes from somewhere else. Although I wouldn't start with "Elsewhere," I wouldn't start with "In [place name]." Why not? Because one of my first broadcast editors (at CBS News), Bob Siller, told me not to do it. He said it's a lazy man's way of starting a story. After his instruction sank in, I realized that anyone could start any story that way: "In Katmandu, Nepal . . ."; "In Timbuktu, Mali . . ."; "In Tippecanoe, Indiana . . ." (But no man can do what Katmandu.)

A place name itself isn't news. What happened in that script is news. So for me, the *in*-lead doesn't make the cut. It's best to go ahead and tell the story as directly as possible. The writer should try to put the place name at or near the top. But not at the end of a long first sentence. And if the writer delays the place name too long, listeners may assume the news occurred in their area. So you can take care of that quickly. At the top: "Denver police say . . ." Or near the top: "Police in Denver say . . ." But "In Denver, the police say . . . " is a nonstarter.

Yet, starting a story with *in* can be acceptable, even desirable in specific circumstances. With a series of fast reactions or related developments, it makes sense to use *in* after an umbrella lead: "The United Nations called on all members today to send food to the hungry people in Starvania. In Washington, President Parker said . . . In London, Prime Minister Munster said . . . In Paris, French President du Jour said . . ."

In that script about the forced sale of a farm, not many people are going to turn up the sound when they hear an item that starts out talking about a distant county. Better: "Protesters [at least this word holds promise of action] in Clinton County, Missouri, tried to block officials from selling a family farm." (Why was the family forced to sell its farm?)

I'm not sure how to rewrite the next sentence in the script because I don't know what an *agriculture protest group* is. Does it protest agriculture? Does it protest the use of the word *agriculture* instead of *farming*? Or are farmers protesting the use of *agricultural implement* instead of *farm tool*?

As for the two *there were*'s in the story's last sentence, let's recast that sentence: "Police [or sheriff's deputies] arrested a few people [protesters? farmers? members of the family?]." I wouldn't take the time to say no one was hurt. It's news that no one was hurt only when the story is about an event in which someone might have been expected to be hurt, yet, remarkably, no one was.

Starting a sentence with *there were* or *there is* is weak. Experts have noted that *there is* lacks substance, that it delays the action in a sentence and shoves the significant verb into a subordinate place, and that it's a dead phrase. There are exceptions, though, like this sentence.

After two *there were*'s in the last sentence of that script, the anchor was dragging. And he began the next item the same way:

> There is a report of poisoned water today, water that may [should be the past tense *might*] have been poisoned by toxic waste. The Interior Department has ordered the closing of . . .

Better: "The government has ordered the closing of a California wildlife refuge because its water may be poisoned. The cause is said to be toxic waste. . . ."

If the refuge had already been closed, I'd write, "The government has closed . . ." Whatever strength that news had was leached out of it by the anchor's first words, *There is.* Also: When the anchor said there's a report, did he mean a reporter has turned in a story about the purported poisoning? Or did the anchor say *report* because it's only a rumor? The story was probably reported by a wire service, so, chances are, the script was based on wire copy. But news agencies aren't in the business of circulating rumors, so his use of *report* was probably thought-free.

As they say euphemistically about a new show in rehearsal that's found wanting, that script *needs work.* That means reworking. Which means rethinking and rewriting. But the outlook for that network anchor's improvement seems favorable. As Samuel Johnson said, "It is only by writing ill that you can attain to write well."

A SCRIPT FIT FOR A CRYPT

Let's look at these ill-fated scripts and see if rewriting can resuscitate them. This script ran on a morning newscast:

> Circus crowds watched in horror as a nine-thousand-pound elephant crushed her trainer to death, then took off thru the streets of Hawaii.
>
> The 21-year-old elephant was shot, then given a lethal injection.
>
> Officials say she was probably spooked by a new circus worker.

If you were news director at that major market television station, how would you react to the script?

1. Would you be so pleased that you'd throw the writer a luau?
2. Would you get spooked and rush through the newsroom like a rogue elephant in *musth* and smash everything in your path?
3. Would you give the writer a lethal injection?
4. Would you inject the script with some life by rewriting it?

If you chose 4, why not rewrite it now and see what you come up with. Stick with the same few facts that appear in the original. You're authorized to add a few plausible factlets. For example, instead of merely echoing the original script and saying the *elephant was shot,* you may want to use the active voice and say a policeman, a zookeeper or a humane society officer shot the elephant. A few inventions like that, nothing fancy or far-fetched. And don't try to top Groucho's Marxmanship: "I shot an elephant in my pajamas. How he got in my pajamas, I don't know." (That may seem irrelevant, but as Groucho said, "Irrelevant never forgets.")

I'll wait while you write. . . . Zzzz. . . . Time's up. Now that you've completed your rewrite, let's look at the original script. If I were telling a friend about the rampage, I wouldn't start by saying, "Circus crowds looked on in horror." (Besides, wasn't it *a* crowd, not *crowds*?) And I would zero in on the action, not the reaction:

"A circus elephant crushed her trainer to death. . . ." I'd want to tell *where* early in the sentence, not at the end. The original says the elephant "took off through the streets of Hawaii." Hawaii is the name of the state *and* the state's largest island. In any case, we don't refer to the streets of a *state* (nor the state of its streets).

The accident occurred in Honolulu, but the story is not *about* Honolulu, so we certainly wouldn't want to spotlight the place name. We want to use it early in the script. But don't start, "In Honolulu today. . . ." We don't start a story with "In [place name]." An excellent network editor once chided me for doing that. Every story originates somewhere. There's nothing arresting about a place name, nothing that stops listeners in their tracks.

Often, broadcast newswriters pick up a piece of wire copy, glance at the dateline (the place where the news service obtained the basic information) at the top and forget that listeners can't see the dateline. So usually we must insert the place name. And if we don't insert it high up, listeners may presume the story is local. In most cases, we can work in the place name at or near the beginning of the first sentence: "Honolulu police shot a wild elephant. . . ." Or "Police in Honolulu shot . . ." But the news isn't the death of an elephant, it's the death of a human. How about "A Hawaiian circus elephant crushed her trainer . . ."? Perhaps, but we wouldn't want listeners to think *Hawaiian* modifies circus or elephant: Hawaii isn't known for growing elephants or producing circuses.

Better: "A circus elephant in Honolulu has crushed her trainer to death. The elephant then bolted out of the circus grounds and charged through the streets."

The first sentence in the original mentioned a *nine-thousand-pound elephant*. I wouldn't highlight the elephant's weight, especially before mentioning *elephant* the first time. A half-tonner can crush someone just as dead as a five-tonner. As soon as you hear that an elephant has killed someone, you don't mutter, "I wonder how much that critter weighs." That's because our mind's eye already sees a jumbo.

The second paragraph of that script begins with the age of the elephant. Who cares about its age? I'd use the age if it had been one day old. Or 100 years old. Or if I had a lot more air time. But every elephant has an age. I'm concerned about people, not pachyderms. Don't worry: I wouldn't call an elephant a pachyderm any more than I'd call a spade an entrenching implement. What about the trainer? I'd certainly use the trainer's sex and age before the animal's.

An Associated Press story that moved the day *before* that script was broadcast identified the trainer as a 37-year-old man. The AP story said the elephant went berserk the *previous* day, at the Saturday matinee. Which means that when the TV station broadcast the story, it was almost two days old. No wonder the script has no time element, like *today* or *yesterday.* Which raises another question: Haven't many listeners read the story in their Sunday papers or heard it on the air already, before the Monday newscast? But perhaps the video—noted on the script—was compelling, at least for the producer.

The AP story, 560 words, says that when the elephant broke away, a dozen people were hurt. But the story doesn't say whether the elephant hurt them, or whether they hurt themselves in their panic to get away. Nor does the story say how badly they were hurt. Even so, the injured are worth including in the script.

The original script's last sentence is acceptable, although *officials* is vague. Were they city, county, state or federal officials—or circus officials—who said the elephant had been spooked by a new worker? The attribution would be improved by another word or two. The AP story is specific.

Now that we've examined the script in the ICU with an ECU (extreme close-up), we see that it's too frail and scrawny to ride the airwaves. Let's hope yours is sturdy, though not elephantine.

My Least Worst

Scripts written by the author

If broadcast news is written on the wind, news scripts are written on tissues. As soon as they've done the job, they're tossed out.

Many newsrooms do hang on to scripts for reference—by insiders. But nowhere that I know of are news script files open to outsiders. When it came time for me to get examples for this chapter, I wanted to find a newswriter willing to share his scripts with strangers and also willing to put up with their criticism—and mine. Eventually, I found one: me.

I've written thousands of scripts for broadcast. And once in a while, I saved a page or two, for no obvious reason—perhaps in the belief that one day I'd find something to do with them. Reprinting my own scripts here offers several advantages: With access to the writer's mind, I can probe his mental processes and get his frank comments on what he thinks went wrong. Also, I'm able to get his ideas on how the scripts can be improved. And if I have a question, he's always on hand. I don't have to write him, phone him, visit him or humor him.

Some of these scripts aren't so bad. Some aren't so good. Some were written under pressure with only minutes to air, and they show it. Some were written with ample time for writing and rewriting—but don't show it. And some, well, see for yourself.

Please read the first script first. Then read my comment next to it. Next, the second script, then my comment. And so forth. So go forth. Here they are, a fistful of scripts that might be called my least worst:

mb

OSGOOD   The New York City marathon was won today by an Italian. He ran the 26 miles in two hours, 14 minutes, 53 seconds. He got a good run for his money and good money for his run. Steve Young has the story:

VTR
[videotape
recorder]   TRACK UP:

My lead-in would have worked just as well without the third sentence. But it has a nice lilt to it and didn't do any harm.

I skipped the name of the marathon winner because the reporter used it. I specified the winner's time because the reporter did not. The reporter did note the amount of the prize, so I didn't have to.

I used the passive voice—*was won*—to set the scene at the outset with the combined *where* and *what* and built up to the *who.* If I had used the active voice—"An Italian won the . . . ," I'd be giving away the key point of the story in the first breath. And when listeners hear that a foreigner has done something, they're probably less interested than when they hear mention of a sports staple widely known at home.

For similar reasons, I try to use the same approach when I write most stories about someone winning a prize: "The Nobel Prize in Chemistry was awarded today to a researcher in Ruritania." After you hear "was awarded today to," aren't you eager to hear who won? Don't you enjoy suspense?

mb

PLANTE   Runner Mary Decker fell short of her goal in the Los Angeles Olympics last summer, but, as Bob McNamara reports from Eugene, Oregon, she's back on track:

VTR   TRACK UP:

It runs nine seconds. No wasted words. All one sentence: short, straight, swift.

mb

OSGOOD   Two Irish boys ran away from
home in Dublin three days
ago, hitchhiked to London
and took an Air India flight
to this country—all without
a ticket or passport. A
policeman at Now York City's
Kennedy airport became
suspicious of them—one 10
years old, the other 13—and
they fessed up. So tonight
they're going back. If they
could write a book on how
they traveled free, it might
be a <u>runaway</u> best-seller.

You had to read a long distance for
a short payoff, so you might call your
journey a *punitive expedition.*

mb

OSGOOD   The U-S boycott of the
19-80 Moscow Olympics
has now come full circle.
The United States stayed
away because of the Soviet
invasion of Afghanistan.
Today, Afghanistan said it's
not going to take part in
this summer's Los Angeles
Olympics. That makes it
eight countries, led by the
Soviet Union, which say they
do not choose to run.

This approach seems preferable to a hard-
news lead, which would not be especially
exciting: "Afghanistan said today it's not
going to take part in this summer's Los
Angeles Olympics." Who cares? Sounds
like another ho-hummer. My treatment
is an exercise in storytelling. A broadcast
newswriter's job is not to philosophize or
theorize, so I did the best I could with a
few facts and a little fancy.

If I could rewrite it today, I'd fix the last
sentence: replace *which* with *that* and
delete *it.*

Ideally, a network newscast would carry
only news that would merit display on
page 1 or page 3 of an imaginary national
general interest newspaper. An exception:
a newsfeature. The Afghanistan story was
printed on sports pages, but I doubt that
any paper carried it on page 1, except in Kabul. (And it probably got a good play there on
Kabul News Network.)

mb

CRONKITE The young woman in the
middle of the McGuire
sisters' singing act was in the
middle again today, this time
before a federal grand jury in
Chicago. The jury wanted to
know about Phyllis McGuire's
reputed romance with an
underworld overlord, Sam
Giancanna. A cameraman
for station WBBM-TV filmed
the courthouse comings and
goings, and Stuart Novins
reports the doings:

OUTCUE:

Until now, no one was aware that I
misspelled "Giancana." I'm glad he never
found out—or I might face a horde of
grumblers. In fact, a mob.

mb

CRONKITE Have you ever looked at a
can of chili con carne and
wondered how much of it
is beans? And how much
meat? Well, maybe before
too long you'll be able to
find out. The government
said today that it's starting a
revision of labeling laws so
shoppers can easily tell just
what's in a can—and how
much of it. Richard Roth has
the story in Washington:

A question lead. And a "you" lead. Rarely
do I write a question lead. More often,
I write a questionable lead. I think this
kind of question, one that every listener
can answer instantly, is acceptable.

If I had written that story straight,
I probably would have started, "The
government said today it's revising the
law on labeling canned goods so you can
easily tell what's inside—and how much
of it."

Too many stories, though, start with
"the government" or talk about the
government. Here was a story that
offered an opportunity to get away from
the standard governmental yawner.
I don't remember whether the wire copy
mentioned chili, but as a chili-eater, I'd

long wondered how much is carne. Or how little. I figured that if I was curious, a lot of other people were, too. So I decided to spice up the lead by turning it into a question.

You grabs listeners by the collar, or by the ear. It's best used when it's almost universally applicable. That's why it sometimes makes sense to write up a postal rate increase this way: "When you mail a letter, you're going to have to pay two cents more." But it makes no sense to use *you* in restrictive contexts: "You're going to have to pay more for a Rolls-Royce." Ninety-nine percent of our listeners aren't going to be buying Rollses, so they're not going to have to pay anything. Used with discrimination, though, *you* can help you.

mb	
CRONKITE	Great Britain is grim about two crises, one with the pound sterling and now one with a sterling pounder, a pounder of drums, that is, whose percussions have prompted wide repercussions. Alexander Kendrick reports:
KENDRICK	TRACK UP:
CRONKITE	The latest medical bulletin reports the operation was a success . . . and Ringo should be an active Starr

again next month. Yeah, yeah, yeah. And that's the way it is. This is Walter Cronkite reporting from Washington. Good Night.

Signs of strain: *pound sterling* and *sterling pounder.* Not to mention *percussions* and *repercussions.*

No, I don't know why I capitalized *night.* (Who cares?)

If I had the power to recall scripts, this is one of those I'd want brought back to the shop for retooling. No fooling.

mb

CRONKITE   When it comes to shops, shoppers and shopping, there's no time like Christmas, no place like New York City and no observer like Charles Osgood:

TRACK UP:

OSGOOD

Another nine-second lead-in. This was a hard one to write because it was one of those annual, or biennial, excursions in search of unusual gifts or givers. Writing a lead-in to a frothy feature is hard because the feature itself, as good as it may be, often defies summarizing in several seconds, or summarizing in a way that arrests listeners. And you don't want to give away the best parts of the correspondent's script.

Although that lead-in was hard to write, almost all lead-ins are hard to write. Only someone who doesn't know much about writing finds writing easy.

mb

REASONER   There's no place like nowhere, but Washington has a tunnel that goes there. Martin Agronsky has the story:

VTR

Six seconds. They don't make 'em much shorter. Or shallower.

mb

CRONKITE Humorist Irvin S. Cobb once
had some fun with the name
of poet Witter Bynner. Cobb
quipped: "'It's been a bitter
Winter,' said Witter Bynner."
But Winter was no laughing
matter today in a large part
of the nation. C-B-S News
Correspondent Harry Arouh
has the story:

WBBM-RR OUTCUE:

If it hadn't been for Cobb and Bynner,
this lead-in could have been shoved into
that tunnel to nowhere.

mb

CRONKITE Americans may think that
the way British play croquet
isn't cricket. But despite an
ocean of difference between
the two groups, they both
play with English on the ball
and mallets for all. Charles
Colllngwood reports from
London:

VTR

At least I didn't talk about "no rest for the
wicket."

mb

CRONKITE Ronald Reagan's positions
are seen by some people
as rigid, so Dan Rather
compares Reagan's rhetoric
and record:

RATHER TRACK UP:

1980 Republican convention. That year
I was churning out so many lead-ins for
videotapes at both conventions, especially
for "bank" pieces prepared in advance,
I don't remember whether this one was
used. So this may be its premiere.

mb

CRONKITE Our country holds age in
high regard in coins, wines
and books—but seldom in
people.
    So age may be an issue in
November, and Andy Rooney
has a new wrinkle:

ROONEY TRACK UP:

This led into a whimsical piece prompted
by the Republican presidential candidate,
Ronald Reagan, whose face was well
wrinkled.

mb

CRONKITE	Andy Rooney has taken a look at—or a listen to—convention oratory, and, needless to say, finds most of it needless to say:
ROONEY	TRACK UP:

If this wasn't used at that convention, it can still be used at the next one, needless to say.

mb

RATHER	Good evening. This is the C-B-S Evening News, Dan Rather reporting. As the British fleet advances toward the disputed Falkland Islands, Britain and Argentina may be moving closer militarily. That's because U-S Secretary of State Haig apparently has not brought the two disputants any closer diplomatically. We have three reports; first . . .

This lead-in was a hodgepodge because it had to provide an umbrella for reports from three correspondents. The use of *may* is weak, but apparently the shooting hadn't started, we had no reporters with the fleet and whatever information we had was probably sketchy.

mb

CRONKITE Two tiny craft managed to meet with pinpoint precision in the infinite depths of space—and the United States took another giant step today toward landing a man on the moon. Gemini-six rendezvoused with Gemini-seven high over the Western Pacific after four hours of maneuvering through light and darkness at 17-thousand, 500 miles an hour. For Gemini-six's astronauts, the day has been a strenuous one:

Too many numbers in the second sentence. "Giant step." Hmm.

mb cont'd. A

CRONKITE Another "first"—the first American musical message from outer space. He was talked into it, in a sense, by the mission control communicator at Houston— Astronaut James McDivitt:

CRONKITE You can't blame him if he can't carry a tune; no room up there.

The first page of this script is missing (don't bother looking for it), but the tag may be worth a look—maybe.

mb	
REASONER	Good evening. America's two astronauts both took a walk today—on the carrier Wasp as it circled off Jacksonville, Florida. James McDivitt and Edward White reviewed their four-day flight, and the space agency released spectacular film of White's walk in space. The pictures were taken by an automatic camera mounted on the spacecraft by White himself and by another camera held by McDivitt. Charles Von Fremd reports:
VTR	OUTCUE:

The first sentence made sense to listeners right away if they already knew that one of the astronauts had taken a highly publicized space walk. By that time, the only people who didn't know were isolates and anchorites (not the kinds in newsrooms).

mb	
REASONER	Outer space and inner grace, star dust and mud. Eric Sevareid has a few thoughts on these and other matters:
VTR	

This lead-in probably ran on an evening when our newscast carried a story about space, the astros' turf.

Writing an introduction to a commentary that skips around without a distinct central theme puts a writer to the test. An anchor's delivery can help him pass.

mb

RATHER   It may be within the letter
of the law, but a letter
from a member of the First
Family has raised some
questions—and eyebrows.
Bill Plante has the story at
the White House:

PLANTE   TRACK UP:

It's good to avoid starting a story or a
lead-in—or a criticism—with an indefinite
pronoun, and it's good to avoid *may*, but
despite these handicaps, it may work here.

mb

KURALT   At a time when the
president is under fire, and
the presidency, too,
it may be helpful to recall
a plain-speaking, peppery
president, a man who
seemed to relish being on
the firing line, a man who
was quick to fire back or
even fire first. And, as Bruce
Morton recounts, he also
was strong enough to <u>hold</u>
his fire—or to <u>light</u> a fire for
illumination and warmth:

I suppose I wrote so much because
I thought the correspondent's script
needed setting up. Whether it needed that
much setting up, I don't know. Whoever
inserted *his* into my script knew his
business. The president was Truman. And
the person who deserves credit for *his* was
probably the anchor himself.

mb

OSGOOD   Tornadoes and
thunderstorms struck the
Southeast today and caused
at least

V/O   two tornadoes in Laurel
county, Kentucky, in the
London area, overturned
mobile homes, toppled trees,
battered buildings, peeled
off roofs, killed cattle and
destroyed or damaged a lot
of other property. At least six
people there were hurt.

If Guinness ever lists the record for the most verbs in one sentence, the second sentence would be a contender. It has seven. Seven good ones. The lead refers to the Southeast, but the only place we had any footage from was Kentucky. Right at the top of the V/O, the script makes clear where the footage was shot.

mb

BRADLEY   Good evening. Hurricane
Allen is gone with the
wind—downgraded to a
tropical storm.
    Its winds greatly reduced,
the storm is now moving
from the Texas coast toward
Mexico.
    But when Allen swept
ashore into Texas from the
Gulf, it caused extensive
damage, though less than
feared.

Gone with the wind? Yes, I was trying for a novel approach.

The last line of the script says damage was less than feared, but between the lines you can read "and less than the producer had hoped for."

mb	
OSGOOD	Weather has been so severe in the Plains states, the temperatures so low, the winds so high and the snows so deep that in some places even highway snowplows have not ventured out.
V/O	Winds in Minnesota reached 60 miles an hour, temperatures fell to 16-below, and with snow whipped into whiteouts, visibility shrank to only several feet. Across the

Plains states, at least eight people have been killed. The National Guard has rescued hundreds of stranded motorists, but many are still snowbound.

The lead-in bounces around in a sort of singsong, but special delivery drove it home. As you read the V/O, you may be able to "see" the footage.

Ordinarily, eight deaths would make the lead, but I think the deaths occurred over several days. And for all I can remember, on that day there might have been no deaths.

This script was written for a Sunday night newscast, but it has no *today*, no *tonight*, no *yesterday*, no *weekend*. With no loss.

mb	
OSGOOD	Capitalism and communism are squaring off in a remote city in China, and it seems that capitalism has got the goods on its rival. David Jackson has the story:
VTR	TRACK UP:

The correspondent told about the emergence of private enterprise and featured busy merchants, which is why I said capitalism *has the goods*. Someone who read the script inserted *got*. If I had ever used *has got* in any English class, I'd never have gotten away with it. But in *The Careful Writer*, Theodore M. Bernstein, a language authority who was an editor of the *New York Times*, wrote, "To see how it adds force, compare *has to meet, must meet*, and *has got to meet*. There cannot be much doubt that *got* in this sense has simply got to win approval."

And that was published in 1968. In 1980, *American Usage and Style: The Consensus* by Roy Copperud said the consensus regards *has got* as standard. For those of us who still think *has got* is redundant, maybe we've got another think coming.

mb

SPENCER   A woman in Woodridge, Illinois, has won what she calls a victory for lefthanded people in a righthanded world: a judgment of 136-thousand dollars from a food store where she worked as a checkout clerk. She's <u>left</u>handed, but the store required her to check out groceries with her <u>right</u> hand. So now the store's <u>left</u> holding the bag.

Although a wire service had moved the story that day, the news was several days old: not fresh, but not yet stale. I did the best I could.

mb

OSGOOD   Only a few years ago, oil was in such short supply that Washington pushed a policy of trying to squeeze oil out of rock. But, as Bob McNamara reports from Grand Junction, Colorado, some companies seem to have dug themselves into a hole:

MCNAMARA   TRACK UP:

To contrast the past and the present, I now think I'd insert *now* after *companies.*

---

mb

SPENCER	One of the most enduring figures of the Old West is the cowboy. But many of the pioneer cowboys have been largely ignored—because they were black. Their descendents, though, have kept the campfires burning and their memories glowing. Sam Ford has the story in Boley, Oklahoma:
VTR	TRACK UP:

To save time, I could have skipped the first sentence and started with *many* (and deleted *of the*).

---

mb

OSGOOD	A new study says children who become hooked on television at an early age often become teenagers who are overweight. And the study by two Boston doctors reports that the more time these teens spend watching T-V, the more weight they put on— making them truly heavy viewers.

Satisfactory.

Although the first line, *A new study says,* is unoriginal and unexciting, it usually does the job. Can you imagine any listener who wouldn't keep listening?

mb	
OSGOOD	Former President Carter arrived in New York City today to lend a hand—in fact, both of them—to help rebuild a burned-out apartment building.
V/O	He came by bus with other volunteers from his hometown Baptist church in Plains, Georgia. On arrival, they talked over their one-week project, sponsored by a religious group. At the abandoned building on Manhattan's Lower East

Side, Mister Carter, an expert woodworker, is going to use hammer and saw to try to make the place fit again.

If you've seen enough TV news, you can almost see the videotape covered by the voice-over: the woodworker himself (Jimmy Carter) getting off the bus, people chatting, the abandoned building. It all fits.

mb	
RATHER	Good evening. The greatest threat to economic recovery, the president said today, is high interest rates. But most of the interest during his news conference seemed to be in what was unsaid. Lesley Stahl has the story at the White House:
	TRACK UP:

Rereading this lead-in reminds me that often a lead-in is merely a stall, playing for time, like preliminary boxing bouts holding the gathering crowd and building expectation until the main event.

mb

CRONKITE   Although this is the main season for charitable <u>giving</u>, investigators have found that some so-called charities are more intent on <u>taking</u>. John Sheahan has the story:

SHEAHAN   TRACK UP:

The contrast between *giving* and *taking* and the emphasis on *taking* (as the last word) give this lead-in its sting.

mb

OSGOOD   This country has about 26-million military veterans, but as the two world wars fade away, more old-timers are answering their final roll call. So the largest veterans' organization, the American Legion, is using new tactics to recruit members for posts whose numbers are no longer legion. Bill Whitaker has the story:

This is the kind of story that needs context and perspective, as one newscaster puts it. So the first sentence sets the scene and the tone. And the last may cause a groan.

mb

CRONKITE	There's a new look in art, and there's more to it than meets the eye. Robert Trout reports
CRONKITE	I suppose you could say, <u>Op</u> goes the <u>easel</u>.

The new look in art was Op Art. Op, short for "optical," created the illusion of movement. Op Art was preceded by Pop Art. But there's no such thing as Mom Art.

The tag is better than the lead-in. But to appreciate the tag, you need to know that while a witness or victim was describing a culprit, a police technician was cranking in features to produce a face on the screen. In this make-believe case, the "witness" (the reporter) carefully described the subject, including his mustache. And the face on the technician's screen turned out to be that of Walter Cronkite.

mb

CRONKITE	A flip that can launch a thousand faces: that's the ability of an amazing new machine. Nelson Benton has the story in Chicago:
VTR	
CRONKITE	Nelson, that man looks like my Walter ego.

I started the script the wrong way. The start may be catchy, but it's wrong to start a story by making an assertion and then adding awkwardly, "That's the ability of . . ." Or: "That's what so-and-so says." Or: "That according to . . ." Or: "That's what happened when . . ." Or: "That's the opinion of . . ." Or: "Dead. That's what Theophilus Thackeray is."

This lead-in might be better: "A remarkable new machine can provide a sketch of someone police are looking for. A technician can flip a lever and launch a thousand faces." Or something like that. But the script, the reporter and the anchor are all beyond recall.

mb

CRONKITE   France long has been a haven for the strange from many lands—heretics, neurotics, the erratic and the erotic. But now France says, "Don't give me your befuddled masses." Bernard Kalb has the story:

With apologies to Emma Lazarus and the Statue of Liberty. Profound apologies.

mb

REASONER   During last Sunday's inaugural demonstration of the Earlybird communications satellite, a Royal Canadian Mounted Policeman broadcast—to the U-S and Europe—a description of a wanted man.

VTR

REASONER   After seeing the international broadcast, an unidentified viewer in Fort Lauderdale, Florida, tipped police that he

recognized LeMay's face as that of a man he knew. LeMay, wanted for bank robbery, was arrested there today aboard his yacht. And once again the Royal Canadian Mounties got their man, this time with the help of Earlybird—and a birdwatcher.

My editor, Ed Bliss, taught me to spell out "U.S.," except when using it as an adjective, as in "the U-S Navy." I don't know why I slipped up here and how it slipped through.

In the tease(r) before the preceding commercial, I wrote, "Earlybird catches its first worm."

mb

PAULEY The outlook for wine in California is again—you might say—rosé. After a 17-day strike, winery workers there have approved a new contract, and they'll start going back to work today—just in time for the peak of the grape harvest. They'll get a 13 percent pay increase in the first year, with smaller increases in the next two.

"Today," Sept. 22, 1980. The editor crossed out the last sentence, apparently because he thought it would tell our viewers more than they cared to know about winery wages—and what the strike was all about.

mb

BROKAW The Shah of Iran has been flown to New York City for medical treatment. The nature of the Shah's illness has not been made public. But a U-S State Department spokesman says the Shah is "quite" sick. He was taken to New York Hospital–Cornell Medical Center. The Shah arrived in New York City on a chartered jet from Cuernavaca, Mexico. He moved to Mexico after he lost his throne in Iran 10 months ago.

"Today," Oct. 23, 1979. No *today* in this story. The Shah landed the previous day or night, so I used the present perfect tense for this warmed-over news.

The first sentence of the script could have been shortened: "The Shah of Iran has arrived in New York City for medical treatment."

mb

GUIDA   Some people making news
today:
Actress Linda Blair:
fined five-thousand dollars,
sentenced to three years'
probation and ordered to
make 12 public appearances
warning youngsters about
the dangers of drugs. Miss
Blair, who starred in "The
Exorcist," had pleaded guilty
to conspiracy to possess
cocaine. No, she didn't say
the devil made her do it.

Some people making news today was
a standing head on "Today" for a short
package about prominent people for
whom we had a still photo, new or old.
The personalities we featured seldom had
made anything definable as news and
seldom that day, but the justification
(if one's needed) was that a wire service
had moved an item that the producer
considered serviceable. After all, the show
must go on.

Someone deleted that last sentence in the
script, maybe in fear of being dispossessed.

mb

GUIDA   Some people making news
today:
Vladimir Horowitz plugs
his ears to muffle the loud
sound at a New York City
disco. Apparently the pianist
prefers pianissimo.

Whoever chose that item must have been
at his wits' end, but when it comes to
filling a two-hour hole, every whit helps.

As Falstaff said about his ragtag band of
soldiers: They'll fill a pit as well as better
men.

mb

GUIDA   Four Secretaries of State
do not make a secretarial
pool. But they do make
an unusual group at a
Washington dinner party.
   The current secretary,
Cyrus Vance, chats
with former Secretaries
Henry Kissinger, William
Rogers and Dean Rusk.
Diplomatically, of course.

When newswriters need to think in
the middle of the night, they should be
forgiven their trespasses and not stripped
of their press passes.

mb

GUIDA   Athlete O-J Simpson, the
long-running star of those
rent-a-car commercials,
is not going to have the
driver's seat to himself
anymore. He's going to
share the chores with Nancy
Lopez. Miss Lopez—a
golfer—has been chosen
to perform by herself and
with him in the rent-a-car
spots—and not just because
golfer Lopez is a long driver.

Another Golden Oldie. I had to write
something. But what ever became of
Nancy Lopez?

---

mb

GUIDA   British pop star Elton John
displays his new thatch
of hair. John had been
almost bald until he started
undergoing hair transplants.
He says he's going to have
two more transplants
to thicken his thatch—
although the head of Britain
is already Thatcher.

Someone crossed out the last phrase,
starting with *although*. And if anyone
reading this knows who, please phone, fax
or FedEx me.

---

mb

GUIDA   Seven persons in
Wilmington, Delaware, have
pointed to a man in court
and identified him as the
bandit who held them up,
a Roman Catholic priest.
But now another man has
come forward, saying that
he committed the armed
robberies, not the priest.
The judge will decide how
to proceed after conferring
today with the prosecutor,
the priest and the penitent.

Once in a great while, the segment called
"Some People Making News" presented
something worthy of being called news.

My Least Worst **211**

> Good morning. Oregon police are searching for a prison escapee who was on board the United Airlines D-C-8 that crashlanded in Portland last night. The escapee was being returned by two guards to the Oregon state prison. 185 persons were on board the plane. In the crash, at least 10 were killed and 45 hurt, five critically. And the escapee apparently escaped again.

That ran on "NBC News Update." It's a second-day lead. I don't put *yesterday* in a lead, but *last night* was necessary here. In the second line, *who was* can be deleted.

Why would a TV script be written across the full width of the page like a radio script? Simple. That's the way the anchor wanted it. The only thing that matters to me is the writing. Did I select the right facts, did I put them in the right order, did I use the right words, did I tell it right? I hope so.

If you think I should have written "185 *people*" instead of *persons*, you're right. Because of my roots in print, I was accustomed to using *people* for large groups or round numbers, and *persons* for exact numbers. When talking, I still say "two persons" or "three persons," and so on. That's what I was taught in school and have not been able to unlearn. Most anchors are "people" persons, and they say "two *people*." But I haven't heard anyone say "one *people*." Yet.

It's easier to be a critic than a newswriter, but anyone who wants to be a better writer should be a keen critic.

"Above all else," the writer Allan W. Eckert quotes his father as saying, "you must be your own harshest critic, your own strictest editor, your own most demanding taskmaster."

And, he said, "If you're honest with yourself in these respects, you will never please yourself entirely. But if you keep trying to do so, you can't help pleasing others."

Your Turn
Test your skills by writing scripts about the stories in this chapter

ow it's your turn. I've said much of what I know about writing, maybe even more than I know, so I'm going to give you a chance to see what you know.

You can do this by rewriting the six Associated Press stories printed in this chapter and comparing them with my rewrites. After you've written the first exercise, read my script, followed by my comments on why I wrote it the way I did. Then proceed to the second story, write it and compare what you've written with what I wrote. Do not write all six stories in a row and then compare them with my scripts. Do one exercise at a time. That way, you may pick up a few pointers you can put to use in your next rewrite.

This isn't a test, nor a drill. Call it an editorial checkup. Or a tune-up. But no matter what you call it, and you needn't call it anything, it gives you an opportunity to try out whatever know-how you've picked up in reading, or riffling through, this book. In this checkup, writing with speed is secondary. What's primary is getting the words right.

In these exercises—and in the newsroom—there is no single "right" version. There may be a few right ways to write a story, but there are an infinite number of wrong ways. My version is just that: my version. It may not be the best possible, even if one script could be designated "best." By now, I should be able to write an acceptable script. Chances are, over the years, I've written more stories than the average newswriter, made more mistakes, had more time to learn and had more opportunities to see how to get it right.

Treat all your source copy here as if it were fresh. Write your scripts for a late newscast. And write your scripts for a city other than the one where the stories are datelined.

Here's the first AP copy. Your assignment: Write a 25-second story. Time limit: none. None because what's paramount here is applying all the tips and rules, not setting a world indoor speed record.

My scripts in this chapter are not intended for use as templates; you needn't hold your story up against mine to make sure it corresponds in every detail. But you should find that you've used most of the facts I did and approximated my pattern. Which gives you considerable latitude (but only 25 seconds' longitude).

OKLAHOMA CITY (AP)—A prisoner being taken by federal marshals from Alabama to California bolted out of a moving plane's emergency exit after landing on Saturday and fled into the darkness, authorities said.

U.S. Marshal Stuart Earnest said the escapee, 44-year-old Reginald D. Still, was en route from a federal hospital In Talledega, Ala., to Sacramento, Calif., where he was scheduled to go on trial on a charge of interstate transportation of a stolen motor vehicle.

Earnest said the plane contained 44 prisoners when it touched down at Will Rogers World Airport. No other prisoners tried to escape, he said.

Still wearing handcuffs and shackles, he leaped out of the plane's emergency exit, onto a wing and then the tarmac as the plane was braking, the marshal said.

One of eight security people on the plane jumped out to chase the escapee, Earnest said.

Federal marshals and local, county and state authorities fanned out across the airport property, southwest of Oklahoma City, in the search.

Prisoners are normally transported by a Boeing 737, but a backup, a Convair 680 propeller, was being used Saturday because the jet was being repaired, authorities said.

The U.S. marshal's service routinely transports prisoners every other day to courts and penitentiaries around the country. The transportation program is based in Oklahoma City, and prisoners on overnight trips often are housed overnight at a federal correctional facility in El Reno, 30 miles west of here.

Here's the way I wrote it:

A plane with federal prisoners was taxiing at an airport near Oklahoma City this evening when a prisoner jumped off and escaped. While the plane was moving down a runway, he bolted through an emergency exit, landed on a wing, leaped to the ground and got away in the darkness, still in handcuffs and shackles.

The plane had been taking him to California to stand trial for theft.

If you've found that one easy, you must have done something wrong; if you start your story by saying a prisoner jumped *out of* a plane or even *off* a plane, many listeners might think the plane had been aloft. I wanted to make it clear the plane was on the ground, so my story takes a few extra seconds to get to the nub.

My second and third sentences are easy to follow (certainly easier than the prisoner was). They're energized by lively verbs, and the sentences flow in one direction. And you can see the action unfold. The last sentence in my script may seem anticlimactic after the exciting escape, but I wanted to let listeners know that the fugitive is not a killer, at least not yet.

▸ I didn't use his name because he's a nonentity, and his name means nothing to listeners.

▸ I didn't use his age because I thought it wouldn't tell anyone anything; everyone has an age. I would have mentioned the age of the lamster only if he were a youngster or an oldster.

▸ I didn't spell out the charge against him because it takes too much time and would be unnecessary.

▸ I didn't say "*car* theft" because a "motor vehicle" could be a car, a van or a truck.

▸ I didn't tell where the flight originated or its destination because those places don't figure in the story.

▸ I didn't identify the plane because it makes no difference whether it's a Convair or an Electra, whether it's a jet or a prop plane, whether it's taking off or landing. Instead I focused on that minute of high drama and moved in close.

▸ I didn't report the number of inmates aboard the plane because the story was about only one. If any other prisoners had tried to escape, I would have said so, but why take time to report what didn't happen? I was pleased to learn that someone has named a "World" airport for Will Rogers, but I didn't mention it lest I run out of time before my story could get off the ground. I'd have preferred to say "tonight," but I didn't know the time of the escape, so I said "this evening." All I knew was that the guy fled into the darkness. But the sun sets early in mid-December; *tonight* might have been wrong; *evening* seemed safer. The wire copy moved at almost 11 p.m., but that doesn't mean the story just broke. It could have been several hours old.

At a session of my broadcast newswriting workshop, I passed out copies of that wire story to the news staff of a TV station and asked everyone to rewrite this Saturday story into a 25-second script for use on a late Saturday newscast. Here's the most inventive lead—and keep in mind that the inmate who fled from the plane was charged with theft:

> When it comes to vehicles, Reginald Still apparently can take them or leave them.

Clever, eh? But what would you think if you were hearing it for the first time, with no previous knowledge of the episode? The real test is, What's a listener to make of it? It's easy for insiders to get a kick out of that lead because we already know the story. For listeners, though, this is the first exposure. So they can't savor the wordplay about "vehicles" and the inmate's being able to "take them or leave them." Sounds more like a final observation than an introduction, an epilogue rather than a prologue. Further, I wouldn't use the escapee's name so early. In fact, I didn't use it all. Why not? No listener has heard of him, no listener need hear of him. If I hear the name of an unknown in a lead, I assume he's a hometowner. In this case, the last name, Still, might worsen any confusion. *Still* is an adverb (meaning "yet"), an adjective (meaning "silent") and common noun (meaning "distillery").

In case you're wondering how that inventive writer handled the rest of the story, here is his script in its entirety:

> When it comes to vehicles, Reginald Still apparently can take them or leave them. Still, an inmate being transferred from Alabama to California, tonight bolted out of a moving plane and fled into the darkness. Police said Still was wearing handcuffs and leg irons when he jumped out an emergency exit. The 44-year-old inmate was scheduled to stand trial on charges of stealing a motor vehicle.

Sounds as if he leaped from a plane in flight. The script doesn't say whether the plane was aloft or on the ground, just that it was moving. *Tonight* would fit better after *plane.* But one of the most important questions of all: *Where* did this happen? No matter what you might think of that lead, the lack of the *where* leaves it nowhere.

How did that writer's deskmates do with the same story? Let's take a look at some of their opening sentences and my brief comments:

> It's the stuff movies are made of . . . a prisoner escape from a moving airplane at an Oklahoma airport.

It's not the stuff good news scripts are made of. Why "movies"? Why not identify the city? Why four periods? Why not a comma or a dash? Why no strong verb, only linking verbs (*is* and *are*) and a verbal (*moving*), which does not behave like a verb? And why turn a good verb, *escape,* into a noun? So that lead gets two thumbs down.

> Right now, the manhunt is on for a prisoner who, handcuffed and shackled, lept from a moving plane.

Right now? That's no way to start this story—or any story I can think of. By the time this story is broadcast, the fugitive might be recaptured, so the manhunt would be over and *right now* would be wrong now. "*The* manhunt" should be "*a* manhunt." "Lept" (spelled *leapt*) should have been changed to the preferred past tense, "leaped." And there's no *where* there.

> Police in Oklahoma City are out chasing their very own Harry Houdini.

Why drag in Houdini? He was a great escape artist, but he died in 1926 and has not reappeared. So now he needs a label: "the master magician Harry Houdini" or something like that. In any case, Houdini has nothing to do with this case.

Use of *their very own* makes it sound as if the person they're chasing is a fellow policeman. No, I'm not going to call that story a Houdunit.

> A plane left Alabama today carrying 44 prisoners to California. When it got there, it had only 43.

That script is missing a lot more than one prisoner.

> Transporting prisoners from one place to another by jet seems to be an escape-proof method. That was until tonight.

Let's not speculate about what *seems* to be. Let's report what we know for sure. Let's tell the news. Right now.

> Police in Oklahoma City are still looking for a prisoner who jumped out of a moving plane.

"Still looking" makes it seem as if the escape was reported earlier and that this is a follow-up. The news is a prisoner's escape. Better: "jumped *from* a moving plane."

> A federal prisoner, handcuffed and shackled, managed to escape from his captors by jumping from a plane tonight.

Where? Over Alaska? "Managed to escape" = "escaped." *Captors?* A captor is someone who has captured a person or animal. If anything, the marshals are losers.

> Federal marshals are wondering tonight how their man got away . . . shackled and in handcuffs.

The writer led with reaction, not action. The news is still the escape. Or Still, the escapee.

> Federal marshals in Oklahoma City are looking for an escaped convict.

Again, reaction, not action.

> An Alabama prisoner made a daring run for it as he was being flown to California.

A running jump?

> Federal marshals in Oklahoma City are hunting for a prisoner who escaped on a wing and a prayer.

He didn't get away on a wing, and he probably was too busy to pray. Which might make this a good place to bail out. Of the dozen or so other scripts on the escape, one or two came close, but I won't inflict any more on you.

The writers? All I'll say, to protect the guilty, is that they work in the Lower 48 (states, not markets).

Now, try your hand at this one, 20 seconds in 20 minutes for a Sunday night newscast.

> LONDON (AP)—Smiling to a cheering crowd, Princess Diana took home from the hospital Sunday her one-day-old second son, Henry Charles Albert David.
>
> The baby, third in line to the British throne, will be known to his family simply as Harry.
>
> Diana, 23, wore a red coat and cradled the infant swathed in a white shawl as she left the hospital 22 hours after a routine birth. Her husband, Prince Charles, 35, accompanied Diana and their new son home to their London residence, Kensington Palace.
>
> The princess blushed as the crowd of about 1,000 people, some of whom had waited through the night outside London's St. Mary's Hospital, waved Union Jacks and called out, "Hurrah, Harry I."
>
> The royal couple's first child, two-year-old Prince William, visited his mother and baby brother for 15 minutes earlier.
>
> William, looking confused by the phalanx of photographers, arrived with Charles, but left holding the hand of his nanny, Barbara Barnes. He gave three small waves to a delighted crowd.
>
> The baby, taken home in a three-car motorcade at the start of a life of wealth, privilege and constant publicity, bears the name of England's famed Henry VIII, who broke with Rome in 1534 because the Vatican would not give him a divorce.

"They chose the name Henry simply because they both like it and also because there is no other member of the royal family at present with that name," said a Buckingham Palace spokesman. "The other names all have family connections."

Prayers of thanksgiving were offered at Sunday church services around the country in the strongly monarchist nation for the birth of Prince Henry, who ranks behind Charles and William in the line of succession. He joins them as a Prince of Wales.

Bells pealed for three hours Sunday across the Gloucestershire village of Tetbury, where Charles and Diana have their country residence, Highgrove House.

The palace said the royal family will call the new prince Harry. The affectionate diminutive is in contrast to palace instructions that William must never be referred to as Bill, or Willy.

The new baby's second name, Charles, is both the name of his father and of Diana's only brother, Viscount Althorp, 21. Albert was the first name of the baby's great-grandfather, who reigned as George VI, and of Queen Victoria's consort.

David, a palace announcement said, was for Elizabeth the Queen Mother's favorite brother, the late Sir David Bowes-Lyons.

David was also one of the names of Charles' great-uncle, Edward VIII, who abdicated in 1936 to marry a twice-divorced American, Wallis Simpson.

"The baby is fine. My wife is even better!" Charles shouted to the crowd outside the hospital after a three-hour morning visit Saturday.

The speed of the announcement of the names of the 6-pound, 14-ounce baby aroused speculation the princess knew from medical tests that it would be another boy.

William's names, William Arthur Philip Louis, were not announced until a week after his birth in the same private ward at St. Mary's on June 21, 1982.

Charles was with Diana, the daughter of Earl Spencer and a former kindergarten teacher whom he married July 29, 1981, throughout her nine-hour labor and the birth Saturday.

Queen Elizabeth II was due back in London next Friday from her Scottish residence, Balmoral, said a palace spokesman, who spoke on condition he not be identified.

The queen smiled and waved to villagers Sunday when she attended church in the nearby Scottish hamlet of Crathie. Prayers were offered for the baby, her fourth grandchild. Her only daughter, Princess Anne, 33, has two children, Peter and Zara Phillips.

The new prince pushes Charles' brothers, Andrew, 24, and Edward, 20, into fourth and fifth in the line of succession. Anne is now sixth.

Yes, this story is dated. In fact, even during marriage, Diana admitted being dated. But for our noble purposes, the story is as good now as the day it was born. It still puts us to the test, gives a workout to our mental muscles and teaches us a few lessons about writing news.

Note that this AP story moved a day after Diana gave birth, but the birth itself had been widely reported on the day of delivery. Most of our listeners probably knew about it already, so our story shouldn't focus on Diana's giving birth. It should carry a second-day lead, yet inform listeners who might not have known about it or who had forgotten. Here's how I wrote it for air:

> **Princess Diana of Britain went home from a London hospital today with her day-old son, Henry Charles Albert David. The new prince will be called Harry. Mother and son were escorted home by his father, Prince Charles. The family's first-born, Prince William, is second in line to be king, and now Harry's third.**

As I look back, I wonder whether I squeezed in too many facts. In my defense, in case you take the offense: I needed the baby's name and his parents' names, and I wanted to point out that Harry was not Diana's first-born. I also wanted to let listeners know why this was more than a mere birth notice, that this baby might be king one day (but not a one-day king). Yet, look at all the facts I succeeded in keeping out.

If I could turn back the calendar, I'd redo the script to distance *day-old* from *today*. So I'd substitute *day-old* for *new*. And I'd delete the second *home;* it's implicit. Also, in the last line, I'd spell out the contraction so as not to hurry Harry. His new standing in the line of succession is too important to speed past.

Although listeners recognize the reference to "Princess Diana," her proper title was "Diana, Princess of Wales." But that sounds a bit starchy.

For the next story, write 20 seconds. Take 15 minutes.

> LONDON (AP)—Smuggled letters from Soviet dissident Andrei Sakharov reveal that he has been mentally and physically tortured by Soviet secret police while in internal exile in the closed city of Gorky, the weekly Observer reported Sunday.
>
> The newspaper said the documents "unmask the careful plan of KGB disinformation," including postcards and telegrams carrying his wife's name, that have for nearly two years suggested Sakharov was living without problems.

Sakharov's stepdaughter, Tatyana Yankelevich, and her husband, Yefrem, received the smuggled letters and photographs in two plain envelopes mailed from an unidentified Western country to the couple in Newton, Mass., the Observer said.

It quoted Yankelevich as saying, "How they got out of the Soviet Union I cannot say, but I know the source, and the source is reliable. They (the documents) have been carefully examined by the whole family, and we are convinced of their authenticity."

Yankelevich, contacted in Newton by The Associated Press, confirmed that he had provided the Observer with the documents. "There were some financial arrangements, but I won't be able to discuss it," he said.

Sakharov, a physicist who led fellow scientists to produce the Soviet hydrogen bomb, has been in internal exile in Gorky, 360 miles east of Moscow, since January 1980.

He became a human rights activist in the 1960s and was ordered to Gorky after he publicly criticized the Soviets' military intervention in Afghanistan in December 1979.

The Observer said the letters, which it will publish in extract starting next week, detail the KGB's ill-treatment of Sakharov. They confirm reports that Sakharov was force-fed during two hunger strikes in 1984 and 1985 and was subjected to mental torture and physical violence while being treated at a Gorky hospital, it said.

The KGB is the Soviet security police and intelligence agency.

Sakharov spent several months on a hunger strike in an effort to get an exit visa for his wife, Yelena Bonner.

The paper said the main document is a 20-page letter written by Sakharov in October 1984 to Dr. Anatoli Alexandrov, president of the Soviet Academy of Sciences. In it, Sakharov appeals for his wife to be allowed to go to the West for medical treatment. Mrs. Bonner was granted an exit visa late last year, and she is now in Massachusetts, where she underwent a heart bypass operation.

Sakharov also describes how he was seized by KGB agents on May 7, 1984, and taken to Gorky's Semashko hospital, the paper said.

Sakharov wrote that hospital authorities "kept me by force and tormented me for four months. My attempts to flee the hospital were always blocked by KGB men, who were on duty round the clock to bar all means of escape," according to the Observer.

It said the letters "contain one of the most vivid testimonies of human suffering ever to have emerged in the Soviet Union."

Yes, this story, too, is dated. But as an exercise it's an evergreen—fresh at any time. We have to deal with a lot of facts here, and, as usual, we have to keep the best and ditch the rest.

Here's how I wrote it.

> A London newspaper says letters smuggled from Soviet dissident Andrei Sakharov confirm that the secret police have abused him mentally and physically.
>
> The paper says the letters knock down what it calls K-G-B disinformation—including postcards and telegrams—suggesting Sakharov has had no problems. He and his wife have been in internal exile, but she's now in this country for medical care.

Why did I write it that way? I led with attribution because I wouldn't assert on my own that Sakharov had been mistreated. Maybe he had been, maybe not. I needed to attribute it. And I know the rule: Attribution precedes assertion. I didn't identify the newspaper; most listeners have never heard of it. And those who have probably don't know whether it's reliable. I, for one, don't know. But I do know better than to take information printed by a newspaper and report it as fact. When I was a newspaperman, I once told a deskmate, in jest, "You can't believe everything you read," and he shot back, "I don't even believe everything I write."

I started my script by attributing the Sakharov story to a London newspaper. Another reason not to identify the paper; the *London Observer* sounds like a London observer.

The wire service used *tortured* in the lead, but I was leery of that. Not that I doubted that the KGB was capable of torture. But why did the body of the story refer to "physical violence" instead of "physical torture"? If the wire story had provided specifics, I might have accepted the word *tortured* without hesitation. I never want to deviate from the facts or go beyond the facts. But what were the facts? All I knew was what the wire service rewriter told me. And all he knew, probably, was what the newspaper said had occurred.

Had Sakharov used the word *torture*? Was that the translator's choice, was it the newspaper writer's characterization? Or was it the wire service's contribution? I didn't doubt that Sakharov had been deprived of his freedom, if it can be said anyone there in those days had freedom. And I'm sure he was treated outrageously. But *torture* is another matter.

If a member of my staff, someone in whom I had full confidence, told me she had learned conclusively that Sakharov had been tortured, I'd accept that. But I'm disinclined to place that much trust in a nameless wire service reporter who's rewriting a faceless newspaper reporter. So after my reasoning—and please don't call it *tortured*—I backed off from the source copy and moderated *torture* to *abuse*. It wasn't just a matter of playing safe, although better half-safe than sorry; it was a matter of my trying to get as close as possible to what was true. Or what seemed true, or at least not untrue.

To simplify the story for the listener, I used only one name, that of the central figure, Sakharov. I didn't drag in a lot of other names that would only divert the listener's attention: his wife, Yelena Bonner; Afghanistan; Gorky; Semashko hospital; his stepdaughter, Tatyana Yankelevich, and her husband, Yefrem; the place where they were living, Newton, Massachusetts. But if you work at a station near Newton, that's another story.

Speaking of other stories—and labored transitions—let's turn to the next story. Please write 20 seconds. Take 15 minutes. Note: This story broke on a Friday but didn't move on the wires until Saturday. You are writing it for a Saturday night audience.

> MINNEAPOLIS (AP)—Drinking five or more cups of coffee a day appears to increase a person's chances of developing lung cancer, according to a researcher who says his study is the first to target coffee alone.
>
> "This is the first time that coffee has been implicated by itself" as a factor in lung cancer, Dr. Leonard Schuman, an epidemiologist at the University of Minnesota, said Friday.
>
> He said the study also found that the effects of coffee drinking and smoking may magnify each other.
>
> Smoking alone increases the risk of cancer tenfold, Schuman said. But men who smoked a pack or more a day and drank five or more cups of coffee had a rate of lung cancer 40 times higher than men who neither smoked nor drank coffee.
>
> Other studies will be needed to determine if the finding represents a cause-and-effect relationship, or is just a fluke finding from one statistical study, Schuman said.
>
> The study didn't ask people to distinguish between regular and decaffeinated coffee, so that's another question that further research might tackle, he said.
>
> Harvard University researchers in 1981 found a statistical link between coffee drinking and pancreatic cancer, but later studies have virtually killed that theory.
>
> Schuman and his colleagues have been studying the dietary habits of 17,818 men, all age 45 and older, and tracking their death rates over the past 18 years.

Even after smoking habits and ages were taken into consideration, those who drank five or more cups of coffee a day were seven times more likely to have died from lung cancer than the men who drank no coffee at all, Schuman said.

"On the basis of this one study, I don't think it's warranted to say 'ban coffee from your diet,'" Schuman said after the findings were reported at a Society for Epidemiologic Research meeting in Chapel Hill, N.C.

However, moderation in the amount of coffee consumed, "like moderation in many other things, might be prudent for many reasons," he added.

"Smoking is still the most important factor in lung cancer," said Schuman. He served on the U.S. surgeon general's blue-ribbon committee of experts in 1964 that concluded that smoking is a major health risk.

Schuman's colleagues in the study are Dr. Robert Gibson of the University of Minnesota-Duluth and Dr. Erik B. Jelke, who now lives in Norway.

Schuman said he didn't know what chemical in coffee might be responsible for any cancer risk, but it presumably would have to enter the bloodstream to reach the lungs.

Here's how I wrote it:

A new study says anyone who drinks five cups of coffee a day, or more, may be increasing the chances of developing lung cancer.

A University of Minnesota scientist says his study is the first to implicate coffee by itself. He also says that if someone drinks too much coffee and smokes, the combined effects may be far worse. But he says investigators must do more research.

That was the kind of medical story that needed attribution early and often. So I started every sentence with attribution. And I avoided *yesterday*. Instead, I started with the historical present tense, *says*. (I'd bet that you didn't notice the word *says* in four consecutive sentences.) I didn't use the scientist's name because listeners wouldn't recognize his name; it would only take time without shedding light. My last sentence alerted listeners to another side of the story by starting with *but*. That's important because it tells listeners that the findings are far from conclusive. The last sentence in the script tends to chip away at the story, but the sentence is important.

If my script is smoother than yours, it may be because I rewrote it for months. And I'm still not sure I have it right.

Next exercise: write this for a Sunday night newscast. Length: 20 seconds. Time: 15 minutes to air; no time to err. As they say in Wisconsin, To err is human, to moo bovine.

KEYSTONE HEIGHTS, FL. (AP)—A 70-foot-wide sinkhole continued growing Sunday after swallowing one house and a carport and forcing evacuation of four homes in a retirement community, officials said.

The hole was about the size of a pickup truck when it was first discovered Saturday in this small town near Gainesville in northeastern Florida, said Mayor William Beam.

Three hours later, it had grown to 30 by 40 feet and had swallowed half of a small house owned by Keystone Heights administrator William A. Erickson.

Two hours later, the house was gone and the owners escaped only with their coats.

The carport of a second house also began slipping into the hole.

"It's still falling in, but gradual; not big hunks of stuff like (Saturday)," Clay County Public Safety director James Corbin Jr. said Sunday.

Corbin said he was not sure if other houses would follow the first house into the sinkhole. But he said the residents evacuated from four homes Saturday were moved as a safety precaution.

"We're preparing for the worst and hoping for the best," Corbin said. "What could you do?"

Clay County Administrator John Bowles estimated the hole was 45 feet deep.

A sinkhole is caused by the collapse of limestone caverns that lose water pressure that supports their roofs.

Much of Florida is susceptible to sinkholes, but central Florida and parts of northeast Florida, with limestone caverns 100 feet or more below the surface, are most vulnerable.

A celebrated sinkhole in Winter Park, near Orlando, grew to an estimated 400 feet across in 1981 and swallowed 250,000 cubic yards of property valued at $2 million, five sports cars, most of two businesses, a three-bedroom house and the deep end of an Olympic-size swimming pool.

Florida law requires that home insurers provide sinkhole coverage.

My version:

---

mb

OSGOOD The swallows have come back
to Florida. No, not the kind
that flock to Capistrano but the
swallows that gulp down homes.

V/O The latest swallow—by a sinkhole—
devoured a home at Keystone Heights,
in northeast Florida. The residents
escaped only with their coats. The
hole is about 70 feet across and 45
feet deep. A sinkhole is caused when
limestone caverns lose the water
pressure that holds up their roofs. The
most vulnerable places are in northeast
and central Florida, where sinkholes
most often pop up—or drop in.

I know: "Confidentially, it sinks." I said
that just to beat you to the pun.

I could have written it as spot news or
a feature. What emerged was a sort of
newsfeature. If I could do it over, I'd move
only after *with*.

Although you were asked to write 20
seconds, I wrote 30 seconds. The reason:
My script had to accompany videotape
that was scheduled in the lineup (or
rundown) for 20 secs. The anchor timed
the lead-in at eight secs., so the V/O ran
22 secs. (Sorry, but I didn't want to leave
secs. out of it.)

To give you an idea how someone else
wrote this story, here's a script broadcast
on network radio. It was based on
wire copy that moved a couple of hours earlier than the copy reprinted above. Length:
30 seconds.

> A sinkhole that's already gobbled up one home and a carport in a Key-
> stone Heights-Florida retirement village is 70 feet wide . . . AND GROWING.
> Keystone Heights is a small town near Gainesville in northeastern Florida.
> The sinkhole first appeared yesterday. It was just a few feet wide but
> began to spread rapidly. Four families have evacuated the area. Sinkholes
> develop when the water pressure that supports limestone caverns drops.
> This happens a lot in Florida . . . especially in areas where rapid develop-
> ment is taking place.

If my approach has any merit, it may be its odd twist. The network
radio script was written as straight news, which may be just as good a
way, or better, to do it. But the first fact the radio script presents—*already
gobbled up one home*—is not new. *Village* has too many attributive nouns,
which serve as adjectives, piled in front of it. Why repeat the name of the
town? No need for *small*. Did the four families evacuate the *area* or their
homes? Also: How deep was the hole?

Last story for you: 20 seconds, 15 minutes.

WASHINGTON (AP)—Amtrak will "starve to death" unless Congress identifies new funding to replace dwindling congressional allocations for the nation's passenger rail service, Amtrak's chairman told a Senate panel Tuesday.

During a Senate Commerce subcommittee hearing, Amtrak President Thomas Downs said funding cuts, combined with Congress' failure to identify a new funding source and allow for operational savings, are squeezing the rail service.

"Without the capital source and without legislative reform, we are dabbling with the edges of disaster for Amtrak," Downs said. "It will actually starve to death over the next five or six years."

Downs' comments came as lawmakers questioned Amtrak's plan to cancel four routes later this year.

"It can't be considered good policy to weaken the overall system in that way," said Sen. Kay Bailey Hutchison, R-Texas, chairwoman of the surface transportation and merchant marine subcommittee.

Downs agreed.

"I don't like losing any element of the system," he said. "I believe it weakens the national system."

But Amtrak faces a $243 million shortfall next year, Downs noted, even as Congress is contemplating a $50 million cut in federal subsidies. In a bid to save $200 million, the rail service has targeted four routes for elimination as of Nov. 10. The lines are:

— Texas Eagle, three-times-weekly service between Chicago, St. Louis, Little Rock, Dallas, Fort Worth and San Antonio, will be discontinued between St. Louis and San Antonio.

— Pioneer, three-times-weekly service between Chicago, Denver, Portland, Ore., and Seattle, will be discontinued between Denver and Seattle.

— Desert Wind, three-times-weekly between Chicago, Denver, Salt Lake City, Las Vegas and Los Angeles, will be discontinued between Salt Lake City and Los Angeles.

— Lake Shore Limited, daily between Chicago, Boston and New York, will be eliminated between Boston and Albany, N.Y.

Asked by Hutchison and Sen. Ron Wyden, D-Ore., if the eliminations could be delayed for six months, Downs replied: "I haven't got the resources to do it . . . I cannot give what I haven't got."

Congress and the Clinton administration have directed Amtrak to achieve operating self-sufficiency by 2002. Even as Congress has cut Amtrak's federal operating support nearly 50 percent since fiscal 1995, lawmakers have yet to earmark a new funding source.

And the rail service continues to await congressional approval of legislation that would allow it to greatly cut energy, labor and liability costs while gaining new freedom from red tape. The bill, which passed the House last year, remains mired in Senate squabbles.

Hutchison expressed support for one proposal: earmarking a half-cent from the 4.3-cent gasoline tax for Amtrak.

My version:

Amtrak says its rail passenger service is approaching the end of the line.

Amtrak's chairman, Thomas Downs, told a Senate subcommittee today that unless Congress finds new money, Amtrak will—in his words—"starve to death."

He said it can keep running for only five or six more years. Congress is questioning Amtrak's plan to cancel four routes this year.

The wire copy tells us far more than we care to know, but we're grateful that it provides a plenteous supply of names, dates, places, numbers and quotations, if not excitement. But that's the nature of most news; it's not the fault of the news agency. A lot of news is humdrum. Our job is to write it the best way we can. And do the best we know how.

That wire copy doesn't have us panting because Downs' statement is self-serving: He's trying to scare up some dead presidents (as slangsters call paper money). And he puts the date of Amtrak's demise at least five years into the future. In fact, into the next century. Between now and then, a lot can—and will—happen.

So the story has no drama, no air of urgency. In the first sentence, the wire copy describes Downs as Amtrak's chairman. But in the second sentence, Downs is Amtrak's *president*. Even if he's both (and he is), we shouldn't use both titles in a script because listeners might be confused—and wind up on a siding. As in every story, you want to keep 'em going full speed down the right track.

By now, you probably see the way I attack a story: I go straight to the subject, go right to a verb and then to the object. Good old S-V-O; just the facts, no frills.

No matter how well you write, don't take someone else's script from an earlier newscast and rewrite it. If the story is newsworthy enough to be broadcast again, get the original writer's source material (perhaps wire copy) and rewrite that. Try to update or freshen it. And tell it in your own words.

The reason you shouldn't rewrite an earlier script: the writer might have omitted or downplayed something important, taken the wrong route or made a factual error. You don't want to be confined to the four corners of that earlier script and risk perpetuating an error. So start anew. And make it new.

Exercise is good for us, so I hope you've learned as much from this chapter—and this book—as I have.

15

All Else
The author discusses writing in Q-and-A with the author

Q. What else can be said about broadcast newswriting?

A. Plenty else.

Q. O.K., let's start with one else: What are the tricks to writing news?

A. The only trick is to know how to write and to understand what you're writing about. And the secret is to make it seem as if it's not a trick.

Q. Huh?

A. We don't engage in tricks or trickery. The writer H. Jackson Brown Jr. put it this way: "Don't waste time learning the 'tricks of the trade.' Instead, learn the trade."

Q. But how?

A. They say, "We always learn from others and end up teaching ourselves."

Q. How can you teach yourself?

A. "Teach yourself by your own mistakes," said the novelist William Faulkner. "People learn only by error."

Q. What about shortcuts?

A. There are no shortcuts, no gimmicks, no quick fixes, no simple steps, no easy answers, no magical cures, no cut-rate, can't-miss techniques, no one-fits-all solutions. "There are no shortcuts to any place worth going," according to the singer Beverly Sills. And you can't become a better writer overnight—even if you work the overnight. As a CD developer said, "ROM wasn't built in a day." And as Nero noted, "Rome wasn't burned in a day."

You can't become a better writer overnight—even if you work the overnight.

If there were one single solution on how to become a better newswriter, it would be, Write, write, write, work, work, work. Work works. The more you write, the more you can write. The more you can write, the more you can learn. And the better you'll write.

Q. Learn from whom?

A. From someone who's better.

Q. What if I'm the best in my shop?

A. "Best in my shop" may be a modest boast: The best may be not much better than the rest. Many newcomers—and old-timers—regard themselves as masters. That's why there are so few masters. The critic Robert Hughes said, "The greater the artist, the greater the doubt; perfect confidence is granted to the less talented as a consolation prize."

Q. What about getting outside help?

A. Most newsrooms don't get outside help. And newspeople, like most other people, find it hard to improve when they have no one to learn from but themselves.

Q. What about learning from writers with more experience?

A. Learn from anyone who knows more than you. The best writers know how much more they have to learn. (At the age of 70, the accomplished French writer Georges-Louis Leclerc, Comte de Buffon, said, "Every day I am learning to write.") Whether you become a writer or a capital W Writer depends on you.

Q. How so?

A. If you want to improve, and apparently you do, you'll have to do it yourself.

Q. Please explain.

A. Experts say good writing can't be taught but can be learned. I disagree with Oscar Wilde's epigram: "Nothing that is worth knowing can be taught."

Q. What do you say?

A. I say writing can be taught and can be learned.

Q. How?

A. By you, as part-time teacher and full-time learner. The author Jacques Barzun says all good writing is self-taught: "Almost any professional writer will tell you that nobody can teach another person to write. . . . But all writers admit that they were helped by criticism; somebody showed them the effect of what they had written—the unintended bad effect. In doing so, the critic pointed out where the trouble lay and perhaps what its cause was. . . . The truth remains that the would-be writer, using a book or a critic, must teach himself. He must learn to spot his own errors and work out his own ways of removing them." You don't learn from success, you learn from failure—examining failure. The billionaire stock trader George Soros says: "To others, being wrong is a source of shame; to me, recognizing my mistakes is a source of pride. Once we realize that imperfect understanding is the human condition, there is no shame in being wrong, only in failing to correct our mistakes."

Q. Any other advice?

A. The author John Ciardi says: "A writer can develop only as rapidly as he learns to recognize what is bad in his writing. . . . [The bad writer] never sees what he has actually written. . . . He does not see because, in plain fact, he cares nothing about it. He is out for release, not containment. He is a self-expressor, not a maker. . . ." And as for the good writer: "His progress toward good writing and his recognition of bad writing are bound to unfold at something like the same rate."

Q. Anything else?

A. For the beginner who asks, "How can I learn to write?" Prof. David L. Grey says the right response is: "Do you care enough to work at it? Or, rephrased: How are your motivation and willingness to accept criticism? Are you willing, literally, to sweat over words? And is your primary purpose random self-expression, or is it to communicate something systematically to someone else? Such a philosophy for writing requires practice and self-discipline, as well as corralling the ego. It demands . . . a willingness to 'grope' relentlessly for the best word and set of words. And it demands active seeking out of the best library and human sources of information and insight."

Q. What else?

A. Listen to the best newscasters and the best reporters, even if it means (sob!) turning to another station or network. Listen carefully. Record newscasts that have the best writing. Play them back. Replay them. Analyze them. And suss out what makes the best writing the best. But don't try to follow the footsteps of a writer you admire. "Find your own voice," says the broadcaster Jeff Greenfield. "Don't be Hemingway, Oscar Wilde, Tom Wolfe; they are taken."

Read some of the books on writing mentioned throughout these pages. Read other good books to deepen your appreciation of good writing and to build up the vast fund of general knowledge needed by newswriters. Read widely, read copiously, read unceasingly. You are what you read, so read, read, read.

Keep in mind an observation by the actress Glenda Jackson: "The only lesson you ever learn is how very difficult it is to act well and how very easy it is to act badly." The same is true of writing.

Q.   Why haven't you mentioned humor?

A.   Funny, thought I had. Humor is hard to write and harder to write about. In news scripts, it's especially fragile. Few news stories lend themselves to humor.

Too much of what's intended as humor in newscasts is contrived and clunky. Most often, the best humor in a newscast depends on humorous aspects of the event itself, not in the newswriter's effort to get a laugh. In fact, most real humor in newscasts produces a smile or a glint of appreciation, not a guffaw. We hear too much on the air that's intended to be humorous but sounds as if it has been pounded out with a sledgehammer. What's needed is the delicate touch of a watercolorist.

"Everything is funny as long as it happens to someone else," Will Rogers said. We might have fun with someone else, but we never should make fun of someone else. Misfortune isn't a matter for jest. We don't make fun of those who've just lost a game, a home or an election.

One last thought about humor: If you write something that's humorous, don't apologize for it. Don't tell your listeners, by word or gesture, that you're uncomfortable with something that's supposed to be humorous. If you're uncomfortable with it, rewrite it. Or, better yet, kill it.

Q.   What about puns?

A.   As a recovering punster, I'm in no position to puntificate. In scripts, I use puns infrequently. They're harder to put across on air than on paper. In print, wordplay sometimes works. But broadcasting is a different playing field. That's because many listeners usually need time to catch on, and we can't call a timeout. A gazette issued by pundits, the

New York Times' in-house monitor, *Winners & Sinners*, set down two good rules on puns: "If in doubt, don't. If anybody nearby winces, definitely don't." The trouble with so many puns we hear and see is that they're obvious or ham-handed, unless, of course, they're our own. So when in doubt, toss it out.

Q.   You haven't mentioned pronunciation.

A.   Pronunciation! It's important in broadcasting because mistakes mean a loss of an anchor's (or reporter's) authority and credibility. The columnist Sydney J. Harris says the 10 words mispronounced most often are *nuclear, realtor, conversant, chaise-longue, harass, lingerie, frequent* (as a verb), *forte, monstrous* and *disastrous*. Several other words that I hear kicked around: *cellulite* (should be pronounced cell-you-light), *covert* (the preferred pronunciation is like *cover* with a final *t*), *dour* (doer, not dower), *lambasting* (as in *baste*), *onerous* (as in honor), *patently* (pay-tently), *schism* (the *sch* is pronounced like *s*) and *long-lived* (*lived* rhymes with *dived*).

Q.   What can be done for writing blocks?

A.   For some newswriters, blocks (including this Block) are a recurring problem. A freelance writer sitting at home can afford the luxury of having a writing block. But broadcast newswriters can't. We have to produce a lot of copy in a short time, often in frantic haste. We can't permit ourselves any hang-ups. So we have to develop inner strength, self-control and devout determination.

If you're stymied by a block and can't get past it, here are several ways to deal with it: Do whatever worked for you the last time you were blocked. Or put your story aside—assuming you're not on deadline—and work on something else while your subconscious works on the original story. Or get up and get a cold drink. Or a hot drink. Or eat early. Or walk around in the newsroom. Or leave the newsroom and take a stroll. Or leave the station and take a run. Splash water on your face. Then go back to your original story and get a move on. Discipline yourself. Tell yourself: "I can do it. I will do it. I must do it, I'm going to do it." Then do it. If you're still drawing a blank, think of your paycheck—blank. If that doesn't work, lower your standards. Or run away and join the circus.

Q.   How do you deal with the blahs?

A.   Don't be blasé. Develop P.M.A. (positive mental attitude). But if newswriting becomes dull for you, if it's no longer interesting or challenging, or never was, maybe you need a change of scenery. Or a new line of work.

Q. How can I learn to write faster?

A. Write more. Speed comes with experience. Meeting deadlines is imperative, but writing fast isn't necessarily a virtue. We're hired as writers, not typists. I can't write without thinking first. So I'm suspicious of speed demons whose fingers fly across the keyboard. Don't they need time to think? Don't they need time to come up with the right word? Don't they need time to figure out how to say it the best way possible? (Do I sound envious?) Warning: Beware of writers who type faster than they think.

Q. What's the best way to avoid mistakes?

A. Write nothing. Usually, the person who makes no mistakes makes nothing. Mistakes are inevitable when writing in a hurry in the hurly-burly. "The greatest mistake you can make in life," the early 20th-century author Elbert Hubbard said, "is to be continually fearing you will make one." Don't let anxiety about mistakes spook you. Your goal should be to turn in copy with zero defects. But if writers always succeeded in doing that, editors could be deleted. Even when writers have someone else checking their copy—editors, producers or anchors—writers mustn't relax their guard against those pesky errors that try to sneak into copy.

> *Warning: Beware of writers who type faster than they think.*

Q. How do you deal with deadlines?

A. Dutifully. How else?

Q. Is there a question you were hoping I'd ask?

A. Yes: "Why bother learning to write well when many superiors, so to speak, don't recognize good writing—and reward bad writing?" My answer is, People who are serious about writing want to write as well as they can. Even the uncommitted don't say, "I want to write just so-so." If you're in the news biz (or any business), you have no business hanging around unless you want to do your best. And who knows? You might wind up working for someone who does know—and require—good writing. In any case, why not be the best you can be? If you're content with mediocrity, you've begged, bought, borrowed or boosted the wrong book.

Q.   Why did you call this chapter "All Else"?

A.   What else? It's a catchall for odds and ends that didn't fit elsewhere, or that deserved different treatment, or that I neglected to put in earlier.

Q.   So why didn't you call it "Odds & Ends"?

A.   I was going to, but then I ran across another book using that title for a chapter.

Q.   How did you happen to think of "All Else"?

A.   On the "CBS Evening News with Walter Cronkite," the three writers were assigned to stories by category: National, International and All Else. Everything that didn't fit into the first two categories—storms, space, disasters, features, plus the other writers' overflow—went into All Else. As a former All Else writer, I thought it would be an apt heading.

Q.   What about zip? The title of this book suggests that the book will tell how to write with zip. Yet you haven't touched on zip.

A.   I might not have been writing with zip, but most of what I've been advising makes for zip. This book's main lesson is that good broadcast newswriting produces copy that's clean, clear and crisp. So if you practice what I've been preaching, you'll write with zip.

Q.   Any afterthoughts?

A.   One thought about *after*—a thought that deserves repeating. If you find *after* in a lead sentence, you should probably rewrite the sentence: Put what comes before *after*. For instance, you first write, "Police are searching for a man in a Santa Claus suit after he robbed a downtown bank." But then you realize that you've put the cart before the reindeer. So you rewrite it: "A man in a Santa Claus suit has robbed a downtown bank." But I wouldn't add *today*. If it had occurred yesterday, we would have reported it yesterday. Besides, my use of the present perfect tense—*has robbed*—rules out the need for *today* in that sentence.

Q.   Anything else?

A.   Yes. If you apply all these tips and rules—and if you apply yourself— you can have the last word.

ll these books have useful information. And some that focus on broadcast journalism offer good advice. I'm not suggesting that you need to buy all of them. But you'd benefit by reading—or dipping into—more than one of them. Even if a book listed here is designated as out of print (out-of-print books are marked with asterisks), it may be available from a book dealer. When I want a book that's out of print, I search for it at www.abe books.com, www.alibris.com or www.amazon.com. And I almost always find it. Another possible source is a public library.

BOOKS ON BROADCAST NEWSWRITING

Although the book you're holding in your hands provides a lot of pointers about writing broadcast news, you might pick up a point or two (or more) from any of these books. One of the authors, Ed Bliss, wrote and produced for Edward R. Murrow. And edited for Walter Cronkite. So Ed has a lot to say, and he says it well. I'm not suggesting that you buy all these books, unless you have a lot of spare space and disposable income.

Beginning Radio-TV Newswriting, 4th ed., by K. Tim Wulfemeyer (Iowa State University Press, 2003).

Broadcast Journalism: An Introduction to News Writing, 3rd ed., by Mark Hall (Hastings House, 1986).*

Broadcast Journalism: Techniques of Radio and Television News, 6th ed., by Andrew Boyd, Peter Stewart and Ray Alexander (Focal Press, 2008).

Broadcast News, 4th ed., by Mitchell Stephens (Wadsworth, 2004).

Broadcast Newswriting: The RTDNA Reference Guide by Mervin Block (CQ Press, 2011).

Rewriting Network News: WordWatching Tips from 345 TV and Radio Scripts by Mervin Block (CQ Press, 2010).

Television Newswriting: Captivating an Audience by Frederick Shook (Longman, 1994).

Writing for Broadcast Journalists by Rick Thompson (Routledge, 2005).
Writing News for Broadcast, 3rd ed., by Edward Bliss Jr. and James L. Hoyt (Columbia University Press, 1994).
Writing News for TV and Radio by Mervin Block and Joe Durso Jr. (CQ Press, 2010).
Writing Right for Broadcast and Internet News by Sharyl Attkisson and Don R. Vaughan (Allyn and Bacon, 2003).

WRITING (GENERAL)

Almost all the books in this category are intended for people who write for print, but they cover many aspects of writing that are of common concern. Although they emphasize the elements of writing for the eye, much of what they say also applies to writing for the ear.

Advancing the Story: Broadcast Journalism in a Multimedia World by Debora Halpern Wenger and Deborah Potter (CQ Press, 2008).
The Associated Press Guide to News Writing, 3rd ed., by Rene Cappon (Arco, 2005).
The Elements of Style, 4th ed., by William Strunk Jr. and E.B. White (Allyn and Bacon, 2000).
The Golden Book on Writing by David Lambuth (Penguin Books, 1996).
On Writing Well, 30th anniv. ed., by William Zinsser (Harper Paperbacks, 2006).
The Practical Stylist: The Classic Guide to Style, 8th ed., by Sheridan Baker (Longman, 1997).
Style: Lessons in Clarity and Grace, 10th ed., by Joseph M. Williams and Gregory G. Colomb (Longman, 2011).
The Suspended Sentence: A Guide for Writers by Roscoe C. Born (Scribner, 1986).
The Use and Abuse of the English Language, 2nd ed., by Robert Graves and Alan Hodge (Marlowe and Co, 1995).
Write Tight: Say Exactly What You Mean with Precision and Power by William Brohaugh (Sourcebooks, 2007).
Writing Tools: 50 Essential Strategies for Every Writer, college ed., by Roy Peter Clark (CQ Press, 2009).
Writing with Style: Conversations on the Art of Writing, 2nd ed., by John R. Trimble (Prentice Hall, 2009).

REPORTING

Before you've written one word of a script, someone has done some reporting—maybe you. If you're rewriting wire copy (from a news service), someone else has already done the reporting. The product of reporting is information, and that's what you need to have before you write one word. Even if you don't do any reporting, you ought to know what it's all about.

The ability to report and gather facts is the heart of journalism, print and broadcast.

Aim for the Heart: Write, Shoot, Report and Produce for TV and Multimedia by Al Tompkins (CQ Press, 2011).

Broadcast News Writing and Reporting, 2nd ed., by Peter E. Mayeux (Waveland, 2000).

Broadcast News Writing, Reporting and Producing, 5th ed., by Ted White and Frank Barnas (Focal Press, 2010).

Crafting the News for Electronic Media Writing, Reporting and Producing (Radio/TV/ Film) by Carl Hausman (Wadsworth, 1992).*

ENG: Television News, 3rd ed. by Charles F. Cremer, Phillip O. Keirstead and Richard D. Yoakam, (McGraw-Hill, 1995).

It Takes More Than Good Looks to Succeed at Television News Reporting by Wayne Freedman (Bonus Books, 2003).

The New News Business: A Guide to Writing and Reporting by John Chancellor and Walter R. Mears (HarperCollins, 1995).

News Reporting and Writing, 12th ed., by Melvin Mencher (McGraw-Hill, 2010).

Professional TV News Handbook by Charles Coates (Bonus Books, 2000).

Radio and Television Reporting by Roy Gibson (Allyn and Bacon, 1991).*

Reporting for Radio by Chuck Crouse (RTNDA/Bonus Books, 1992).

Television News, Radio News, 4th ed., by Irving Fang (Rada Press, 1985).*

Writing for Television, Radio and New Media, 10th ed., by Robert L. Hilliard. (McGraw-Hill, 2011).

EDITING

Writers need to be their own editors. They can't count on having their copy edited by an editor, let alone a good editor. So it makes sense for any writer to learn how to edit. A word to the wise is usually insufficient, so let me say again: Learn how to edit.

The Editorial Eye, 2nd ed., by Jane T. Harrigan and Karen Brown Dunlap (Bedford/ St. Martin's, 2004).

Getting the Words Right: How to Revise, Edit and Rewrite, 2nd ed., by Theodore A. Rees Cheney (Writers Digest Books, 2005).

Line by Line: How to Edit Your Own Writing by Claire Kehrwald Cook (Cengage Learning, 1990).

GRAMMAR AND USAGE

If your grammar is sloppy, you gotta clean up your act. These books can help. What you say and how you say it are paramount for your own standing in the broadcasting world. Besides, you don't want to upset any listeners. Many of them are knowledgeable about grammar. And some are quick to write to a newsroom to complain.

Several years ago, a talk show host in Kitchener, Ontario, was interviewing me on the air. I don't think we were discussing grammar, but he said more than one listener had complained about his grammar. So I told him, "If you can't stand the heat, get out of Kitchener."

The American Heritage Book of English Usage (Houghton Mifflin, 1996).

American Usage and Style: The Consensus by Roy Copperud (Van Nostrand, 1980).

The Borzoi Handbook for Writers, 3rd ed., by Frederick Crews and Sandra Schor (McGraw Hill, 1994).

The Careful Writer: A Modern Guide to English Usage, 2nd ed., by Theodore M. Bernstein (Free Press, 1995).

Dictionary of Contemporary Usage, 2nd ed., by William and Mary Morris (Harper and Row, 1992).*

A Dictionary of Modern English Usage by H. W. Fowler, edited by David Crystal (Oxford University Press, 2009).

Garner's Modern American Usage, 3rd ed., by Bryan A. Garner (Oxford University Press, 2009).

The Good English Guide by Godfrey Howard (Macmillan Reference Books, 1993).

Handbook of Good English by Edward D. Johnson (Facts on File, 1991).

The Language of News: A Journalist's Pocket Reference by Jack Botts (Iowa State University Press, 1994).

Modern American Usage, rev. ed., by Wilson Follett (Hill and Wang, 1998).

Modern English Usage, 2nd ed., by H. W. Fowler, revised and edited by Sir Ernest Gowers (Oxford University Press, 1987).

Painless Perfect Grammar: The National Grammar Hotlines Most Frequently Asked Questions by Michael Strumpf and Auriel Douglas (Bandanna Books, 1997).

A Pocket Guide to Correct Grammar, 3rd ed., by Vincent F. Hopper, Cedric Gale and Ronald C. Foote, revised by Benjamin W. Griffith (Barron's, 1997).

Practical English Usage, 3rd ed., by Michael Swan (Oxford University Press, 2005).

Webster's Dictionary of English Usage (Merriam-Webster, 1994).

Webster's New World Guide to Current American Usage by Bernice Randall (Simon and Shuster, 1988).*

Woe Is I: The Grammarphobe's Guide to Better English in Plain English, 3rd ed., by Patricia T. O'Conner (Penguin Group, 2009).

Working with Words: A Concise Handbook for Media Writers and Editors, 4th ed., by Brian S. Brooks and James L. Pinson (St. Martin's Press, 1999).

STYLEBOOKS

Stylebooks deal with the basic work rules for a newsroom, rules set down mainly for uniformity. Stylebooks do not deal with writing style.

Newsrooms should have, at the very least, the *AP Stylebook*. As a reference book, it encompasses rules, spelling, grammar and usage. It even lists some of the most popular abbreviations used in texting and IMing like BRB (be right back), G2G (got to go) and ROFL (rolling on the floor laughing). The 470-page *AP Stylebook* also has a section on business guidelines, a section on sports guidelines, a punctuation guide and a briefing on media law.

The Associated Press Broadcast News Handbook, compiled and edited by Brad Kalbfeld (McGraw Hill, 2000).

The Associated Press Stylebook and Libel Manual, 45th ed., edited by Darrell Christian, Sally Jacobsen and David Minthorn (Basic Books, 2010).

BBC News Styleguide, by John Allen (London: BBC Training and Development, 2003). Available at www.bbctraining.com/pdfs/newsstyleguide.pdf.

Broadcast News Style Guide edited by Keith Leslie (Broadcast News, 1997). [Broadcast News is a unit of The Canadian Press.]

Broadcast News Writing Stylebook, 4th ed., by Robert A. Papper (Allyn and Bacon, 2009).

The Economist Style Guide, 10th ed. (The Economist Books, 2010).

Los Angeles Times Style and Usage Guide, compiled by Kathy Gosnell (Times Mirror, 1995).

The New York Times Manual of Style and Usage, rev. and exp. ed., by Allan M. Siegal and William G. Connolly (Three Rivers Press, 2002).

Reuters Handbook for Journalists by Ian Macdowell (Butterworth-Heinemann, 1992).

The UPI Stylebook, 3rd ed. (United Press International, 1992).

U.S. News & World Report Stylebook for Writers and Editors, 7th ed. (U.S. News & World Report, 1994).

Wall Street Journal Guide to Business Style and Usage (Simon & Schuster, 2002).

Washington Post Deskbook on Style, 2nd ed., compiled and edited by Thomas W. Lippman (McGraw-Hill, 1989).

REFERENCE

Every writer should have one book within reach: a good dictionary. And another book not far: a good thesaurus. The online dictionaries and thesauruses I've seen don't measure up to the best in print. My favorite is the American Heritage hardcover desk dictionary. It features the opinions of a usage panel and contains hundreds of usage notes.

The Webster's New World Dictionary says it is the official dictionary of the Associated Press, the *New York Times* and the *Wall Street Journal,* among other news organizations. If the *AP Stylebook* is silent on a question such as which of two alternate spellings to use, then the AP goes with the one listed as preferred in AP's official dictionary.

American Heritage Dictionary, 4th ed. (Houghton Mifflin, 2006).
Dictionary of Concise Writing, 2nd ed., by Robert Hartwell Fiske (Writer's Digest Books, 2006).
Merriam-Webster's Collegiate Dictionary, 11th ed. (Merriam-Webster, 2006).
Random House Unabridged Dictionary, 2nd ed. with CD-ROM (Random House, 2007).
Roget's International Thesaurus, 6th ed. (HarperCollins, 2002).
Webster's New International Dictionary, 3rd ed. (G. and C. Merriam, 2002).
Webster's New World Dictionary, 4th ed. (Simon and Schuster, 2004).

HISTORY OF BROADCAST NEWS

A solid history of broadcast news—TV and radio—was written by a newsman, Edward Bliss Jr., who had a strong background in both media. Disclosure: he was my editor on the "CBS Evening News with Walter Cronkite." Fuller disclosure: Ed and I became friends. The other books in this section will help journalists judge what is news.

Deciding What's News: A Study of CBS Evening News, NBC Nightly News, Newsweek and Time by Herbert J. Gans (Northwestern University Press, 2004).
The Elements of Journalism by Bill Kovach and Tom Rosenstiel (Three Rivers Press, 2007).
Now the News: The Story of Broadcast Journalism by Edward Bliss Jr. (Columbia University Press, 1991).